PRAISE FOR
THE GEN Z FREQUENCY

'Youth culture is always moving, changing and evolving. This book delivers well-researched, actionable strategies and tactics that focus on alignment and value creation with that culture. Many books talk about Gen Z, but this is a definitive playbook for modern marketers and business people to authentically engage an emerging generation.' **Stefan Heinrich, Head of Global Marketing, ByteDance (TikTok – formerly musical.ly – and Vigo Video)**

'Finally, a book that not only understands the complexity and vivaciousness of my generation, but also gives practical insights into how brands connect, market and build community with us. It provides an insider's view into our mindset and teaches brands how to build trust with a generation notorious for scepticism.' **Natalie Riso, Content Marketing Strategist, Studio71, and two-time LinkedIn Top Voice at age 21**

'An essential read for business leaders due to the fact that Gen Z sets the benchmark for every other generation now in regard to trending consumer behaviour. Witt and Baird not only do a great job laying out every area that brands need to focus on when it comes to Gen Z: transparency, culture, media, marketing, community and influence, but the layout of the book itself makes it Gen Z by design with its TL;DR chapter summaries. Ignore at your own peril.' **Geoffrey Colon, Senior Marketing Communications Designer, Microsoft, and author of** *Disruptive Marketing: What growth hackers, data punks, and other hybrid thinkers can teach us about navigating the new normal*

'Witt and Baird leverage their combined decades of experience in the youth culture space with actual research on Gen Z to create an essential playbook that is full of strategic insights, compelling anecdotes and relevant data. For any brand or organization hoping to reach Gen Z, *The Gen Z Frequency* is your new required reading.' **Anastasia Goodstein, SVP of Digital Innovation, The Ad Council, and author of *Totally Wired: What teens and tweens are really doing online***

The Gen Z Frequency

How brands tune in and build credibility

Gregg L Witt and Derek E Baird

KoganPage

First published in Great Britain and the United States in 2018 by Kogan Page Limited

2nd Floor, 45 Gee Street	c/o Martin P Hill Consulting	4737/23 Ansari Road
London EC1V 3RS	122 W 27th St, 10th Floor	Daryaganj
United Kingdom	New York, NY 10001	New Delhi 110002
www.koganpage.com	USA	India

© Gregg L Witt and Derek E Baird, 2018

The right of Gregg L Witt and Derek E Baird to be identified as the authors of this work has been asserted by them in accordance with the Copyright, Designs and Patents Act 1988.

ISBN   978 0 7494 8248 0
E-ISBN 978 0 7494 8249 7

British Library Cataloguing-in-Publication Data

A CIP record for this book is available from the British Library.

Library of Congress Cataloging-in-Publication Data

Names: Witt, Gregg L., author. | Baird, Derek E., author.
Title: The Gen Z frequency : how brands tune in and build credibility / Gregg
   L. Witt and Derek E. Baird.
Description: New York : Kogan Page Ltd, [2018] | Includes bibliographical
   references and index.
Identifiers: LCCN 2018030634 (print) | LCCN 2018033545 (ebook) | ISBN
   9780749482497 (ebook) | ISBN 9780749482480 (pbk.)
Subjects: LCSH: Branding (Marketing) | Consumers' preferences. | Advertising
   and youth. | Consumer behavior.
Classification: LCC HF5415.1255 (ebook) | LCC HF5415.1255 .W578 2018 (print)
   | DDC 658.8/27—dc23

Typeset by Integra Software Services, Pondicherry
Print production managed by Jellyfish
Printed and bound by CPI Group (UK) Ltd, Croydon, CR0 4YY

GW

For Torrin, Talisen, Traesin and Eyela Witt
— my Gen Z tribe

And to all young people who question authority while
working to find the answers.

DB

If I've learnt anything during the process of writing this
book, it's that Gen Z is going to change the world. Thank
you to all the young people who were willing to talk with
me during the writing of this book and for helping me
tune in to the Gen Z frequency.

CONTENTS

ABOUT THE AUTHORS

Gregg L Witt

Gregg L Witt's tireless pursuit of the youth culture thread has been a long and winding road. Never content to just 'know it when he sees it', Witt has dedicated his career to a focused examination of the wisdom and authenticity inherent in today's youth culture, while guiding others on how they might, respectfully, do the same. With over 16 years of experience in consumer insights, influencer programme management and marketing activation, Witt is a renowned cultural marketing strategist and national public speaker. He is EVP of Youth Marketing at Motivate Inc., where he leads insights, strategy and influence marketing campaigns for brands targeting youth culture. In 2016, he was named a Top Youth Marketer To Follow by *Inc. Magazine*. Some of Witt's clients have included Autodesk, AwesomenessTV, FunnyOrDie, HBO, Nissan, Partnership for Drug-Free Kids, Procter & Gamble, Qualcomm and Walt Disney World.

Derek E Baird

Writer, social media expert and youth-culture trend spotter, Derek E Baird's professional vocation centres around the intersection of demography and technology: specifically, entertainment media and the ways that teens, kids and their parents use powerful social platforms in their everyday lives.

His immersive youth marketing and product strategy work has led to work with Yahoo!, Facebook and the Museum of Tolerance. A dedicated advocate for cultural, gender and racial diversity in youth media and entertainment, he is an adjunct professor at Pepperdine University Graduate School of Education and Psychology and a recipient of the Disney Inventor Award.

FOREWORD

Initially, I had just seen the book cover when I was given the honour of writing the foreword. Yes, I *do* judge a book by its cover. Now having read more, let me just say, this book is absolutely golden – and I mean that literally and figuratively.

Sure, as a marketer and storyteller I can point out the importance and impact this modern, highly entrepreneurial, negotiatrix segment is already having on our digital marketing landscape. I can bullet point some key differences between this cohort and Millennials, Gen X and any other preceding generation. But I rather come to you as a maniacal mother of two teenage boys. A parent whose greatest daily adventure consists of tuning in to the plurals (or 'pluralist generation') mastermind to understand why they do the things they do the way they do them. I fail more times than I'd like to admit.

I'm grateful. *So* grateful for this book.

Gregg and Derek are not just experts in the youth culture and brand marketing field. I acknowledge them as Sherpas. This narrative hand-holds you through the treacherous, uncharted territory that is effective communication with Gen Z, exposing raw truth about the shortcomings and challenges all of us are facing today as marketers, brands or agencies when trying to land the most relevant youth marketing message. Be comforted in the fact that our guides offer the must-have essentials to survive this foreign land, and ensure you proceed carefully at every step.

Beyond comforted, be enthusiastic at the '*un-learnings*' you will experience that will help shift paradigms that may have been fossilized by past generations or marketing ideals.

This is a book for explorers – marketers, communicators, strategists and creatives – who seek to build the indispensable skill set to triumphantly grab and keep Gen Z's attention for the long haul. As all of the above, this book has been illuminating (and a little bit of a fundamental wake-up call), forcing me to rethink, re-strategize and reposition myself and content for better results both at work and at home.

So go forth, dear reader, and learn the ways of the Sherpas and the mysterious terrain of the youth culture. Consider Gregg and Derek's own journey, their pitfalls and successes. Tune in to the Gen Z frequency with the tools they so generously share and discover the uniqueness of this newly formed expanse that is begging to be explored and understood.

Miri Rodriguez,
Storyteller at Microsoft

PREFACE

Successful brands reaching Gen Z all have one thing in common: they know how to get on the same wavelength as their target audiences.

What is the Gen Z frequency? The short answer is that it's the wavelengths or frequencies that young people use to communicate and express themselves. The more comprehensive answer is this: Gen Z has a generational voice, their own frequency, yet that unified voice is made up of many distinct voices. Each youth segment, group and subgroup – right down to the individual – has a voice that identifies what makes it unique, is formed by its ideas, likes and dislikes, interests, and motivations… essentially, all the things that make up their particular slice of the world. Each of these voices or frequencies tells an important story that helps us to understand Gen Z as a whole. The trick is to hear and resonate with these unique voices and frequencies within the generational cacophony, and understand that Gen Z is not simply one homogeneous whole.

Born between 1996 and 2011 (approximately), Gen Z may not have reached full maturity, but they are sophisticated and nuanced in how they approach their world. To truly listen and communicate we have to put in the work and pay attention to these groups, learn their cultural specificities, and understand what they want and need. Only when we become skilled at tuning in and communicating on the frequencies of our brand's targeted audiences, can we start to build the relationships with youth consumers that result in collaboration, loyalty and success.

Consumers and brands communicate – or fail to communicate – with one another, in a multitude of ways: video, images, voice, text, virtual and real world experiences. Despite all this communication, however, it isn't always immediately obvious what is and isn't working, and why. Is your brand receiving positive or negative attention? Are you getting enough attention? Brands talk about being part of the conversation with youth culture, but the types of content, experiences, and channels deployed are ineffectual if you are not aligned with youth audiences. Alignment is the key to effective communication – especially with Gen Z – and it comes from listening in closely, and contributing to the conversation.

In *The Gen Z Frequency* we offer a wealth of information and tools that guide you towards alignment and engagement with youth culture. An authentic connection is critical – successful brands tune in to the frequency of Gen Z. No business is exempt.

ACKNOWLEDGEMENTS

Writing a book while juggling work and family life is – without doubt – a monumental challenge. One that took many people and an unwavering dedication to overcome. We simply cannot thank everyone who took part in the creation of this book enough.

There is no real way of tuning in to the frequency of Gen Z without their collaborative involvement. Therefore, a major thank you goes to everyone who participated on the national Gen Z advisory board and those who made it possible. The depth of responses to questions, candid points of view and creativity helped shape and validate all aspects of this book. They were the voices that informed and inspired us most throughout the process, and the ones who kept our thoughts in check. Special thanks to Sofia Lowenstein, friend and English Department Chair at the School for Entrepreneurship and Technology, who so generously worked with us in the beginning to pilot the initial advisory board in San Diego.

An equal amount of thankfulness is owed to the many Gen Z entrepreneurs, influencers, creators and managers for the interviews, marathon texting conversations and, most importantly, for their thoughtful and unfiltered advice to brands. We extend honorary fist bumps to Gen Z trailblazers: Jake Skoloda, Sam Park, Richard YoungJun Kim, Ruvim Achapovskiy, Natasha Takahashi (the Chatbot queen), Connor Blakely, Jenk Oz and Kodie Shane for going above and beyond amid their busy schedules.

We owe the deepest gratitude to Susan Stanley, who took the initiative (and literally all of her free time) to help us navigate the challenges encountered while working on this book. More specifically, we are thankful for her help in organizing thoughts, for manuscript editing expertise and for overall project management. Her role was heroic, and appreciated.

A tremendous thank you is due to Zoe Oksanen, who contributed as both a peer and an editor, from real-time edits during her kids' football games to late nights helping review and improve chapters, especially during the last stages of the book.

We are also thankful for the expert co-conspirators we are fortunate enough to call our friends and colleagues, who allowed this book to incorporate far more than just the perspectives of two youth marketing and digital media professionals. While there isn't room to name everyone we interviewed, quoted or flooded with e-mails, phone calls and texts, we would like to call out the following: Rich Antoniello, Founder and CEO at Complex Media; John Davidson, Head of GameStop Partnerships; Geoffrey Colon at Microsoft; Dan Winger at LEGO; Sebastien Marcq; Charlie Buffin, Co-Founder at MC Projects and Brent Rivera Talent Management; Fran Richards, RJ Kraus and Scott Tilton from Hookit; Sara Unger from Civic Entertainment Group; Steve Berra, President at The Berrics; Adam Wilson from Carhartt; Kevin Wilkins; Nick Tran from Hulu; Michael Abata; Jim Louderback from Vidcon; Steve and the late Barb King at Landscape Structures; along with Kevin Macnamura and Sandy Bodecker at Nike for helping us share their story. We'd also like to thank Miri Rodriguez for the honour of her beautiful foreword, amazing storytelling and the best cheetah pants in the business.

Mike Carnevale, dear friend and master creative, who understood our vision and created the hand-drawn artwork and design style of all things visual in this book. Your time and dedication are immensely appreciated, and we can't thank you enough. A big thanks as well to Grant Brittain for your wisdom and friendship over the years, a lifetime of iconic skateboard photography and usage of the legendary Bones Brigade Four Handplants photo on the Animal Chin Ramp. High fives forever to our former partners Cindy and Keith White at Immersive Youth (acquired by Motivate, Inc. in 2016).

Special thanks go out to Trevor Hansen, CEO, and Marcia Hansen, Founder, at Motivate Inc. – a specialized insights, strategy and media activation agency driving ROI through cultural alignment – for believing in us, and enabling the leadership necessary to build our youth culture practice as part of the Motivate family.

We couldn't have written a book about Gen Z without having a broader, quantitative look at youth trends, which is why we are grateful to KidSay – our youth insights partner – for providing access and collaborative analysis throughout the research and writing process.

Thank you especially to Ryan Scofield, Bob Reynolds, Terence Burke and Carolyn Callen.

It was a great pleasure to work with the team at Kogan Page, who patiently guided us through the process. Jenny Volich, our commissioning editor, who found us and believed in the project from the start. Charlotte Owen, our development editor, who supported us every step of the way to the finish line, along with Kogan Page publisher, Chris Cudmore, who made this book a reality.

Derek E Baird would like to thank Charlotte Owen at Kogan Page for her editorial eye and guidance in writing this manuscript; thank you to John Saveland for donating his time to provide feedback, insight and peer review; thank you to Jarrod Walczer for generously allowing me to use part of our Gen Z and Dear Evan Hansen research in this book; thank you to Gregg for inviting me on this journey, and thanks to everyone else I talked to during the writing of this book for their contributions, inspiration and support.

Gregg L Witt would also like to express his gratitude to the skateboarding community, which led him to find his passion, motivated his pursuit of business and connected him with some of the most remarkable people within youth culture and beyond. Lastly, and most importantly, thank you to my mom and dad, Julie and Terry Witt, for their unwavering faith in my business endeavours since the age of 16, and to Mary Baldwin and Dave Hennis for being there since day one.

Introduction

Are you tuned in to Gen Z?

Let's face it: youth marketing isn't always 'likes', hearts and unicorns

After 20 years of sitting on both the brand and agency side of the table, we know at first hand that there is no such thing as a holy grail of youth marketing solutions, or some quick fix that will perfectly reach and engage Gen Z. This group is the largest and fastest-moving cohort that we have worked with to date, and as a group they have minimal tolerance for companies that haven't taken the time to get to know them. Rather than lose credibility, we treat this audience as actual people, align with them and actively contribute to the culture they're building. Follow our lead and connect with this group; whether you're a global company or a small startup, the same rules apply. In our time spent working with brands across many industries, we've seen enough evidence to know that true alignment is at the root of every successful youth-focused initiative.

Who are we and why should you listen?

Gregg Witt is a renowned cultural marketing strategist and national public speaker. He is Executive Vice President of Youth Marketing at Motivate Inc., where he leads insights, strategy and creator partnerships for brands targeting Gen Z, LGBTQ and multicultural consumer segments. In 2016, he was named a Top Youth Marketer To Follow by *Inc. Magazine*. Derek Baird specializes in kids, family and teen digital strategy and innovation as a consultant. A dedicated advocate for cultural, gender and racial diversity in youth media and entertainment, he is an adjunct professor at Pepperdine University Graduate School

Figure 0.1   Estimated percentage of Gen Z population in the United States, based on Nielsen Total Audience Report

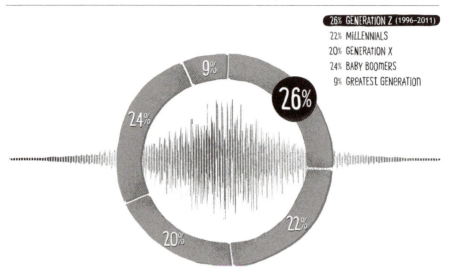

26% GENERATION Z (1996–2011)
22% MILLENNIALS
20% GENERATION X
24% BABY BOOMERS
9% GREATEST GENERATION

SOURCE Data from Nielsen (2017). Illustration by Mike Carnevale

of Education and Psychology and a recipient of the Disney Inventor Award. Over the past two decades, we've worked with a diverse array of companies, from pioneering startups and non-profit organizations to global corporations such as The Walt Disney Company and Yahoo!. We've consulted with the world's largest advertising agencies and founded two leading youth marketing agencies. We also work as strategic advisers with KidSay, one of the most respected authorities in youth research and innovation in the country. Their annual trend-tracking study is used by many leading brands to stay ahead of the curve in the highly dynamic youth market. Our work with KidSay is notable, as it enables us to have our fingers on the pulse of youth trends and behaviours in near real time, helping us to foresee hundreds of significant fads and trends, including Minecraft, fidget spinners and the rise of YouTube, Instagram and musical.ly (now TikTok). We've integrated many of these insights on youth culture throughout this book.

Research that fuelled *The Gen Z Frequency*

In order to establish a strong foundation for this book, we wanted to challenge what we knew about Gen Z and to get immersed in the most current version of this evolving generation. The objective was to explore what it means to really get on the same wavelength with young people in order to tune in and build credibility. We knew it would mean practising what we preach to client partners: 'don't go it alone', when it can be done better with audience feedback and participation in youth culture. We started the research process by conducting qualitative and quantitative research over a six-month timeframe during 2017–18.

The first phase was to create a youth advisory board, which we piloted in partnership with SET High School (School for Entrepreneurship and Technology) in San Diego. Originally the SET Advisory Board was made up of 140 students, and was active over a few months in 2017. The pilot was successful and informative, so we created another, this time expanding the scope to be more nationally representative, and choosing markets that balanced the conservative regions with the more avant garde (Austin, Chicago, Minneapolis, New York City, Ohio, San Diego and Seattle). In order to have a closer dialogue and more of a community feel, we interviewed and hand-selected 61 participants, which allowed the board to be manageable in size yet broad enough to catch a wide range of perspectives. Participants were aged 13–18 to capture the midrange of the generation and represented a mix of talents and personalities to encourage interactions and stimulate energy within the group, as well as develop a strong sense of mission.

Our interactions with the board included a monthly themed survey, in-person and mobile video-based interviews, and ongoing iterative feedback on the perspectives, methods and strategic frameworks presented in this book. The qualitative research focused on the following objectives:

- To better understand their hopes and fears.
- To take a deeper look at their media consumption preferences.
- To assess shopping habits: online vs physical stores.
- To gain perspectives on environment, social change, ethics and privacy.
- To further explore what cultural trends are shaping their lives.

Some of the most insightful findings were revealed by the more creative, thought-provoking themes, such as 'what brands suck, and why?' and 'if you could only choose five brands for the rest of your life, which would you pick and why?'. One thing we've learnt over the years is this: 'ask boring questions and you get boring data'.

In order to gain a broader perspective, our next step in the process was to leverage KidSay's Trend-Tracking data to observe the quantitative, bigger picture view of youth trends, and to see how our qualitative research stacked up to the larger sample size (6,000 annually). Indispensable research also came from interviews with the respected youth culture influencers and creators with whom we have established relationships. Influencers have a deeper understanding of the youth audience than most people, as they are interacting with those audiences in an ongoing capacity, and we find them to be an integral part of our practice.

Finally, to match our findings with market realities we conducted 43 interviews with accomplished marketers, business owners and researchers who play various roles in the youth market. The goal was twofold: to have them weigh in on our findings and points of view, and to share their unfiltered opinions in the form of advice to our readers. When we analysed all of the collected findings together, we identified five central themes that came up repeatedly in one form or another; they represent the challenges that we address throughout the book.

- Gen Z tends to reject companies without a clear and relatable brand story and content.
- Gen Z is concerned about having their privacy protected, being listened to or respected by brands, and the reliability of brands they choose.
- Gen Z seeks brands that connect with their passions and interests and contribute to their lives, or support them in what they are trying to do.
- Gen Z wants more brands that inspire them to push forward, to reach further to achieve their dreams, and to find and inspire new and unique solutions that empower them.
- Gen Z looks for brands to provide experiences that create community, a place of belonging, or something for them to be part of, or that they can share and be excited about.

Here's what you can expect

In **Chapter 1**, we consider some of the problems and challenges that brands and their agencies face when trying to connect with or market to tween, teen and young adult consumers. It's not easy, but we are all in the same boat. There can be very high immediate costs of failing to run authentic, relevant campaigns, as well as significant long-term implications of getting it wrong. We illustrate this with the story of a brand that continued their pursuit of a particular youth subculture over *several decades*, until they finally succeeded. The identity of this tenacious global brand may surprise you.

Chapter 2 starts to uncover the Gen Z identity – who they are, how they communicate, where they can be found, and what it is like to grow up in this generation. By digging in to who they are and what has shaped them and their behaviours, we start to understand how to approach them.

Chapter 3 offers some essential guidance to help you prepare your brand for success in the youth market. We look at the foundational 'truths' that help brands connect with Gen Z and cultivate a deeper understanding of the Gen Z mindset. In this chapter, we ask you to complete a five-part youth brand readiness audit, which will help you to identify any assumptions or obstacles that need to be addressed in order to succeed.

Chapter 4 begins with a discussion of youth culture in the age of individuality, and the challenge this creates for brands. Next, we cover the need for brands to evolve their segmentation methods in order to discover the target audiences that will work best with their brand. Whether you're just starting out, expanding your reach or just can't see the best path, we help you reconnect to yourself and your audiences, from general to niche groups and back again. You'll find here a comprehensive tool to help you connect with the like-minded segments that align with your brand *and* offer commercial viability.

In **Chapter 5** we talk about how to design and execute collaborative research strategies to reveal Gen Z's unspoken insights, so we are clear on how they can be actionable. We also talk about the recruitment strategies and the techniques and tools that we use to make our youth research methodologies engaging, effective and 'non-researchy'.

We end with a case study and an interview that illustrate the benefits of collaborative research.

Chapter 6 is all about building an effective youth engagement strategy playbook. We will guide you through the essential components, as well as explore the core strategies that align brands with Gen Z audiences. This is the culmination of all the work done in the previous chapters and sets you up for success.

Chapter 7 walks you through social strategies and tactical considerations for effectively reaching and engaging young consumers. We will cover practical ways to tune in to social, influence and emerging technologies such as virtual and augmented reality as well as some of the unwritten rules of social engagement that can make or break a brand's online presence. For brands using influencers in the United States, we also touch on the latest Federal Trade Commission (FTC) influencer guidelines so that you can make sure your brand is on track.

Chapter 8 is all about content. We revisit the Truths from Chapter 3 and apply them to content planning and strategy, and we look at how to incorporate voice and tone for each social platform. From hashtag selection to social platform vanity URLs, we cover the key elements every brand needs to consider when planning a content strategy that will resonate with Gen Z.

Chapter 9 outlines the key strategies required to build a functioning, vibrant and healthy online community with an emphasis on Gen Z. We cover content moderation, the importance of social reporting, community management roles and online privacy, including the US Children's Online Privacy Protection Act (COPPA) and the European Union's General Data Protection Regulation (GDPR). The case studies in this chapter will help you see the concept of online community management from a wider perspective.

Chapter 10 will get everyone responsible for your brand's bottom line to pull up their chairs and listen attentively. We present EMV (earned media value) as an important way to evaluate the performance of your brand's Gen Z-focused social and influence marketing campaigns based on actual engagement instead of assumptive impressions.

In **Chapter 11** we present our conclusion. We sum up what we've talked about throughout the book, and think about next steps, ideas and youth initiatives.

Finally, in the **Epilogue** we leave you with a few real-life stories from the youth marketing trenches. Some were successes, others failed, but each one helped to get us where we are today.

Aligning with youth culture is not an easy task, but this book will guide you through many of its complexities in ways that we have found to be successful. We will ask you to take a hard look at your brand, to identify any assumptions you may have, reassess your strategies and explore new ways to collaborate with this highly individualized generation. Even with the deepest insights and experience, youth marketing remains a challenge. Over the course of time, we've seen, *and made*, a lot of mistakes, but as a result we've learnt how to listen better to youth audiences and to communicate on their frequency. Each client, category, assignment, problem, timeline, budget and team personality is unique and poses a unique set of challenges, but what they all have in common is a need for alignment and connection with youth audiences. *The Gen Z Frequency* will act as your guide, as you...

Tune in and build credibility with Gen Z.

Reference

Nielsen (2017) [accessed 15 March 2018] The Nielsen Total Audience Report, *Nielsen Insights*, 12 July [Online] http://www.nielsen.com/us/en/insights/reports/2017/the-nielsen-total-audience-report-q1-2017.html

A true story of finding youth culture relevance

01

The more the world continues to become centred and focused around subcultures and tribes, the more it makes sense for brands to support and fuel those subcultures that in turn rely on those brands. The brand's capability to empower young consumers drives passion more than advertisements or empty narratives. It isn't just about imaging in terms of the product, but what the brand stands for that's important to youth culture.

GEOFFREY COLON, 2017, DESIGNER OF MARKETING
COMMUNICATIONS, MICROSOFT, AUTHOR OF *DISRUPTIVE MARKETING*

Embracing the conflicts with youth culture

Companies all over the world face similar challenges when targeting youth culture, but what makes understanding today's young consumers so difficult or elusive? While we were all young at some point, unless we are under the age of 21 in 2018 we are not a part of Gen Z. We can only gather second-hand intelligence, no matter how immersed we get. Gen Z is growing up in the world that *we* created, but they of course see it from a very different perspective. Some researchers have described youth culture as embodying values that are 'in conflict with those of the adult world' (Patil, 2014). How can adults connect authentically with a culture that is in conflict with them? There is undoubtedly a conflict of interests and priorities that needs to be overcome, but there are also many unexpected similarities and shared values. Look past your assumptions about youth culture and listen to this cohort when they tell you how they experience the world. See it from their perspective; embrace the conflicts or face the consequences.

We'll start this book with an example that illustrates some of the common principles that apply when connecting to a younger audience – principles that cross generations from Gen X to Gen Z. You don't have to throw away everything you know about young consumers and start again with each new group. (We are still talking about human behaviour, after all.) If we can establish a basic understanding of what works for youth culture across generations, we can more adeptly explore how an individual generation – whether Gen Z or another – develops and expresses their own identity, have their own conflicts and are a unique puzzle to solve.

No business is exempt from cultivating relevance

This is the true story of what one of the largest sports brands in the world went through to become the influential youth brand it is today. We are talking about Nike – now one of the most respected names in skateboarding and streetwear. Yet it wasn't always that way. In fact, Nike had to work through several evolutions before it could earn the acclaimed role it now has in youth culture. To understand the huge transformation it underwent, we have to jump back to the 1970s, when the brand first started to notice skateboarding.

Nike started its relationship with skateboarding casually, without any official athlete endorsements or sponsorship deals. It just 'flowed' boxes of shoes to support some of the popular skateboarding teams of the day, such as Alva, G&S and Powell Peralta. At most, Nike was involved in some competitions and events, and had some limited visibility in the scene. However, its presence in skateboarding had all but dried up by the late 1980s/early 1990s when skateboarding's popularity began to wane. Nothing much changed until 1995, which saw the debut of the ESPN X Games (the Extreme Games at that time) and was the year that action sports, which include skateboarding, hit the mass market. It was also the year that Nike became seriously interested in this burgeoning sport.

After sponsoring the 1995 X Games, Nike advertised in the top two skateboarding magazines during 1996, but it didn't go over well with many skaters. Then, during the 1997 X Games, it launched a beautiful, award-winning ad campaign – 'What if' – to promote its skateboard products (Blümlein, Schmid and Vogel, 2008). The mass-market ads asked the question, *What if* other sports were treated like skateboarding, and featured golfers and tennis players being hassled by the police, the way street skaters notoriously were (and still are)? While they were clearly in support of skateboarding, the ads failed to connect authentically with the skateboard community. This was in large part because the brand simply hadn't put enough time and investment into the culture, and the culture, in turn, wasn't ready to be courted.

In 1998, Nike launched its first dedicated skate line featuring state-of-the-art skateboarding shoes (Blümlein *et al*, 2008). It was completely different from any Nike skating presence before, and, as far as many core skaters were concerned, it was off the mark. The shoes debuted at the X Games that year in California to a lukewarm reception. Norm MacDonald (former general manager of Ultimate East, a division of Ultimate Distribution, a leading Canadian distributor) told us in 2018 that, 'The first pair of "skate" Nikes I saw were given out for free to officials and VIPs at the X Games in Mission Beach. Can't remember the year... I gave mine away.' Jaya Bonderov, a top professional skateboarder (and X Games Medallist), who at the time was a sponsored athlete for the original Nike skateboarding team, was obligated to publicly wear Nikes only, but even he had a hard time finding a model he could skate in. (This is according to co-author Gregg Witt, who saw at first hand what did and didn't work with Nike's first skate-shoe designs and initial market presence. Witt was also a partner at Adrenalin Skateboards with Bonderov.)

Nike's product line was cancelled after just 12 months (Robertson, 2004). It was still way off target, but it was also undeterred. It wanted the market, and so it would soon get back in the ring a little wiser.

Just don't expect to build a youth audience overnight

Entering a new market segment isn't easy for anyone, no matter how big or how successful a company is. If a segment is hard to reach, like skateboarding – a culture that is highly resistant to involvement from mainstream companies – the stakes only get higher. The skateboarding industry was initially populated by brands that came from *within* the culture: shoe brands such as 4CE, Aera, Axion, C1RCA, DC, DuFFS, DVS, Etnies, Emerica, éS and Sens. At the time, these smaller brands eclipsed Nike because, historically, anything even remotely mainstream was viewed with suspicion among the skate community.

When Blazers, Dunks and Air Jordans became go-to skateboarding shoes in the 1970s and 1980s, it was primarily because they were available, reasonably priced and had good board feel. In *The Search For Animal Chin* (IMDb, 2016) – an iconic skateboarding movie classic from Powell Peralta in 1987 – the final scene culminates in four of the most globally known skaters performing simultaneous handplants. Three out of four are conspicuously wearing Nike Air Jordans 1s. One of the pro-skaters, Lance Mountain, reported that many skaters at the time had been getting shoes from Vans, but the supply had dried up a bit, and the Bones Brigade (the team in the movie) were out of shoes, with the exception of Tony Hawk (back right). When a box of Air Jordan 1s arrived at Powell Peralta, Lance, Steve Caballero and Mike McGill liked them and put them to use (Palladini, 2009). Despite being a part of this iconic skateboarding moment, Nike was not engrained in the culture and it took another 25 years before Nike dominated the market.

Figure 1.1   Bones Brigade Animal Chin Ramp Four Handplants

SOURCE Photo courtesy J Grant Brittain, legendary skateboarding photographer. Illustrative element by Mike Carnevale

See trends before they undercut your plan

It was becoming evident that Nike's big-brand status could be an obstacle to acceptance by skateboarding culture, and that it would be more effective to get to know skateboarders at a grassroots level. In 2001, Nike partnered with Savier, a startup footwear brand from Portland, Oregon. Technically, Savier was an independent subsidiary, but it launched with Nike money and had full access to Nike's technology labs. Savier's president had even worked for Nike (and Burton Snowboards) before deciding to start his own skate-shoe company. It was a neat package that benefited both parties: Nike could keep a toe in the market without riling its detractors and Savier could operate with financial backing, but with little to no day-to-day oversight from the shoe giant. They both kept the partnership quiet.

At first, business looked good. With the playground of Nike's technology lab and factories, Savier developed some cool, functional features that skateboarders appreciated. Both pro and amateur riders made up the in-house test team, and they all received the development shoes and tested the technologies. Nike consistently held roundtables with the team and skaters from the community to discuss the colours and designs.

Savier formed close relationships within the community and focused on growing the market at a grassroots level. It supported local and amateur skaters across the country with products, hosted contests, helped repair public and DIY skateparks and even traded new Savier footwear in exchange for people's old shoes at events (right on the spot). Sales reps were at events to sell, but were also responsible for helping support the scene nationally. Legitimate skaters who were highly respected in the culture worked with them, the market was paying attention and they were fully immersed in the culture.

However, something wasn't quite right. As some of the smaller footwear brands were having trouble delivering on their technology and starting to fade, a trend towards low tech–low price began. Savier, by contrast, had great-quality technology, but its high-tech look and price point were not in tune with market trends.

For all the exhaustive grassroots community building, youth-culture brand positioning and the support of skateboarders, Savier had missed the mark on its *product*. Or, more accurately, the market had shifted away from the product it had. If it changed and followed the trend, it would be copy-catting, or always playing catch-up. Despite its great connections and acceptance by the skate community, in 2004 Savier closed its doors.

Establish a core audience and deepen the connection

Meanwhile, something interesting was happening. Nike was quietly pursuing its own brand-named skateboarding division, while simultaneously trying to figure out the real skateboarding culture. Launching Savier was a smart and versatile move by Nike to help work in and support the skateboarding scene: if it succeeded, great! If it didn't… well, it wasn't really them anyway. The full Savier/Nike connection was inevitably discovered, and it actually helped to blaze the trail for the legitimacy of Nike SB (Nike Skateboarding).

While still heading the soccer division at Nike, Sandy Bodecker (as of 2018, Nike's VP of Special Projects) had been watching action sports grow and wanted Nike to be a part of it, but it wasn't his main area of expertise. In 2000, he started to investigate the culture more deeply and met with Robbie Jeffers, who managed the Stüssy skateboarding team and was highly respected in the skate and streetwear communities. At first, Jeffers felt as mistrustful as the rest of the community, but Bodecker's commitment impressed him, and they agreed on three non-negotiable points:

Listen: Bring back the Nike Dunk.

Co-Create: Let the community (skateboarders) be involved in the shoe design process.

Commit: Invest in developing the right product and building the audience for a minimum of five years.

Jeffers became the Nike skateboarding team manager and sought out four pros who could ride *and* contribute to the development of the culture. Team member Richard Mulder has said that what got him to even consider a brand like Nike was that, 'They approached us from a place of humility. . . They didn't pretend to know it all' (Robertson, 2004). Nike SB was conceived.

Mulder, along with Reece Forbes, Gino Ianucci and Danny Supa, was known and deeply respected within the core street skateboarding scene: each was recognized as a 'skater's skater'. They all supported the Dunk and were actively consulted as the models were developed, and then sent boxes of test shoes to make sure the shoes were right. The ambassadors of skate were listened to, and Nike delivered a skate-centric product. These original four – and many after – became very invested in the partnership as a result of this process. 'The riders were very important to the process', Bodecker says (Robertson, 2004). 'This was an all-hands-on-deck effort with the early crew and it was the combined commitment to connect with, listen to and support the core community. That was the catalyst that helped get the ball rolling.'

Nike SB was launched with the 'Colors By' series in March 2002. Each of the four Nike SB Dunk Lows had a colour and material combination chosen by one of the four team riders. The Dunk was a shoe that skaters had originally chosen to skate in, and in bringing it back Nike had tuned in to the relationship that had been there all along. There were history and nostalgia associated with the shoe, as well as the skate-specific performance updates to the shoe by pro riders.

Later that year, Nike teamed up with Supreme, a retailer and street wear brand that at the time catered specifically to skaters and skate culture. Supreme took skate culture seriously, and incorporated collaborations with punk and hip-hop musicians, artists, designers and photographers. Production runs remained small to keep its gear exclusive and exclusively within the culture, where it belonged. In September 2002, Nike and Supreme released two colourways of the Dunk Low Pro SB, creating something that was exclusively for skaters, street culture and sneakerheads alike.

Nike SB launched as more of a skate lifestyle brand with a market-compatible low-tech, street-style vibe. It also chose to sell almost exclusively at independent shops, which reinforced its commitment to skate culture. The skate community took notice, and the Dunk started selling. The effort had limited national sell-through because the company was targeting a smaller, specific core market. Nike didn't want to come on too strong, but rather blend into the culture. It was committed to tremendous tactical change, and to a long-game approach. Its product was completely focused on skateboard culture: the support, ads, shops, artists, influencers – everything – all came from and were directed towards the community. Nike, effectively, became woven into the fabric of skateboarding. This was the key step in building the relationship that would eventually make it synonymous with skateboarding.

In 2004, Nike signed some big names in the skateboarding world: Paul Rodriguez and Lewis Marnell. This was shortly followed by its sponsorship of Stefan Janowski, Brian Anderson, Omar Salazar, Eric Koston and even one of the most influential skaters of all time – Lance Mountain – all by 2009. Nike sponsored collaborations with artists and musicians popular in skate culture (see the box below).

Notable brand collaborations

Stüssy, Huf (Keith Hufnagel), NYC graffiti legend Futura, and Brian 'Pushead' Shroeder (who created legendary graphics for Zorlac Skateboards and *Thrasher* Magazine). The collab with Staple resulted in a shoe so rare that those lucky enough to get one had to be sneaked out the back of the store and secretly into a taxi so they wouldn't get robbed. Bands loved by the culture, such as DelaSoul, Slayer, The Melvins and Dinosaur Jr., were all commemorated with a Dunk. In 2005 Nike and *Thrasher* Magazine collaborated on a Blazer, which commemorated an illustration that appeared on the magazine's cover in 1981. Beer brands were memorialized, wine companies were featured, and there was even a marijuana-inspired shoe called the Skunk, colabbed with artist Todd Bratrud of Consolidated Skateboards. The irreverent humour of skateboarding was immortalized in the 'Fallen Idols' pack of shoes, which were devoted to iconic controversies such as the 'PeeWee Herman' and 'Vanilla Ice' (Gordon, Engvall and Bengston, 2013).

The collabs that Nike formed between its Dunks and the characters and stories from street and youth culture were incredibly well received by the skateboarding world, but also, impressively, in the world at large. In fact, the Dunks became so big with sneakerheads and other segments that it was hard to tell who was buying more (VICE Sports, 2017). By 2013, Nike had gone from inconsequential to 55 per cent of the North American skate market alone, and skate-boarding, as a result, got a massive boost that brought it to a wider global audience (Gwilliam, 2014).

Ultimately, everyone makes mistakes; even an $11 billion company with plentiful assets can miss the mark. Not every organization, however, is able to come back from mistakes, assess, learn and keep trying until they get it right. That process takes courage, dedication and a laser-focused endgame in mind. Today, Nike is a company that is known for being highly tuned in to youth culture. It sets the bar when creating a skateboard legacy that Gen Z recognize and respect, and continues to partner with youth culture in revolutionary ways. What follows is a list of takeaways that reflect on the lessons of Nike's journey.

TL;DR *(too long; didn't read)*: chapter takeaways

- **Develop meaningful relationships with youth segments that align with your brand, and commit to them over the long haul.** Trends come and go in cycles. Adjusting your level of audience support is understandable, but baling out when markets are down can have serious negative implications – don't do it.

- **Let go of assumptions: what you think is true may not be to Gen Z.** Ask yourself, what do you deliver that young people need or want? Are you filling a needed gap in the marketplace; are you educat-ing or entertaining them? If you're not offering real value, then it might be wise to rethink your plans.

- **Identify what authenticity means to youth segment/s before trying to be *authentic*.** Don't just jump on a bandwagon and think you can belong to a culture. Authenticity can't be faked or bought.

- **See trends coming before they undercut your plan.** Employ or part-ner with cultural insiders to stay ahead of emerging trends that will impact the market: trying to play catch-up is a risky business for companies of any size.

- **Move with the frequency, be flexible, but stick to your core audience.** Collaborate with people and partners that align with your brand and help deepen the connection with your targeted youth audiences. As you expand and grow, avoid disrespecting the youth culture foundation that got you there.

References

Blümlein, J, Schmid, D and Vogel, D (2008) *Made for Skate: The illustrated history of skateboard footwear*, Faux Ami, Germany

Gordon, D, Engvall, N and Bengston, R (2013) [accessed 14 March 2018] The 100 Best Nike SBs of All Time, *Complex* [Online video] http://www.complex.com/sneakers/2013/06/the-100-best-nike-sbs-of-all-time/entourage-dunks

Gwilliam, A J (2014) [accessed 14 March 2018] What Does the Death of Nike Snowboarding Mean for the Future of Skateboarding? *HIGHSNOBIETY* [Online] https://www.highsnobiety.com/2014/10/13/what-does-the-death-of-nike-snowboarding-mean-for-the-future-of-skateboarding/

IMDb (2016) [accessed 19 March 2018] The Search for Animal Chin [Online video] www.imdb.com/title/tt0378720/

Palladini, D (2009) *Vans: Off the wall: Stories of sole from Van's Originals*, Abrams, Inc., New York

Patil, S (2014) [accessed 8 May 2018] A Sociological Perspective of Generation Gap, *International Journal of Innovative Research and Development* [Online] http://citeseerx.ist.psu.edu/viewdoc/download?doi=10.1.1.883.6420&rep=rep1&type=pdf

Robertson, J (2004) [accessed 14 March 2018] How Nike Got Street Cred: The $11 billion company overcame its corporate image to win over the fiercely independent skateboarding market, *CNN Money* [Online] www.money.cnn.com/magazines/business2/business2_archive/2004/05/01/368253/

VICE Sports (2017) [accessed 14 March 2018] Presented by Nike SBL: Fifteen Years of SB Dunk – Stories from the Inside Out [Online video] https://www.youtube.com/watch?v=K4Jsmg2oYH4

Gen Z

A sociological perspective

02

Don't call us anything. The whole notion of cohesive generations is nonsense.

KIERNAN MAJERUS-COLLINS, 2018, AGE 22, DEMOCRATIC PARTY
CHAIRMAN, LEWISTON, MAINE (BROMWICH, 2018)

Tuning in to Gen Z

Every new generation has a desire to evolve from the one before and Gen Z is no exception. This unique, mobile-first demographic, raised on technology and unprecedented access to information, is impacting every facet of society. Anyone who wants to succeed in marketing, educating, or connecting with Gen Z will need to be tuned in.

We explain how throughout this book as we share key insights, strategies and tactics that your organization can deploy to build credibility and tune in with the unique cultural preferences of Gen Z. While you're learning these approaches, we also encourage you to look beyond merely viewing Gen Z as a set of statistics in a spreadsheet or target demographic that enhances your bottom line and get to know Generation Z, their culture and as people (AwesomenessTV, 2017).

Along with the foundational demographic information you'll find in this chapter, we introduce you to Jenk Oz, the youngest Gen Z CEO in Britain; you'll learn how students in Ireland are using virtual reality (VR) in their classrooms; and we share why the Tony Award-winning Broadway musical 'Dear Evan Hansen' resonated so deeply with US youth culture. If that sounds like a diverse collection of information, just wait until you meet the individuals who are creating the culture of this dynamic and rising generation.

The Gen Z frequency

To understand Gen Z, you must first understand their lives, digital habits, struggles, role models, cultural touchstones, how they manage Fear of Missing Out (FOMO) and figuring out where they fit into a rapidly changing world. However, most of what sets this generation apart is an unrelenting relationship with information, media consumption and mobile technology. During the past few years, we have conducted hundreds of interviews with Gen Z kids, tweens, teens and young adults and have distilled our findings into a list of youth culture attributes. These generational markers are the identifying traits of what will be the most significant global demographic shift in history.

Gen Z generational markers

- **Independent:** Gen Z is willing to work hard for success vs the 'be discovered' mentality prevalent among their older Millennial siblings.
- **Diverse:** As a global cohort, Gen Z is open to all ethnicities, races, genders and orientations. They expect to see those values reflected in their brands, classrooms and media.
- **Engaged:** Gen Z is very politically aware and actively involved in supporting environmental, social impact and civil rights causes. They are focused on making the world a better place and want to align with organizations dedicated to making a difference. Activists like Malala Yousafzai are their role models.
- **Knowledge managers:** Often misrepresented as having a 'short attention span', Gen Z has developed an ability to quickly filter the mass quantities of information that appear on their screens and decide what is worthwhile and what should be filtered and discarded.

- **Pragmatic:** Raised by Gen X parents who experienced a similar childhood shaped by a recession, Gen Z are choosing more pragmatic careers (for example, selecting a legal profession instead of trying to be a YouTuber influencer), are financially conservative and are avoiding the social media privacy pitfalls of Millennials.

- **Personal brands:** Unlike Millennials who tended to overshare on social media, young people are managing their presence like a brand; privacy matters and contributes to the popularity of ephemeral social media apps such as Snapchat and Instagram.

- **Collaborative:** Whether it is in the classroom using Skype with students in another country, playing eSports on Twitch or team sports in their backyard, Gen Z has learnt early in life the importance of collaboration in both local and distributed (or virtual) environments.

Defining Gen Z

The bulk of this generation, born approximately between 1996 and 2011 and currently in their teen years, are a group yet to be fully defined. For Gen Z there is no definitive date, but this range is the broadest accepted in the industry.

Gen Z culture

Overwhelmingly, the primary driver of (most) Gen Z life is finding a balance between their offline and social media identities. Often this results in the creation of multiple social media personas that are a hybrid of both their aspirations and the reality of their offline lives. Fuelled by easy access to social technologies, streaming media, external cultural and demographic forces, in some ways their childhood is shorter than for previous generations. Yet in others, they remain 'kids' longer than previous generations of teens, with a trend towards delaying behaviours associated with adulthood, such as drug use, sexual activity and driving.

However, one of the major differences between the offline actions of previous generations and the online actions of the youth in this mobile age is the way the internet can now take whatever information they post and amplify it way beyond their immediate group, and potentially even turn it viral. For some, this *social media amplification* is about propelling them into being internet famous, but for the majority, social media offer a way to be validated. Ultimately, this aspect of being seen and heard and belonging to something bigger than oneself is one of the core motivators for Gen Z.

Raising Gen Z: same behaviours, new tools

As social media natives, this is the first generation in human history that views behaviours such as status updates, texting, selfies, social networking, mobile devices and 'information at your fingertips' as an everyday part of life. In many ways, Gen Z is experiencing many of the same behavioural patterns that their parents did as kids; they are just using different tools and technology to create the same artefacts of youth culture as their parents, siblings and peers.

Think of it this way: you may have had a phone (the one with the cord that you could only use in your house and had no web access); they have a mobile phone (the one without a cord and 24/7/365 web access). You perhaps made home movies using a camcorder and shared them on your VHS player; they make videos on their phone and upload them to YouTube, Instagram TV and Snapchat. You took pictures with a Polaroid and shared them with friends; they take pictures with their phone and publish them in real time to Instagram. You made mixtapes; they make playlists on Spotify, Apple Music or YouTube. You hung out at the mall with friends; they hang out with friends and online communities on Houseparty, Snapchat and Instagram with friends. In the end, they are exhibiting the same behaviours but using different tools to meet their need for self-expression.

A few short years ago, students wrote a mean thing about other kids on the bathroom wall, and the school janitor quickly removed it. Now bullying is shared on Twitter, Snapchat or Instagram, and it is seen by a wider audience and has a more significant emotional impact. One thing is clear: the *ways in which* Gen Z youth consume information and communicate are fundamentally different from earlier generations. For this cohort, all forms of media are a social experience that can be shared with the tap of a finger.

Gen Z: a phenomenon without borders

Data from Population Pyramid (2017) show that the current population of Gen Z is estimated to be a little more than 1.9 billion, or 27 per cent of the global population. As of 2010, the population of Gen Z globally was 1.86 billion (Population Pyramid, 2017). With the exception of the United States, some of the most significant Gen Z growth is taking place in countries that are either developing or underdeveloped countries.

According to a 2017 study by the World Bank, 42 per cent of the world's population is under the age of 25, with most of that growth taking place in South Asia and sub-Saharan Africa, comprising almost half (525 million) of the global youth population (Khokhar, 2017). When it comes to reaching Gen Z, it's critical that you adopt a global mindset. Your next significant market opportunity may be in Lagos, not Los Angeles or London. Listed below are the top 10 countries by Gen Z's percentage of total national population. The supporting statistics included are each country's total Gen Z population and its percentage of the global Gen Z population:

India

– 2017 Gen Z population total 373 million
– 2017 percentage of global Gen Z population 20%

China

– 2017 Gen Z population total 260 million
– 2017 percentage of global Gen Z population 14%

Nigeria

– 2017 Gen Z population total 68 million
– 2017 percentage of global Gen Z population 4%

Indonesia

- 2017 Gen Z population total 65 million
- 2017 percentage of global Gen Z population 3.5%

The United States

- 2017 Gen Z population total 62 million
- 2017 percentage of global Gen Z population 3.4%

Pakistan

- 2017 Gen Z population total 61 million
- 2017 percentage of global Gen Z population 3.3%

Brazil

- 2017 Gen Z population total 50 million
- 2017 percentage of global Gen Z population 2.7%

Bangladesh

- 2017 Gen Z population total 46 million
- 2017 percentage of global Gen Z population 2.5%

The Philippines

- 2017 Gen Z Population Total 33 million
- 2017 percentage of global Gen Z population 1.8%

Mexico

- 2017 Gen Z Population Total 33 million
- 2017 percentage of global Gen Z population 1.8%

SOURCE Adapted from Population Pyramid; Singh, 2017

Research conducted in 2017 by Sapient, a global consulting firm (which considered Gen Z to range from 1995 to 2010), also found that most of the growth in the younger segment of the Gen Z population is coming from developing and underdeveloped countries. For example, the 2017 research from Sapient points out that in 2010, as much as 43 per cent of Nigeria's population are classified as Gen Z youth, while in Germany this demographic youth group accounted for only 13.5 per cent of the total populace (Singh, 2017).

Figure 2.1   The percentage of Gen Z in each of the selected country's populations

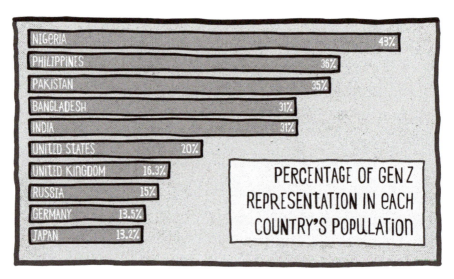

NIGERIA — 43%
PHILIPPINES — 36%
PAKISTAN — 35%
BANGLADESH — 31%
INDIA — 31%
UNITED STATES — 20%
UNITED KINGDOM — 16.3%
RUSSIA — 15%
GERMANY — 13.5%
JAPAN — 13.2%

PERCENTAGE OF GEN Z REPRESENTATION IN EACH COUNTRY'S POPULATION

SOURCE   Data taken from Singh (2017). Illustration by Mike Carnevale

Spotlight: Malala Yousafzai, Gen Z activist

One of the most well-known Gen Z icons is Pakistani schoolgirl Malala Yousafzai, who at the age of 11 started an anonymous diary documenting life in northwest Pakistan's Swat valley. In 2009, there was a ban on girls' education. In her diary, she expressed her desire to continue going to school and for all girls around the world to have the right to an education.

As reported by the BBC (2017), her diary was published (anonymously) and her story immediately captivated the world. It also enraged the Taliban. Her identity was eventually exposed and in October 2012 she was shot during an attack on her school bus. After the shooting, she and her family relocated to England, where she not only recovered but also became an advocate spokesperson for the rights of girls around the world. Moreover, the world noticed.

In 2013, she released her autobiography *I Am Malala* and was named one of *TIME* magazine's most influential people. In 2014, Malala was awarded the Nobel Peace Prize, the youngest and first Pakistani and Gen Z person to win the prestigious prize. For many Gen Z members, Malala is a real-life heroine who has inspired countless numbers of girls around the world to stand up for their rights and be engaged in the world (BBC, 2017).

For Gen Z, diversity matters

For Gen Z, diversity is more than a buzzword. It is their reality. The most current US Census noted that there had been a 50 per cent increase in bi-racial youth since 2000, up to nearly 4.5 million (US Census, 2010a). The outcome of a sharp rise in multiracial marriages in the United States, Gen Z is the most diverse and multicultural of any generation in the United States. Fifty-five per cent are Caucasian, 24 per cent are Hispanic, 14 per cent are African American and 4 per cent are Asian (US Census, 2010b). Moreover, the number of mixed white-and-black bi-racial and the number of bi-racial white-and-Asian grew 134 and 87 per cent respectively (US Census, 2010a). In the first decade of the 21st century, the Hispanic population continued to grow at four times the rate of the total US population. This demographic shift towards racial diversity will continue to impact the views and perspectives of this generation (Nielsen, 2017).

The most significant influence on their attitudes towards race was the election of Barack Obama as the President of the United States. Propelled into office, mainly by a substantial turnout of youth voters, his election set a precedent and expectation that anyone could grow up and become the President of the United States, regardless of race, gender or background. For Gen Z youth under 15, Obama was the only president they knew until Trump. That consciously and unconsciously shaped their understanding of opportunity and equality. This is not just a phenomenon in the United States. In 2016, Sadiq Khan was elected as the first Muslim mayor of London.

However, for Gen Z, the idea of diversity has also transcended race. Once almost absent from all mass media, LGBTQ+ (Lesbian, Gay, Bisexual, Transgender, Queer and others) characters and stories are now commonplace in movies, TV and popular culture. Even terms such as 'gender fluidity' and gender-neutral pronouns are a part of mainstream youth culture (Valens, 2017). A significant number of schools we visit have a student in gender transition. It's a reality that would have been unimaginable as early as five years ago. As the first generation to grow up in an era when same-sex marriage was considered the norm, equality for their LGBTQ+ friends and family is non-negotiable. Social media platforms such as Tumblr and Twitter have also provided many teens and tweens with access to online communities where they share, learn, support and connect with LGBTQ+ youth outside their immediate circle of friends and family.

Because of this new openness and acceptance of sexual orientations and gender fluidity, youth are feeling more comfortable to embrace the sexual orientations of friends, parents, family and, in many cases, themselves. The key takeaway for marketers to remember is that marketing to these communities is not a right; instead, it is something that must be earned by listening and learning about the many facets of the community, being a brand upstander, creating opportunities for authentic connection and inspiring everyone to be more accepting.

Gen Z, technology and media

Gen Z has a relationship with the internet that is different from previous generations. It is a place where they communicate with their friends, share content and spend their free time, but it is also a research tool and a voice. Armed with a mobile device and a social media megaphone, this generation will use Google to fact-check brands, determine if the product has good reviews, or find out if something is real or 'fake news' in real time. For brands, this means being thoroughly Googled, which is how Gen Z will determine if that brand has any credibility. Brands need to be 'Google-proof!' For example, if your brand is testing on animals or is not being an upstander for LGBTQ rights, they will find out and hold you publicly accountable on Instagram, Facebook and Twitter. Also unlike older internet users, and contrary to what you may hear on the news, this generation cares deeply about privacy. For example, research conducted by the National Cyber Security Alliance in 2017 found that teens and young adults are more proactive in managing their digital footprint than older adults (Raicu, 2016).

Spotlight: Jack Andraka, Gen Z inventor

In many ways, Jack Andraka is a typical high school student who likes to hang out with his friends, drink chocolate milk and wear red Nike sneakers. However, Jack is no ordinary teenager. As a freshman, Jack invented a test that can detect early onset pancreatic cancer and won the Smithsonian American Ingenuity Award and the Intel International Science and Engineering Fair.

Jack's test, the first of its kind for pancreatic cancer, can detect the disease with just a drop of blood. That breakthrough has led to a flourish of interest from the scientific community along with several patents, TED talks, and talks at international ideas festivals (Tucker, 2012).,At just 17, this young inventor is making scientific breakthroughs that will save lives and change the face of cancer research. Jack is an example of how Gen Z, even at such a young age, isn't afraid to take on and find solutions for significant problems.

Gen Z is constantly connected

Mobile phones are *the* essential piece of technology in Gen Z life. It is the gateway to all things that matter to them (social life, texting, social networking, music, friends, pictures, video and more). The mobile phone is their 'social oxygen' around which all aspects of youth culture revolve. Moreover, the age of smartphone ownership has aged down to the point where it is not unusual to see third graders with cell phones in their school backpacks. The vital role of mobile devices is especially evident for youth living in urban and rural areas where they do not have access to broadband internet service. Minority youth in the United States, for example, bridge the digital divide using mobile devices to connect with their peers on social networking platforms such as Facebook, Instagram and Twitter and engage with online communities, school work and fandoms (Palley, 2012).

However, this is also true outside of developed nations such as the United Kingdom or Australia. Research conducted by Sapient in 2017 reported that Indian telecom Juxt found that in many emerging markets, such as China, India, Egypt and other African countries, mobile devices are bridging the broadband divide. In India, for example, over 10 million people use mobile phones as their primary access point to the internet, with the majority of those living in rural areas (Singh, 2017).

Gen Z is 'always on'. A study by the Kaiser Family Foundation (KFF) (Kaiser Family Foundation, 2012) found that US kids between 8 and 18 spend an average of 6.5 hours a day absorbed in media. All totalled, it comes to 45 hours a week (KFF, 2012) spent watching TV or streaming videos, playing video games, posting photos, listening to music and surfing the social web – more than a full-time job.

As a result of this constant connection, Gen Z has learnt to become expert multi-taskers. For example, they do not just watch TV or stream videos on Netflix. That is a passive activity. Instead, they will 'watch TV' and videos on YouTube in real time with friends and fire back commentary via text messaging, social media platforms such as Tumblr or Twitter and creating and sharing visual narratives (screenshots, GIFs, video clips). The primary downside to being 'always on' is sleep deprivation. This generation is attached to social media, and many of them are sleeping with their phones close at hand and texting at all hours of the night, with resultant increased levels of anxiety (Hunt, 2017).

Above all, social media is like a lifeline for maintaining and strengthening relationships with Gen Z. They use social networks to strengthen their existing 'real world' relationships, not to connect with strangers. For most, communication does not necessarily mean having a verbal conversation. A 'conversation' can mean anything from an Instagram 'Heart' to comment on Snapchat or a text message. In *Gen Z: Digital in their DNA* (Palley, 2012), a study of 800 youth in the United States and the United Kingdom reported that most of the Gen Z youth attached more importance to digital connections than to money, music and movies.

They are perpetually connected to their peers, friends, teachers, parents and content through social media apps on mobile phones. Their experience with mobile technology and content creation resources, online communities and digital media encourages them to be open to more diverse backgrounds.

How Gen Z uses visual social media

Gen Z navigates their social media anxieties by relying on visual-centric social media, such as GIFs, memes and emoji, to provide visual interpretations of shared cultural experiences and project their own emotions into their social media feeds (Walczer and Baird, forthcoming 2018). The use of visual descriptors allows them to collaboratively solve their collective and individual problems, learn new knowledge and coping skills from one another, and provide peer-to-peer support. They also serve as avenues to embrace more empowered positions of digital citizenship on topics some may find difficult to talk about or express at home or in school (Highfield and Leaver, 2016).

Spotlight: Gen Z pop culture – *Dear Evan Hansen*

When viewed through the lenses of popular youth culture, the hit Broadway musical *Dear Evan Hansen* provides educators, and marketers, with a unique perspective on the role that visual social media and visual narrative artefacts play in the lives of Gen Z youth (Walczer and Baird, forthcoming 2018). *Dear Evan Hansen* (DEH), the winner of the 2017 Tony for Best Musical, is the story of a teen named Evan Hansen, played by Tony Award-winning actor Ben Platt, who, like many Gen Z, faces a daily struggle with social anxiety. In mid-2016, as DEH began to bubble up in the popular culture, teens around the country simultaneously engaged with communities on Tumblr and Instagram to share how DEH felt like a mirror of their unfiltered emotions and unspoken anxieties on the pressures of popularity and social media.

The musical struck a nerve and resonated with many youths, who saw in Evan Hansen the first authentic portrayal of their daily reality. DEH quickly became a cultural phenomenon and spread using the community hashtag #YouWillBeFound. In short, through Evan Hansen many youths felt as if they had found their tribe. Many teens suffer from the effects of social media bullying and anxiety in silence (Pappas, 2015), and for many of them, DEH was the first piece of popular culture that made them feel that they were not alone in experiencing these feelings. In many ways, *Dear Evan Hansen* became a form of self-care, with members of the community (aka 'Fansens') combining fan art, social media and hashtags

(#YouWillBeFound) to create self-care memes. They distributed them on Tumblr, YouTube and Instagram as rallying points to combat cyberbullying directly as well as other issues, including depression, anxiety, self-harm and suicide.

The key takeaway here is that youth recognize the power they have when they self-organize and remix themes into digital visual stories that suit their platform preferences and community identities. Social media provide them with a platform to express their feelings as well as help other teens struggling with social anxiety issues. This phenomenon is both relevant and timely, as Lady Gaga's anti-bullying initiative, *The Born This Way Foundation*, recently launched *The Kindness Project* with the cast of *Dear Evan Hansen* to talk about the impact of bullying, kindness and mental health.

> Note: adapted from the forthcoming (2018) *#YouWillBeFound: Leveraging 'Dear Evan Hansen' on Instagram and Tumblr to combat cyberbullying and empower teens* (Walczer and Baird, forthcoming 2018).

Gen Z speak emoji. Do you?

Emojis, the once-obscure collection of smiley faces and cartoon poop, have migrated their way into pop culture, brand communications, the tweets of pop stars, and brand advertising. You might be wondering what they all mean and how a brand should use them. The bottom line is: there is no straightforward answer. There's no translation for a wave next to a heart next to a laughing cat! In fact, that is part of what made emojis so popular with youth culture in the first place.

The truth is, Gen Z use emojis to tell a story or convey emotion, but in many cases they are merely a digital artifact that is used to make a conversation more visually appealing and tell a story. Deployed strategically, they can also be used as an emotional barometer to lighten the mood, provide an emotional context to avoid the misinterpretation of text-only communication, or reflect the seriousness or sadness of an event (Highfield and Leaver, 2016). The key here for brands is to use them sparingly and in an authentic context. As discussed previously, the worst thing a brand can do to its credibility and authenticity with Gen Z is try to be someone it is not.

Gen Z and fandoms

In today's world, brands can no longer expect to reach Gen Z by relying on traditional or one-way marketing channels (print, TV or radio advertising) alone. An effective alternative is to learn to engage with fandoms and online communities. A fandom, if you are wondering, is a group or community built around a mutual affinity for a book series (Harry Potter), TV show (*Riverdale*), the movie (*Star Wars*), artist (Camila Cabello) or other pop culture artefact (*Dear Evan Hansen*). These fandoms are fuelled by a combination of pop culture, social media and the use of a standardized, distributed hashtag which allows members of the fandom to self-identify as a fan, find others who share the same passion, validate their decision to join the fandom and, through the creation of social media artifacts, drive their fandom into the mainstream.

For many tweens and teens, joining a fandom means they get to collaborate with others while working to shape their own identities; find, create and participate in communities; set goals; and negotiate the ways brands, marketers and educators reach them. Fandoms are an integral part of the Gen Z identity, providing young people with a community of supporters who share their love for certain stories, characters and fictional worlds. The members of the fandom create meaning around works of fiction and make them a reality. When evaluating the idea of fandom, it is essential to redefine our concept of what constitutes a legitimate 'social system' or 'social interaction' (Baird, 2016a).

Moreover, because the fandoms are created on the internet, it opens the fandom to making connections across the globe. Anthropologist Lori Kendall (2002) spent years researching the dynamics of online social identity, fandoms and community, and concluded that members of fandoms have 'intact social systems and highly charged social relations'. Fandoms are created organically when real people connect with a character, content or story. As a brand, your job is to find authentic ways to celebrate and support a fandom that pops up around your content, without co-opting or directing the community culture. Think about what visual narratives or memes or other content assets you can create to help your community and make the fandom move forward.

Spotlight: Jenk Oz, Gen Z entrepreneur

Jenk Oz is a young actor, entrepreneur and musician with access to events, experiences and celebrities that his friends could only dream of. That's not all. As Britain's youngest CEO, Jenk is using iCoolKid – a digital media platform aimed at Gen Z – to share these experiences and create content, social media and a community that he designed with his generation in mind. The core brand message of iCoolKid is to encourage other young people to be passionate about their interests and hobbies and to make their dreams a reality.

Jenk started iCoolKid in 2014, when he was eight years old, as part of a school project to share the 'cool things' he was doing outside school. His newsletter grew from something he shared with his friends at school into an international website being embraced by kids from across the United Kingdom, United States, India and around the world. iCoolKid is now a digital publishing, media, consulting and production company providing original content for Gen Z. As CEO, Jenk manages a team of professionals who produce articles, previews, reviews and features, as well as original music. As the face of the iCoolKid brand, Oz attends all the coolest pop culture events, movie premieres and live events, and conducts interviews backstage with A-list celebrities such as Idris Elba. In 2017, Jenk was invited to speak at TEDxYouth in Harlow, Essex. In his presentation, Jenk shared his strategies for getting your ideas out of your head and building them into a real company.

Jenk is a harbinger of a dynamic generational cohort that is ready to roll up their sleeves to create and build a future filled with media that reflect what's most important to them. For Gen Z, it seems, the sky's the limit. Jenk is representative of both the entrepreneurial spirit of Gen Z and an example of how they are building their own brands through the efficient and strategic use of social media. Brands need look no further than the type of content being created by iCoolKid to learn what type of content and social media interaction resonates with youth audiences.

Educating Gen Z

The innate digital learning styles of this generation include fluency in digital media, online communities, guided mentoring, video games or collective reflection via social media platforms (Baird and Fisher, 2010). To actively engage learners in the classroom, educators should focus on providing content that allows the pupil to understand the context of the learning objectives while utilizing various forms of social media and emerging technologies such as virtual reality (VR) and augmented reality (AR).

Understanding and incorporating these digital learning experiences into your frontline and online curriculum will increase student motivation and enhance the delivery of instruction while meeting the needs of today's digital learning styles (Baird and Fisher, 2010). The use of mobile devices in the classroom should be directly connected with their personal experiences and authentic use of technology outside school. The key is to create an experience that will allow them to access information, communicate collaboratively, and create content using mobile devices and new digital skills such as VR and AR technologies in the classroom.

Gen Z digital learning attributes

- **Interactive**: Use interactive, engaging content and material that motivates them to engage through the creative use of social media, conceptual review and community feedback. Gen Z also expects to find, use and 'mash-up' various types of web-based media, such as audio, video, multimedia, edutainment and educational gaming/simulation.

- **Student centred**: Shifts the learning responsibility to the student and emphasizes teacher-guided instruction and modelling. Customized, interactive and social media tools, and ability to self-direct how they learn.

- **Situated**: Reconcile classroom use of social media with how technology is used outside the classroom. Use of technology should be tied to both authentic (learning) activity and intrinsic motivation.

- **Collaborative:** Learning is a social activity, and students learn best through observation, collaboration, and intrinsic motivation and from self-organizing social systems comprised of peers in either a virtual or in-person environment.

- **On demand:** Gives the ability to multitask, handle multiple streams of information and juggle both short- and long-term goals. Access content via different media platforms, including mobile, PC based, or another handheld (portable) computer device.

- **Authentic:** Deploy active and meaningful activities based on real-world learning models. Industry-driven problems and situations should be the focus and require reflective elements, multiple perspectives and collaborative processes for relevant applicable responses from today's student.

SOURCE Adapted from *Digital Learning Styles 2.0: Digital, social, and always-on* (Baird, 2006).

Teaching Gen Z with emerging technologies

Technologies such as VR and AR provide Gen Z with opportunities to engage in a social, collaborative and active learning environment (Baird, 2018). In an evaluation report on the MissionV Schools Pilot Programme in Ireland, Dr Conor Galvin, a professor at University College School of Education, found that the use of VR technology in the classroom showed a real benefit in tackling students' social issues (Baird, 2017). For example, Galvin points out that the students struggling to be included in their classroom were able to become accepted by their peers because of their technology skills. Integrating the VR project into the curriculum allowed shy students to 'come out of their shells' and boosted confidence in students who were previously lacking in confidence in their maths skills.

While it is still a relatively new technology as far as its educational context is concerned, there are already some great AR experiences available for educational uses. For a generation that's been raised on interactive technologies, bringing AR into the classroom and curriculum can also help encourage active engagement and contribute to student retention (Baird, 2016b). For example, AR helps students who are visual learners gain a better understanding of the concepts that the teacher has explained in class lectures or that they have read about in traditional textbooks. AR is also a valuable assessment tool, allowing students to demonstrate proficiency in a variety of subjects.

AR is also a useful pedagogical strategy to enhance learning with flashcards, pop-up books or textbooks embedded with interactive media. It's clear that AR is rapidly finding its way into 21st-century classrooms. For example, Google is using its Google Cardboard VR viewer for schools, creating original content through its Google Expeditions Pioneer Program which takes students on a virtual tour of the ocean, historic sites and more (Baird, 2017).

One thing is clear: as Gen Z move from the classroom to the workforce, it will be increasingly essential to deepen our understanding of these burgeoning digital learning styles and prepare educational and training programmes (online and off) to meet them on their own territory (Baird, 2018).

Spotlight: Gen Z – virtual reality in the classroom

Students at St. Kieran's, a school in the Irish town of Broughal, recently went on a field trip to Clonmacnoise, a nearby ancient monastic site with historic ruins. Nothing unusual or exceptional about that, right? What makes this school field trip surprising, though, is what the students did when they came *back* to the classroom. The students, part of a VR pilot programme in Irish schools, used the MissionV VR platform to create a virtual model of the Clonmacnoise ruins in OpenSim and then viewed it using Oculus Rift headsets.

In this VR Clonmacnoise example, these 10–12-year-old students utilized technology (maths, scripting, 3D modelling, programming), creative thinking skills (archaeology, history, design) and social skills (project management, collaboration, face-to-face interaction) in a constructivist-based project environment to create a VR experience (Ó Muíneacháin, 2014). In short, for Gen Z, it is not just about technology, it is about relationships. Social interaction will continue to be at the heart of any active Gen Z offline (traditional) or online (learning) or virtual learning environment (AR or VR). Brands that want to embrace these emerging AR/VR technologies in new products, marketing, and campaigns need to be aware of the role that content creators and VR developers play regarding media literacy and creating experiences deemed factual by Gen Z audiences (Baird, 2018).

TL;DR: chapter takeaways

- **Identify ways your brand can have 'non-verbal' conversations with Gen Z.** What types of digital artifacts (GIF, meme, emoji) can you use to enhance the conversation?

- **Consider strategies that capitalize on the growing global generation.** With a majority of Gen Z living in developing countries, do you have a mobile-only strategy to reach Gen Z consumers in India, Nigeria and other countries where mobile devices are the only way to connect?

- **Review your marketing campaigns from the past three years.** Do the young people in your advertising and content reflect the diverse (racial, gender, orientation) populations that comprise Gen Z?

- **Conduct social listening for your brand on social media platforms such as Instagram and Twitter, or online forums such as Reddit.** Find out what Gen Z is saying about your brand, organization or educational institution.

- **Don't treat Gen Z as one monolithic target market.** Every sub-segment within this diverse generational cohort has different needs, wants and frequencies, even when they share common values such as inclusiveness.

- **Where Gen Z is concerned, mobile is the great leveller, providing brands with access to nearly every consumer in the world.** Your ticket to entry starts by developing mobile-first marketing communications and engagement strategies with youth culture.

- **Gen Z is already producing incredible changemakers such as Jenk Oz, Malala Yousafzai and Jack Andraka.** Their stories give brands a preview of the leading edge of a generation with unprecedented access to digital media, knowledge and ambition. YouTube and other global digital communities will bring many more changemakers to the forefront.

- **Comprising 25 per cent of the US population, Gen Z is going to be larger than Boomers, Xers and Millennials.** Gen Z is set to influence nearly 600 billion dollars of family spending and will comprise 40 per cent of consumers by 2020.

- **Gen Z is a global phenomenon.** Marketers should look to emerging markets such as Nigeria, Southeast Asia and Mexico for opportunities to reach Gen Z.

- **The democratization of media, means of production and distribution of content has shifted power to the youth audiences and creators themselves.** Gen Z consumes social content often – going there as a first option over 'traditional media'. This makes social platforms like YouTube, Snapchat, Twitch, Instagram, and other rising and emerging platforms, legitimate competitors to major digital media companies.

References

AwesomenessTV (2017) [accessed 15 October 2017] Gen Z: The Audience You Can't Ignore [Online] https://awesomenesstv.com/genz/

Baird, D (2006) [accessed 23 September 2017] Learning Styles 2.0: Digital, Social and Always On [Online] www.debaird.net/blendededunet/2006/04/learning_styles.html

Baird, D (2016a) [accessed 2 September 2017] Identity & Member Roles in Online Communities [Online] www,medium.com/@derekeb/identity-member-roles-in-online-communities-3efdea78fc20

Baird, D (2016b) [accessed 2 September 2017] The Social Life of Virtual Reality Learning [Online] www.debaird.net/blendededunet/2016/01/how-virtual-reality-encourages-active-learning.html

Baird, D (2017) [accessed 25 September 2017] Top Educational Virtual Reality Experiences: Virtual Reality Pop [Online] https://virtualrealitypop.com/top-educational-virtual-reality-experiences-ae323d04951e

Baird, D (2018) [accessed 9 January 2018] Student Perspectives on Virtual Reality (VR) in the Classroom [Online] https://virtualrealitypop.com/student-perspectives-on-using-virtual-reality-vr-in-the-classroom-76d5839444fe

Baird, D and Fisher, M (2010) [accessed 22 September 2017] Neomillennial User Experience Design Strategies: Utilizing Social Networking Media to Support 'Always on' Learning Styles [Online] http://journals.sagepub.com/doi/abs/10.2190/6WMW-47L0-M81Q-12G1

BBC (2017) [accessed 19 September 2017] Profile: Malala Yousafzai [Online] www.bbc.com/news/world-asia-23241937

Bromwich, J (2018) [accessed 13 March 2018] We Asked Gen Z to Pick a Name. It Wasn't Gen Z [Online] https://www.nytimes.com/2018/01/31/style/generation-z-name.html

Highfield, T and Leaver, T (2016) [accessed 24 December 2017] Instagrammatics and digital methods: studying visual social media, from selfies and GIFs to memes and emoji, *Communication Research and Practice* **2** (1) [Online] https://doi.org/10.1080/22041451.2016.1155332

Hunt, E (2017) [accessed 12 September 2017] Teenagers' Sleep Quality and Mental Health at Risk over Late-Night Mobile Phone Use [Online] www.theguardian.com/lifeandstyle/2017/may/30/teenagers-sleep-quality-and-mental-health-at-risk-over-late-night-mobile-phone-use

Kaiser Family Foundation (KFF) (2012) M2: Media in the Lives of 8–18 Year Olds [accessed 19 September 2017] https://www.kff.org/other/report/generation-m2-media-in-the-lives-of-8-to-18-year-olds/

Kendall, L (2002) [accessed 11 October 2017] *Hanging Out in the Virtual Pub: Masculinities and relationships online,* University of California Press [Online] www.ucpress.edu/book.php?isbn=9780520230385

Khokhar, T (2017) [accessed 15 September 2017] Chart: How is the World's Youth Population Changing?, World Bank [Online] www.blogs.worldbank.org/opendata/chart-how-worlds-youth-population-changing

Nielsen (2017) [accessed 21 October 2017] Youth Movement: Gen Z Boasts the Largest Most Diverse Media Users Yet [Online] www.nielsen.com/us/en/insights/news/2017/youth-movement-gen-z-boasts-the-largest-most-diverse-media-users-yet.html

Ó Muíneacháin, C (2014) [accessed 18 September 2017] Irish Kids Create a Virtual Reality, Explore it in Oculus Rift [Online] www.technology.ie/irish-kids-create-virtual-world-explore-using-oculus-rift-video/

Palley, W (2012) [accessed 29 September 2017] Study: Gen Z Immersed in Technology, J Walter Thompson Intelligence [Online] www.jwtintelligence.com/2012/09/data-point-gen-z-immersed-in-technology/

Pappas, S (2015) [accessed 8 July 2017] Social Media Cyber Bullying Linked to Teen Depression, *Scientific American* [Online] www.scientificamerican.com/article/social-media-cyber-bullying-linked-to-teen-depression/

Population Pyramid [accessed 1 October 2017] [Online] www.populationpyramid.net

Raicu, I (2016) [accessed 8 August 2017] Young Adults Take More Security Measures for Their Online Privacy than Their Elders, *Recode* [Online] https://www.recode.net/2016/11/2/13390458/young-millennials-oversharing-security-digital-online-privacy

Singh, S (2017) [accessed 21 September 2017] Generation Z: Rules to
Reach the Multinational Consumer, *Sapient* [Online] www.sapient.com/
content/dam/sapient/sapientnitro/pdfs/insights/TR1_GenZ.pdf

Tucker, A (2012) [accessed 23 September 2017] Jack Andraka:
The Teen Prodigy of Pancreatic Cancer, *Smithsonian
Magazine* [Online] www.smithsonianmag.com/science-nature/
jack-andraka-the-teen-prodigy-of-pancreatic-cancer-135925809/

US Census (2010)) [accessed 11 October 2017] Population Characteristics
(P20) [Online] https://www.census.gov/prod/www/population.html#p20

Valens, A (2017) [accessed 29 December 2017] The Future is Fluid:
Generation Z's Approach to Gender and Sexuality is Indeed
Revolutionary, *Daily Dot* [Online] https://www.dailydot.com/irl/
generation-z-fluid/

Walczer, J and Baird, D (2018, forthcoming) #YouWillBeFound:
Leveraging 'Dear Evan Hansen' on Instagram and Tumblr to Combat
Cyberbullying and Empower Teens

The five foundational truths of youth marketing

03

In the past, young consumers had to endure brands talking at them via campaigns created by adults, and broadcast on adult platforms they couldn't be any less interested in listening to. Today, the conversation has changed. Brands can't get away with talking at their audience anymore, they can't even get away with talking to them, they have to talk with them, the way real human beings do. Brands have to know that their most valuable weapon – particularly with this elusive demographic – is their ability to listen. There has to be an exchange of thoughts and ideas. Only then can brands produce and present what is needed and wanted by the very people they're trying to cater to in the first place. If a brand can do that, they're going to make it. If they can't, then it's a roll of the dice.

STEVE BERRA, 2018, PRESIDENT AT THE BERRICS

Is your brand ready for the truth?

The truth. We all say we want to hear it, but can we accept it when we do? Sometimes the truth means we need to get out of our comfort zone and take risks. It can mean hearing things we'd rather not hear. Often it can paralyse us into doing nothing at all rather than heading into unknown territory.

The truth doesn't need to be so daunting, though. In fact, when it comes to building brands and consumer audiences, there are several 'truths' that ring true over and over again. We've distilled these down to five foundational guideposts that we refer to when working with brands. In fact, we apply these Truths to everything we do, because they lay the foundation for how we think and act long before even starting to plot a strategy or put a marketing programme into action.

The Truths are simple. You will have seen them before, but you might not have considered how they build upon each other, creating a linear, practical way to tune in and build credibility with youth culture. Don't be fooled by the Truths' simplicity – the magic is in their application.

The five foundational truths of youth marketing

- Identity
- Trust
- Relevance
- Possibility
- Experience

These foundational youth market Truths (Figure 3.1) are the starting point for understanding and defining your relationship with any audience; however, they are particularly relevant to guiding youth-focused initiatives, because they acknowledge how Gen Z connects

Figure 3.1   The five foundational youth marketing truths act as an equalizer to help brands tune in to the frequency of Gen Z

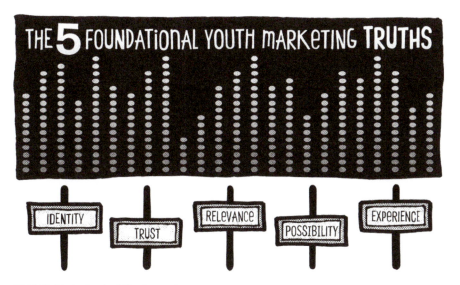

SOURCE Illustration by Mike Carnevale

with brands. Yet we rarely find that all of them are well executed, or even practised together in one harmonious approach. If you want to be relevant to Gen Z, build these Truths into your own process, so that you can leverage your unique differentiators, learn how to communicate them effectively to your audience and stay firmly cemented in the realities of youth culture.

Throughout this chapter you will hear many perspectives on the Truths from the young people who participated in our advisory groups and surveys, and from the influencers and brands we interviewed. As you read on, we've provided a set of questions at the end of each section that make up a Youth Market Readiness Audit. It is designed to help you assess the preparedness of any organization seeking to connect with youth culture. Use our digital audit tool to put your brand to the test and see how you score at **www.genzfreq.com**

Truth 1: Identity

Gone are the days when brand identity is built with a bullhorn. We all know that brand identity is now the sum of every consumer experience, but that doesn't mean covering the spread of fragmented media with one brush stroke. In our opinion, context is just as important as content. It's about brands boldly proclaiming a belief in why they exist in the first place, then proving it in ways that shape-shift within the medium and the context of media. In other words, prove that you are who you say you are in as many ways as you can.

ADAM WILSON, 2018, FORMER DIRECTOR OF BRAND MARKETING
FOR CARHARTT, NORTH AMERICA

Brands need an identity young people care about. To find that identity, you need to go far beyond your service, product and packaging and really determine *who* you are and *what* you represent to Gen Z. It's the differentiator between successful brands, with strong audiences and proven staying power, and those that struggle to find their path. If you can build an identity Gen Z respects and cares about, you will have taken a significant first step towards the bigger goal of brand–audience alignment.

It's easy to see when a brand is genuine because they really have something they stand by, rather than just marketing products to us. I don't think brands are going to be successful if they don't put their heart into it.

Daniel P, 2017, age 16

Ask yourself these questions: Why does my brand exist? What do we really care about? Are we truly aligned with the audience we want to connect with? Do we actually have a story that Gen Z connects with and can participate in? Yes, we ask a lot of questions, but the answers to these questions will lead you closer to what matters to Gen Z. With a genuine, compelling and entrenched foundation, your brand can withstand the ups and downs of the market or trend cycles. Once you've established your identity, stay committed to your core principles and beliefs – know what is non-negotiable and what can morph and evolve with your audience.

Perception challenges identity

We all put a filter on reality. How one person sees something can differ hugely from how another person does. The concept of perception is critical when discussing a brand's identity. 'There is an internal perception (the brand as the supplier sees it) and an external one (the brand as it is present in the memory of consumers and customers)' (Franzen and Moriarty, 2009).

We need to ask ourselves if our internal perception is accurate, and learn how to rise above any bias so we can be open to the reality of how our product may be received in the outside world. By getting ourselves out of the way, we can see Gen Z clearly and position brands the way we want them to be perceived.

In order to do this, we need to know what informs Gen Z's perceptions of the world. Once we understand what fuels Gen Z's opinions and preferences, we can better understand what motivates them. If we want their attention, we need to figure out how to appeal to them from *their* perspective. This is how you build strategies that work in reality and not just in the boardroom.

Today's youth are the social media generation. It has never been so easy for young people to explore a brand's values and determine if they are values that they wish to support. I cannot think of an easier or more effective way to have your brand resonate in the minds of Gen-Z than have values that they align with. The truth of the matter is in this world not only do you need to convince youth to purchase your product. You need to them to pick you.

Jake Skoloda, 2017, age 18, CEO Millennial Ad Network

Does your brand resonate with youth culture?

As we've outlined in Chapter 2, Gen Z is a large and global demographic. The whole cohort, however, is made up of many groups and identities that are continuously evolving, and we have to know which groups and identities are the best match for our brand. This leaves brands with a dizzying array of options to consider and ways to position themselves. Yet, it is so important to be dialled in to these identities, or what may seem like a small detail for a brand can become a big problem for a misidentified group within Gen Z. An appeal to one group may alienate others, so brands have to prioritize: do they water down the message to be more broadly palatable, but possibly less compelling overall? Or do they prioritize one group over another, based on the group's alignment with the brand, or the commercial viability of the group? There is no easy solution, but we recommend that a brand start with a core group affiliation that is the best fit, and build from there.

If you only appeal to Gen Z in the larger context, you lose opportunities to connect to the more influential and passionate groups within the whole. In fact, you may even be ignored for failing to respect those groups. Because some groups are more nuanced, we recommend that you don't alienate some as you try to appeal to others.

How do we maintain our core identity in an evolving and challenging market?

An important part of your identity is knowing what you are not. Ask yourself: What is most you? What is somewhat you? What is less you? Sometimes even brands with ultra-clear identities can become distracted. When challenged by competitive threats, market fluctuations and trend cycles, brands should revisit their core values, beliefs and personality to get back on track, rather than reach for something new, which can weaken their story. Sure, brands need to evolve, but they need to stay anchored to their core identity as they do, or risk chasing audiences and trends. It takes confidence and courage to define yourself and stand behind that definition, rather than editing yourself in response to market pressures. Yet, fall into the trap of choosing something that might quickly boost sales over something that is truly you, and you may compromise your relationship with youth culture – you'd be trading a quick buck for the greater value of a long-term investment.

Youth Market Readiness Audit: Identity

Establishing a strong, authentic and honest identity is a non-negotiable step for *any* brand. When we work with clients, our first step is to address their brand identity as it relates to their audience segment. Before moving on in this chapter, you should be able to discuss and confidently answer the following five questions that comprise the Identity section of the Youth Market Readiness Audit.

Identity checklist
1 What is your brand's 'Why', and what need do you fill in the market?
2 Why should youth culture be interested in your brand?
3 When you look at your core beliefs, do they align with the needs and desires of Gen Z?
4 Is your core promise believable for youth culture?
5 What does your brand do to establish an emotional connection with youth culture?

Truth 2: Trust

Trust? It's everything. When it's there, when it's really there, that's how a brand gets brought to life, protected and defended, grown and shared in the most authentic and powerful way possible. Trust takes belief, belief takes faith, and faith takes nurture and care. It takes more than a product, a promise, or a campaign. We work to earn trust in everything we say, everything we make and everything we do. Period. This is an important lesson I learned early on and continue to bring with me wherever I go.

NICHOLAS TRAN, 2017, MARKETING EXECUTIVE AND THOUGHT
LEADER AT GLOBAL CONSUMER ELECTRONICS BRAND

Building trust is *absolutely critical* when building consumer relationships. The process, while it might not always be easy, doesn't need to be complicated. Through our experience helping brands connect with their targeted youth audiences, we have learnt that building trust comes down to a simple equation: Transparency + Authenticity = Credibility. By avoiding pretence or deceit and being true to core beliefs, consumers will trust in your promise, reliability, and the strength of your company.

The science of trust

The role of trust in consumer–brand relationships has been championed in the advertising industry since the early 1990s and has been studied extensively in behavioural and chemical science. A 2012 study by Krueger *et al* on the neuro-chemical aspect of trust begins with the connection to behaviour. 'Trust as a critical social process is indispensable in friendship, love, families, and organizations. It facilitates interpersonal relations and permits reciprocal behaviors that lead to mutual advantages for cooperators during social and economic exchange' (Krueger *et al*, 2012). In other words, in order to build a genuine relationship with Gen Z, your brand's identity has to be trustworthy and invoke an emotional connection.

> When we build trust and bond, our bodies release a chemical that drives us to deepen the relationship on both sides. We commit to Gen Z while they commit to us. When we earn trust, we reinforce brand loyalty. But it's more than just feel-good – it actually creates a chemical reaction in our bodies. [T]he neurochemical oxytocin (OT) is synthesized in the human brain when one is trusted or simply treated well. The OT molecule, in turn, motivates reciprocation. The release of OT signals that the other party is 'safe' to be around and that cooperative behavior

will not be exploited… the synthesis of OT motivates people to treat the other party 'like family' (Crosby and Zak, 2015).

Earning trust takes time. You can't develop a relationship overnight with Gen Z any more than you could with a friend. Brands need to approach sales and marketing with thoughtfulness towards the needs and desires of their audience. This way, they have the best chance of being brought into the circle of trust. If you are not palpably committed, Gen Z will move on.

> Brands break my trust by failing to listen and underestimating people who support them, by creating products that are unreliable, or by making a negative impact on society. I hate when companies use pop culture influences just for financial gain.
>
> Devan T, 2017, age 16

Trust is critical to any consumer, and Gen Z is no different

As a brand, positioning yourself as an authority to Gen Z is definitely not advisable. You stand a much better chance of earning your way in as a trusted friend, with no pretence of control. The modern relationship between youth consumers and brands is a symbiotic one, rooted firmly in identity and trust. It goes both ways, or not at all. When brands do lead, it's only because Gen Z's trust in the direction of their leadership is tried, true and absolute. Trust lowers the barrier to acceptance and creates a safe environment – which means they may just choose you over the hundreds of other products they will see today.

Youth Market Readiness Audit: Trust

Just as we took an Identity audit when we addressed brand positioning, we ask that you to do the same for Trust. Before moving on in this chapter, you should feel confident in your answers to the following five questions that comprise the Trust section of the Youth Market Readiness Audit.

Trust checklist

1   Why should young consumers trust your brand?
2   Do you proactively build relationships with your audience?
3   What are you doing to reinforce your relationship with youth audiences?
4   Are you transparent about your business practices?
5   Does Gen Z view you as an ally or an authority?

Truth 3: Relevance

Staying relevant with Gen Z requires brands to stay on the pulse of everything happening in culture. And not just a gut check a few times a year... it requires a daily pulse of what this audience is talking about, feeling and connecting with emotionally. From politics to pop culture, Gen Z admires brands who are willing to engage in timely conversations.

MICHAEL ABATA, 2018, CULTURAL AND CONSUMER FUTURIST

You've established who you are and why you matter (your identity) and you've begun to earn Gen Z's trust. The next step is to establish relevance, but how do we go about it? Why does one brand have Gen Z standing in line for hours waiting for a new product to drop, while other brands are discounting product just to drive a few visits to their site? For a brand to be relevant, they have to bring something – whether that's product services, content or entertainment – of unique value to consumers, at exactly the moment it is useful, critical or applicable. When a brand does this, it takes on the role of friend and resource, making sure that needs are taken care of.

What is relevance? Giving back, standing for something, creating products and content relevant to the new school, that's linked to your brand and [done] at lightning speed.

Kodie Shane, 2018, age 19, rapper and singer

A prime example of the power of relevance is the rise of Fenty Beauty by Rihanna, the cosmetics line for all skin tones by music star Rihanna (www.fentybeauty.com). In 2017, it was celebrated not only because of the popularity of and devotion to Rihanna, but because it finally provided a mainstream product to a notoriously underserved population, at a time when diversity was being increasingly embraced in popular culture. It was irresistibly relevant to young consumers, who themselves are an increasingly diverse population, and who, we have found, applaud brands that want to make a difference in the world.

> Don't go by what you think you know about teens, because most likely you will end up advertising to stereotypes, not people. We are not mindless beings who don't think about the harsh adult stuff. We discuss the failings of our country just the same amount as we discuss what we're going to wear for Halloween. Here's some advice: create a style that appeals to us, collaborate with cool brands we enjoy, and try acting like a friend that others want to follow and be like.
>
> Abigail W, 2018, age 17

Are you immersed in the world your audience cares about, and the way they experience the world? Have you thoughtfully taken their circumstances into consideration when you develop products or communications for them?

Youth Market Readiness Audit: Relevance

You've completed the Identity and Trust Audit, now it's time to do the same for Relevance. Before moving on in this chapter, you should be able to discuss and confidently answer the following five questions that comprise the Relevance section of the Youth Market Readiness Audit.

Relevance checklist

1 What makes your brand relevant to Gen Z?
2 When it comes to products and services, are yours relevant to young consumers?

3   Are you in tune with the attitudes, behaviours and perceptions that matter to your target youth audience?
4   Is your brand accessible to Gen Z when and where they need it?
5   Does your brand connect Gen Z with their peers or anyone who inspires them? Are you helping to elevate their status and build community?

Truth 4: Possibility

Find a creator – a real creator, not a fake one – that speaks to and inspires the audience you're after. Partner with them for six months, a year or longer with a goal of becoming a true member of that creator's community. Don't tell them what to say – instead enable them – and through them their community – to go places, do things, discovery possibilities. Become part of that creator's community, but let the creator chart the course, set the sails and choose the destination. You're not buying media, you're not running a campaign. You're joining a community. Be respectful, be generous, but mostly keep your mouth shut. With the right match between creator, community and brand the results will be amazing.

JIM LOUDERBACK, 2018, CEO VIDCON

Gen Z is at a stage of their lives where possibility surrounds them. They are in the most volatile, hormone-bathed crucible of change imaginable, and are trying to figure out who they are, who they want to be, and how to look cool doing it. Whether they are aware of it or not, they are desperately in need of inspiration and guidance. This is where brands step in. Brands can help Gen Z to experiment with different identities, and can lay the groundwork for young consumers to aspire to be the person they want to be in the world. Brands can help Gen Z find options and opportunities to keep them inspired and moving forward. For some, it may be about discovering things that interest them, for others it might mean escaping an identity imposed on them by family.

Brands can invest in the future by inspiring Gen Z today

If a brand truly wants to inspire Gen Z, it needs to create the potential beyond the moment of purchase, so that consumers imagine how an offering could impact their life going forward. One way brands do this is by helping their audience explore, learn about, and experiment with their world. To *do*, not just be. This creation of possibility can be a strong brand distinguisher. Every product has a list of features and benefits, but in a sea of competition it is the story around the product that resonates and gets remembered. If you can make consumers feel that new things are possible, you'll leave a lasting imprint. Fill their minds with possibility, and they will keep coming back for more.

> Supreme makes me feel like anything is possible, 'cos they started as New York skaters [and went on] to become one of the world's biggest clothing brands. And they were themselves. They were unique, and had their own identity.
>
> Santiago S, 2017, age 15

Needs motivate consumption

Gen Z often sees brands as a way to express a multifaceted identity. They communicate who they are to others, in large part, through association. Products themselves may be simple – like a t-shirt – but when they come from a particular brand, they convey much more information than just whether or not they fit, for example; they are now a part of what the brand represents. When a consumer chooses a brand, they choose to be aligned with what that brand means or promises. Gen Z may look to brands to give them the opportunity to express what they are struggling to express on their own.

Why do we choose between two products that are essentially the same thing? Consider AH Maslow's theory of human motivation (Figure 3.2). Maslow believed that, 'Man is a perpetually wanting animal' (Maslow, [1943] 2000). Human needs can be classified in a hierarchy that must typically be satisfied in order. From basest to highest, the needs that must be satisfied are physiological, safety, love/belonging, esteem and self-actualization (Maslow, [1943] 2000).

If we reconsider the t-shirt, it is, at its most basic, a sleeved tube that will cover your torso, after all. If you are cold, it may keep you

Figure 3.2   Maslow's hierarchy of needs

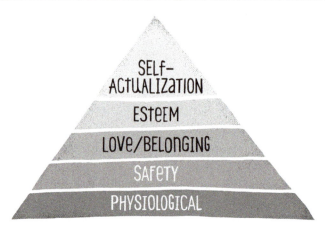

SOURCE Illustration by Mike Carnevale

warm (physiological), if you are in public, it may keep you from feeling exposed and vulnerable (safety). Any t-shirt does this, so what else is it? Why is the customer really buying a new t-shirt when they already have 10 at home? The new shirt clearly provides something those shirts don't. Maybe a brand is popular, and associating with it makes the wearer feel as if they are a part of something (love/belonging). Perhaps the brand is exclusive and the wearer gets a boost to their sense of self (esteem). It could be that the brand or message on the shirt stands for something that the wearer believes represents their true self and helps them say, 'This is me!' (self-actualization).

No matter what a brand represents, it can influence youth consumers who are looking for opportunities to fulfil their personal needs. If we identify compatible audience segments and are able to connect, we can investigate and discover what motivates them both intrinsically and extrinsically. This helps us understand what they want and how we can help them achieve it. If Gen Z aspires to a world where workers are treated fairly, for instance, a brand's support of fair trade can imbue their product with the promise that this t-shirt was made in a fair trade factory, and that when you wear it you are helping people exit a life of poverty. If your brand can cover each stratum of Maslow's human motivation triangle, and your product has the ability to deliver and satisfy on all these levels, then you are well on your way to tuning in effectively and building credibility within youth culture.

Youth Market Readiness Audit: Possibility

Is your brand ready to deliver possibility to Gen Z? Before moving on in this chapter, you should be able to discuss and confidently answer the following five questions that comprise the Possibility section of the Youth Market Readiness Audit.

Possibility checklist

1 Do you know what motivates your youth audience? How can your brand help meet their needs?
2 Are you doing anything to help young people re-imagine themselves and take advantage of new opportunities?
3 How can your brand bridge the gap between youth culture and current, emerging and future trends?
4 How are you inspiring Gen Z to overcome obstacles and excel, even when things seem impossible or too difficult?
5 What are you doing to encourage and inspire young people to reach beyond what is currently possible, and start to create their future?

Truth 5: Experience

*A fundamental part… perhaps **the** fundamental part of humanity is to derive meaning from our existence, in the broader context of the universe. Gen Z is coming of age in a time period where we are constantly given digital reminders that we are not alone. An individual experience, recorded on a Snapchat or Instagram story, is almost immediately integrated into a broader 'story' pooled together by hashtag or geographic location. Technology has given us the tools to show us, in real time, that we are one piece of a much larger puzzle. Brands need to become part of this larger puzzle, and contribute to the overall experiences of this generation.*

SARA UNGER, 2018, SENIOR VICE PRESIDENT,
CULTURAL INSIGHTS AND STRATEGY, CIVIC ENTERTAINMENT GROUP

Supreme (www.supremenewyork.com): if ever a brand has created an experience that is greater than the sum of its parts, it's this brand. Typically, young consumers are impatient, like the rest of us. They don't like waiting for a video to load, or for anything longer than a swipe or tap away. So why will Gen Z wait in line for hours at Supreme for a new product to drop? According to Jeff Carvalho, executive editor of www.highsnobiety.com, 'They want to be in the line. The line is the new community. When 200 to 300 kids are lining up outside of a store,' he continues, 'it's because they want to be part of something' (La Ferla, 2017). Those who wait in line not only get first dibs at an elite selection of products – they also get a seat at a very elite table. While picking up their t-shirt, they are also connecting with other like-minded fans and feeling part of a larger community.

Gen Z is used to sensory overload and craves it. They want to be surrounded by experiences that make them feel alive and connected. Supreme (and many other brands that have been successful at creating the right experiences for Gen Z) understands this. While it garnered trust by creating alliances with artists, photographers, athletes and more who resonated on just the right frequency for the youth consumer, it also knew it needed to take that to the next level by providing the right experience. It is doing something right, because 20 years later, you'll find discerning young consumers still waiting in line at its door.

Today, successful brands are creating experiences that invite their audience to become part of the story. They want to be part of the conversation, not just talked to. A good experience builds community, encourages interaction and builds brand loyalty. For more on digital and emerging experiences, see Chapter 6, where we explore more on immersive experiences.

> Snap lenses are awesome for times when I have to wait or am bored or nervous. You can look at anything and pick a theme and make it totally different in real time. It's pretty fun by myself, but with my friends it's the best.
>
> Matt W, 2017, age 16

Youth Market Readiness Audit: Experience

Our final audit! Before moving on in this chapter, you should be able to discuss and confidently answer the following five questions that comprise the Experience section of the Youth Market Readiness Audit.

Experience checklist

1 Are you providing memorable experiences for young people across social, digital and real-world environments?
2 What are you doing to build community and create a true sense of belonging for young people?
3 How are you leveraging relationships with creators, influencers or celebrities to heighten the brand experience for your audience?
4 If a young person has a negative experience with your brand, what action steps are in place to assess and improve future interactions?
5 Do the branded experiences you offer align with the unique characteristics of the target youth culture audience?

TL;DR: chapter takeaways

- **Youth culture is a complex convergence of subgroups; a concerted application of the Truths is critical to building consumer–brand relationships.** Take the time to reflect on the Truths as they relate to your brand and situation, then complete each Youth Market Readiness Audit. Your answers will be used in Chapter 4 as you go through the Youth Culture Alignment Framework, and again in Chapter 6 as part of the foundation for the Youth Culture Engagement Playbook.

- **Identity: Define and position your brand in ways that contribute to youth culture.** The brand stories should be unique, audience-relevant, and something Gen Z can and wants to participate in.

- **Trust: Be trustworthy, dependable, and earn the respect of youth culture.** Transparent business practices, consistency and reliability are the actions needed for Gen Z to consider you an ally.

- **Relevance: Know what matters within youth culture, and actively forge relationships that deepen the connection.** Deliver on what Gen Z needs and wants, when and where they expect it, and make them look cool in the process.

- **Possibility: Determine what you can uniquely offer that opens up the realms of possibility for Gen Z.** How can your brand inspire young people to define themselves, to reach beyond the present and yearn for the future?

- **Experience: Create positive and meaningful experiences that connect your brand with the broader stories in youth culture.** Deliver unique and memorable experiences across channels that contribute to the overall experiences of this generation in all its manifestations.

References

Crosby, LA and Zak, PJ (2015) [accessed 13 March 2018] The Neuroscience of Brand Trust, *American Marketing Association, Marketing News*, 24 September [Online] https://www.ama.org/publications/MarketingNews/Pages/the-neuroscience-of-brand-trust.aspx

Franzen, G and Moriarty, SE (2009) [accessed 13 March 2018] *The Science and Art of Branding*, Taylor & Francis, London

Krueger, F, *et al* (2012) Oxytocin receptor genetic variation promotes human trust behavior, *Frontiers in Human Neuroscience* **6** (4), doi:10.3389/fnhum.2012.00004

La Ferla, R (2017) [accessed 14 March 2018] The Cult of the Line: It's Not About the Merch, *The New York Times* [Online] www.nytimes.com/2017/08/03/fashion/waiting-in-line-supreme-streetwear-merch.html

Maslow, AH ([1943] 2000) *A Theory of Human Motivation*, Classics in the History of Psychology [Online] http://psychclassics.yorku.ca/Maslow/motivation.htm

Further reading

Fehr, E *et al* (2005) Oxytocin increases trust in humans, *Nature*, **435**, pp 673–76 [Online] http://www.nature.com/nature/journal/v435/n7042/abs/nature03701.html?foxtrotcallback=true

Forbes Agency Council (2017) [accessed 13 March 2018] How should influencers and brands authentically build trust? Six professionals offer advice, *Forbes Community Voice*, 21 June [Online] https://www.forbes.com/sites/forbesagencycouncil/2017/06/21/how-should-influencers-and-brands-authentically-build-trust-six-professionals-offer-advice/#3ce6fb2573fc

Hunter, M (2012) [accessed 13 March 2018] What's with All the Hype – A Look at Aspirational Marketing, *The Nordic Page*, 14 July [Online] https://www.tnp.no/norway/global/3059-whats-with-all-the-hype-a-look-at-aspirational-marketing

Mersom, D (2016) [accessed 13 March 2018] From Dr Martens to Supreme: What Makes Urban Brands so Alluring? *The Guardian*, 16 July [Online] https://www.theguardian.com/cities/2016/oct/07/dr-martens-supreme-urban-brands-vans-stussy

Roberts, A (2017) [accessed 13 March 2018] Bad news brands: consumers could probably live without you, *Clickbiz*, 7 February [Online] (https://www.clickz.com/bad-news-brands-consumers-could-probably-live-without-you/109334/?_ijcid=1508033288063|1.1147618225.1508033125506.-59a0668d

Suleymanova, Y (2015) [accessed 13 March 2018] Consumer Aspirations and Luxury Brand Management, *Suley Group*, 3 September [Online] http://suleygroup.com/index.php/suley-university/item/7-consumer-aspirations-and-luxury-brand-management/7-consumer-aspirations-and-luxury-brand-management

Aligning with youth culture in an era of individuality

04

Historically, in order to be labelled as 'cool' by a commonly accepted standard, young people used to try very hard to be clones of each other allowing for only slight variations when dressing, listening to music or even deciding who to admire and emulate. That has all changed, now I think young people have done away with the herd mentality that used to dominate high school hallways. They are getting comfortable developing their own sense of style across the board and most importantly, their own voice. For this very reason, understanding and including smaller groups of like-minded young people will be needed to successfully interact with youth going forward.

JENK OZ, 2018, FOUNDER ICOOLKID.COM, BRITAIN'S YOUNGEST CEO

There is a reason why Mountain Dew collaborates with established street artists, why Levis works with urban youth to fund and build DIY skate spots, and why Milk Cosmetics creates unique product collections with established lifestyle brands such as Burton Snowboards. It's because they know that making deeper connections is crucial to alignment with youth culture. Today's young people are highly individualized and making culturally relevant connections is non-negotiable. If you want to be noticed, followed and garner attention, align with the most relevant groups within youth culture.

In our experience, successful alignment with youth culture depends, in part, on segmentation focused on psychographic and situational context. What does this mean, exactly? We find that many brands default to demographic, geographic and behavioural targeting as their primary filters because they are more convenient, but the reality is that relationships are built in the personal realm. We still use demographic segmentation, such as age, gender and ethnicity, as a starting point to help us organize consumers who are more likely to be a good match with a brand. The ultimate priority, however, always has to be the segmentation that helps us *understand* youth culture – not just *organize* it.

In this chapter we discuss the challenges we come across when working with Gen Z and the confines of traditional segmentation, then tackle them head on with our Youth Culture Alignment Framework. It's a simple – yet highly effective – approach that helps brands identify and align with the seemingly infinite subcultures and lifestyles within Gen Z, through clear, actionable steps.

Hyper-individualization is the norm: Gen Z expects unique

Let's take a closer look at the title of this chapter: 'Aligning with youth culture in an era of individuality'. The concept of 'individuality' has been evolving for nearly all of recorded history. In the 17th century, the concept of the individual was championed and celebrated in the fields of art, literature, religion and science, and fed the Age of Enlightenment. More recently, Baby Boomers were called the 'Me Generation' and Millennials labelled as 'Generation Me'– individual to the point of being stereotyped as incredibly self-absorbed. The idea of individualism doesn't belong definitively to just one generation, however. In fact, it belongs on some level to every generation, according to Clark University Professor Jenson Arnett (Director of the Clark Poll of Emerging Adults). 'There's a space that's opened up in the 20s that is the most individualistic time of life… I describe it as the self-focused time in life… they have fewer social rules and obligations – the freedom to be self-directed'(Arnett, 2014).

In 2018, Gen Z is definitely pushing the idea of individualism, sometimes to the point of hyper-individualism (McKibben, 2007). We have observed that Gen Z *defines themselves* as being more highly individualized than previous generations, through direct observation, ongoing dialogue and project collaboration (which we conduct through our network of young consumers, influencers and co-creators). This perception is important. Whether they truly are the most individual generation of our time or not is almost a moot point if they believe that they are. In addition, when you consider how much exposure they have to the world via the internet and social media, at a time when they are creating their sense of self, they have more options and raw materials to choose from than any previous generation.

Regardless of studies and statistics, if we are to understand Gen Z's perspective, we have to recognize their *self-perception* as the most unique generation. A 2017 report by AwesomenessTV found that, 'Growing up in a time when *intersectionality* is the buzzword du jour, [Gen Z] perceive identity on a spectrum – a complex, ever-evolving construction of self rather than a static set of demographic descriptors... Now we are faced with an arsenal of niche, interchangeable and hyper-specific labels...' (AwesomenessTV, 2017). In fact, there seem to be an infinite number of hybrid subcultures that young people can zero in on and claim as 'home'. No identity is too specific or personalized anymore; it can all be made-to-order. Being highly individualized is no longer a barrier to entry or to societal acceptance. They might easily be accepted *because* of their individuality, instead of being excluded for it.

In 2017, Chloe French, a British Gen Z writer, described her own experience of her generation. 'I have found my move to uni quite empowering. Where I can finally dress head-to-toe in pink like I always wanted to growing up, without the fear of getting heckled like I would if I wore it at home in Derby... Despite the lack of large gang subcultures in the youth of today, what we are is (for the most part) resoundingly accepting, in fact, we outwardly encourage individuality – that's something we can all be proud of' (French, 2017).

Today's youth celebrate their differences with less judgement or hesitation than previous generations, but it goes beyond just self-expression. Gen Z needs a more flexible identity, because they have to adapt to more variety and situations in their lives. Identity is less and less conveyed by a static, stereotypical 'persona' and more by a fluid, evolving, ever-changing condition (AwesomenessTV, 2017).

We've all been in situations where we bring a different side of our personality forward to blend with the person or group involved, whether that's our parents, our boss, our peers or our partners. This is adaptation. Gen Z will try to match themselves to their current situation just like everyone else. Yet, to those in this life stage, coming up with the right personality may be even more intense, because they are discovering and defining themselves, not just toggling between more solidified personalities like adults might do. Gen Z is blending characteristics like the moving pieces in a kaleidoscope; not just switching hats. A teenage male entrepreneur who enjoys knitting in the back seat while he and some friends drive out to Coachella is no longer seen as having an identity crisis – he's making an identity statement.

If Gen Z is this blend of continuously changing characteristics that ebb and flow depending on the situation, then their consumption patterns are probably similar. As brands that want to connect, we need to understand and adapt to these moving targets, but how can brands cater to so many changing personalities? How do we connect with such a diversified, morphing group?

A brand's likelihood of building a commercially viable audience with today's young consumers is in direct relation to a brand's ability to *identify* and *connect with* the right spectrum of groups within youth culture. In other words, those that will desire and value what that brand represents. Relying on demographic targeting can be like casting a net into the water and crossing your fingers. A segmentation method rooted in the lifestyles of youth culture puts the emphasis on skill over chance.

Traditional demographic targeting models are outmoded

Segmentation is saying something to somebody instead of saying nothing to everybody...

LEVINSON AND GODIN, 1994

Traditional targeting models are outmoded – *especially* in youth culture. If we really want to target today's individualistic consumers, then demographics and other less personal approaches need to be part of a more culturally based segmentation approach. We see a lot of polarized opinions in our industry, where some groups continue to pursue shotgun marketing while others shout, 'Demographics are dead! Long live the individual!' Yet neither of these is a useful position for developing successful youth-focused initiatives that work in the real world. We need to take both the micro *and* the macro view into account.

Some companies rely primarily on demographic-based segmentation. There's comfort in concrete statistics that can be organized and analysed, as opposed to the more complex dynamics of psychographics and situational context. Although demographic targeting alone has become a less effective activity, demographics are still an important part of the way we start to filter for groups within Gen Z.

On the other hand, some advertising industry professionals argue that demographics are dead, and that today's consumer trends can't be predicted or understood by typical demographics. We believe that the 'demographics are dead' theory is too dramatic and blurs the edges of the truth. It's a buzz-phrase that might get views when published, and makes some question their approach, but do the proponents of this theory really believe that demographics are useless? Does age, gender, ethnicity or income no longer matter? We can tell you, right now, that they do to those who are in the trenches of youth marketing. Some make the argument that Gen Z has more freely defined identities, leading to consumer behaviours that defy traditional demographics such as age, gender and income. While there is some truth to this argument, it doesn't make demographics wholly unusable. Rather than kill demographics, these consumer behaviours require them to be redefined in new terms – dictated by the consumer, technology and the present moment.

There is definitely more potential demographic overlap today between the purchasing behaviours of different groups. Take a 40-year-old male and 15-year-old female, for example. Both consumers may buy an Imagine Dragons album, a new smartphone and an acai bowl, but there are also just as many differences between them. It makes sense to address those differences by applying demographics. (You can always remove the filter to see the commonalities that different ages and genders share.) Whether a consumer is male, female, lesbian, gay, transgender or queer (LGBTQ) will always influence their needs and preferences. Add in factors such as age-related developmental changes, and you can see how age and gender will always matter. In fact, rather than pronounce demographics as dead, we need to emphasize complementary filters – *not* rely on demographics as the primary audience filter.

CASE STUDY   Demographic targeting gone BADD (Brand Audience Disconnection Disorder)

In the autumn of 2016, a national clothing retailer came to us wanting to better understand the Gen Z mindset, and to learn why its influencer campaigns weren't working, despite having partnered with celebrity content creators. The content was great, and even received a moderate amount of engagement, but the brand just wasn't positioned to capitalize on it. After spending time getting to know the brand, their team and their situation, it became clear that their youth positioning needed some fundamental work if influencer marketing – or any advertising for that matter – was going to positively impact the brand. Up until that time, they had limited their youth targeting to 'students', but their marketing just wasn't hitting home. In other words, they had a real case of BADD (or Brand Audience Disconnection Disorder as we call it around the office). Here is an abridged version of the discovery questionnaire we sent them, along with some of their responses. You can see the challenges the brand was facing at that time.

Client Discovery Questionnaire

Question 1: Can you identify your targeted teen consumers and briefly describe what you know about them?

Answer: 'Currently, we only have anecdotal insights and feedback from the retailers. We know they prefer style, slim fit, super skinny, top looks/styles, and that parents accompany teens.'

Question 2: Does your brand divide young consumers into segments and subgroups?

Answer: 'We have not done audience segmentation beyond "teen boys". All creative is aimed at teen boys. Messaging has been targeting teens. Secondary messaging has been targeting parents. Currently we do messaging, not segmentation.'

Question 3: Does your brand have a 'bull's-eye' consumer profile within the youth segment?

Answer: 'At present, we do not have a "bull's-eye" defined. We know: Boys aged 16–18, we also know parents play a key part for the awareness piece, but we're unsure how they play into the purchasing decision.'

Question 4: What motivates young consumers who support your brand? What do they care about?

Answer: 'We do know it's all about the look, skinny fit. For example: boys want slim fit, mom says "are you sure that is skinny?" Boy says, "YES!" Price and convenience are also key factors.'

It was apparent that the national retail clothing company had trouble connecting because it tried to tackle too large of a cohort with an outmoded demographic segmentation approach. It simply didn't lead them to any real understanding of who their actual audience was. There was no basis for building a relationship with these potential customers, beyond selling them a particular type of clothing. We listened, prioritized the foundational issues, and devised a strategy for course correction. By seeking out youth audiences in their own niche cultural environments and effectively leveraging the company's social channels to talk to them, we were able to help the brand tune in to their frequency. As a result, the brand has now established the segmentation alignment they needed and built targeted relationships that allow marketing programmes to thrive.

Embrace the diversity, stop chasing the cohort

There is no such thing as a Mass Mind. The Mass Audience is made up of individuals, and good advertising is written always from one person to another. When it is aimed at millions, it rarely moves anyone.

FAIRFAX M CONE, 1952, FOUNDER, FOOTE, CONE & BELDING
ADVERTISING

When we see brands trying to appeal to an entire generation or a big segment as though it's an organized controlled environment, we call it 'chasing the cohort'. The reality is that Gen Z is comprised of blending, clashing and evolving cultures. It is a diverse whole, not a homogeneous whole. Today's youth are well aware of their power and sway as consumers, and don't tolerate being lumped together as if their individuality didn't matter. If we approach Gen Z as a homogeneous entity, and fail to listen to and appeal to the multitude of *'cultural, interest and lifestyle segments'* that comprise it, we are doomed to a limited view of their world. We will fail to identify and appeal to the diversity behind their decision making and buying power. Chasing the entire cohort as if it's one big animal is to lose sight of the myriad opportunities for connection, insight and opportunity. Instead, take the time to tune in to all of the frequencies, and Gen Z can be a powerful ally.

How to find and align with youth culture audiences

You've got to start and own the conversation. When we built Complex, big publishers weren't paying attention to sneakers, design, or hip-hop but that was our passion and we built deeply vertical communities around those passion points that we've been able to leverage and scale. Now niche culture is driving mass culture because these kids are large groups of super passionate fans that define the way the mass perceive brands and products.

RICH ANTONIELLO, 2018, FOUNDER AND CEO OF COMPLEX MEDIA

Every brand incorporates some degree of segmentation, but *how* we segment can make or break our ability to align with youth audiences. We've been aligning brands and culture for so long that, when asked how we did it, we realized we had never formalized our process. This led to the development of our Youth Culture Alignment Framework, which takes the user through a series of steps that help them to segment their audience with the goal of optimized audience alignment, rather than being limited to a demographic or behavioural approach.

To start, we use traditional segmentation filters to help subdivide groups that are too big and diverse to tackle as a whole. An example of this would be to pare all of Gen Z down to female teens with a select, disposable income from suburban Kansas City. Once we've applied these demographic, geographic and behavioural filters, we can narrow this select group into more culturally relevant subgroups using psychographic and situational filters. For example, this might result in a subgroup of the Kansan female teens that are die-hard cosplay fans, console gamers and high school seniors. Knowing that the females have these particular interests, habits and an upcoming transition out of high school provides a wealth of context. We can now develop strategies based on the aspects of their lives that compel them the most, *and* provide content and experiences that connect to their passion and situation. This human connection helps us to develop more effective strategies. When carrying out initial segmentation, demographic, geographic and behavioural factors are all important, but they don't truly connect us to our audience just by narrowing the field. Once you focus on the cultural groups, subgroups, and even the smallest splinter groups that make up your audience, then brand–audience alignment becomes clear to see and easier to access.

The Youth Culture Alignment Framework: a practical approach to modern segmentation

We've explored many of the challenges that brands face when seeking alignment with young people. Our solution to these challenges is our Youth Culture Alignment Framework – a youth-specific approach to consumer segmentation that revolves around a hybrid of psychographics and situational context – making the process clear and the goal attainable.

Demographic and geographic filters still provide good directional information, and behaviour graphics help show us patterns such as *how* and *when* people purchase, consume and use products and services. Yet these levels of segmentation don't get us closer to the *heart* of the consumer. Psychographic and situational context filters tell a markedly different story. While they may be more abstract, they reveal the personal and human side of our audience. Psychographic and situational context can help us understand what motivates consumers. They give us the personal insight necessary to make an emotional connection by getting to know consumers as people. In fact, over years of helping clients build successful relationships within youth culture, we've learnt that this is the most effective way to identify appropriate groups and make authentic connections. Data collected from demographic studies or machine-driven algorithms can help us predict consumption patterns based on history, but these are not the insights that will help us cultivate relationships with young people, especially with anyone under 13. (Privacy laws such as the US Children's Online Privacy Protection Act (COPPA) and the European Union's General Data Protection Regulation (GDPR) severely restrict the collection of data on minors without parental consent. We delve deeper into COPPA, GDPR and Australian privacy laws in Chapter 9.)

Youth culture segmentation filters and examples

Activities: Those who identify according to activities such as: music, entertainment, work, reading, swimming, hacking, painting, binge-watching, football, video games, etc.

Interests: Those who identify according to interests such as: LGBTQ, #BlackLivesMatter, eSports fans, technology, science, collecting.

Brand and content affinities: The brands that youth subgroups relate to, and the types of content they consume.

Opinions: Those who identify with opinions such as: social issues, censorship, environment, teen pregnancy, privacy rights, equality, diversity, politics, religion, economics, etc.

Situational context: Those experiencing life situations such as: live events, prom season, testing periods, frequent travel, certain types of weather, etc.

The list above provides a useful way to organize segmentation filters in a way that helps us to see Gen Z as a convergence of individuals, instead of an age-defined whole. This perspective allows us to tune in to the frequency of the groups, subgroups, micro groups and splinter groups that make up the complexities of Gen Z culture (Figure 4.1), and will help you identify which are most relevant to your brand. When completed, the framework should provide you with a list of aligned audience groups that are a logical and specific starting place for research and strategic planning. (Throughout this chapter, rather than list groups, subgroups, micro groups, splinter groups and so on, we will refer to any subdivision of Gen Z as a subgroup, unless otherwise specified.)

Figure 4.1 A visual representation of youth culture complexity

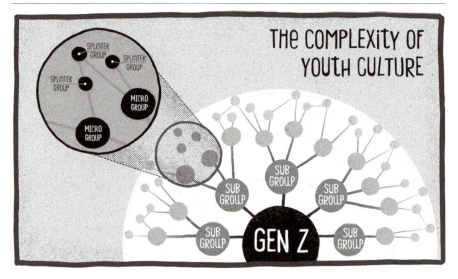

SOURCE Illustration by Mike Carnevale

Preparing to use the Alignment Framework

The Youth Culture Alignment Framework builds on the generational understandings and Truths we covered in Chapters 2 and 3 of this book, so before you jump in, we suggest you refresh your memory on a few key points:

1 Have you developed a youth-relevant brand identity? In Chapter 3 we emphasized the importance of a strong and resilient identity that young people care about, and explained that part of this identity is knowing what role you play in the youth culture. This may be a new project for you, or just an opportunity to dust off your brand book and check your brand's pulse if you are an established company already.

2 Can you improve your brand's potential to build relationships with young people? Based on the results of the Youth Market Readiness Audit from Chapter 3, you should have a good indication of your brand's ability to impact the youth market. Were you able to respond to the questions with confidence? Did your answers stimulate ideas and improve how you approach youth culture? Do you feel that your brand is prepared for the challenges of engaging Gen Z? If no, we suggest working through the questions until the answer is yes. If yes, let's continue and keep fine tuning as you go.

3 Are you targeting youth segments that fit your brand identity? Are you targeting too broad an audience? Make sure you've started some initial segmentation (demographic, geographic, behavioural), and that you have begun to lay the foundational groundwork before you move forward through the framework. With this in place, it will be much easier to think about targeting youth audiences from a cultural alignment perspective.

Stages of the Youth Culture Alignment Framework

- Stage 1: Youth culture segmentation needs analysis
  - Purpose: determine the extent of your targeting needs.

- Stage 2: Brand and youth personality match
  - Purpose: help brands identify the consumer qualities they should look for in compatible youth and brand-relevant consumer subgroups.

- Stage 3: Youth subgroup opportunity identification and prioritization
  - Purpose: develop a list of subgroups that share key personality traits and characteristics with your brand, and determine their alignment and commercial viability for your brand.

- Stage 4: Optimal youth audience definition
  - Purpose: analyse the relationship of alignment and viability and explore how it creates areas of opportunity for your brand.

The four stages of the Youth Culture Alignment Framework

Stage 1: Youth culture segmentation needs analysis

Purpose: determine the extent of your targeting needs.

We don't always have to segment down to the smallest subgroup. The level of audience segmentation depends on both the identity and the needs of the brand, combined with the product or service provided. To determine how extensively we should segment, we need to look at the relationship Gen Z consumers have with a particular brand, as well as with the product or service (referred to henceforth as 'offerings').

At a stage of life where self-exploration and identification are in high focus, Gen Z is highly attuned to what an association with a product or brand might say about them. For example, products such as toothpaste or hand soap (less specialized) will likely say less about who they are, whereas clothing, footwear, smartphones and technology choices (more specialized) can make or break their social identity. It comes as little surprise, therefore, that they are more likely to invest emotionally in their choice of smartphone cases and accessories because these items reflect their personal identity. In turn, a smartphone accessory brand will have to work harder to win Gen Z over because the stakes are much higher. If a brand wants to gain trust, it will need to find and align with influential subgroups. It's important to understand how much your brand and its offerings matter to your audience, as it lays the groundwork for adjusting your segmentation and providing the right product, to the right people, at the right time.

How it works

Step 1: Determine if your brand and offering have more of a broad (mass) or niche segment appeal

Read through the factors and elements in Figure 4.2 and consider how they apply to your brand and offerings. There are aspects of your brand and its offerings that could have a broader appeal, and aspects that will have a more niche appeal. We ask you to rate your brand and offerings, or a particular offering, from the perspective of each factor or element. Use a scale of 1–4, where 1 is more niche and 4 is broader. These do not have to be absolute statistical certainties; the purpose of the worksheet is to guide you to better understand what your brand's audience segmentation needs might be. Have multiple team members complete the worksheet and compare outcomes. The results of this will be entered into Figure 4.3.

Figure 4.2   Use this rating system to help determine the extent of youth culture segmentation needed *(Rate each item's appeal to a more niche or broad Gen Z audience. Use a scale of 1–4, where 1 is more niche and 4 is broader)*

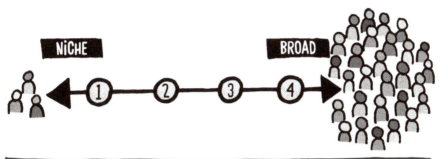

BRAND STORY AND HERITAGE	1	BRAND ASSOCIATIONS (PEOPLE and PARTNERS)	3
PURPOSE OF BRAND	4	CAMPAIGN AND CONTENT THEMES	3
LOGO AND IDENTITY STYLE	2	ACCESSIBILITY OF BRAND OFFERINGS	2
BRAND MESSAGES	1	PRODUCT FEATURES AND FUNCTIONALITIES	4
USER EXPERIENCE	4	DESIGN AESTHETICS	2

(These numbers are for example only)

SOURCE Illustration by Mike Carnevale

Step 2: Determine the extent and variety of targeting that suits your brand and offering

Specific segmentation needs vary according to how niche or broad an appeal your brand and a particular offering or offerings have when considered together. Graph the results of Figure 4.2, by placing a marker for each '4' rating you chose in the '4' ring of Figure 4.3. Do the same for each rating number, placing the '3's in the '3' ring, and so on. The results will help you determine your targeted segmentation needs and the combination of group types that may work best for your brand. This is not an absolute guide, but a starting point for a segmentation approach that is focused on alignment with youth culture.

Figure 4.3   Organize youth segments by their appeal rating to help determine variation by group type

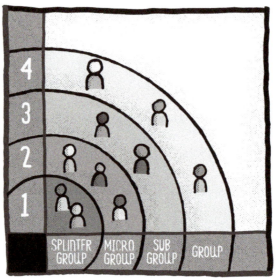

(These numbers correspond with the numerical examples in Fig 4.2)

SOURCE Illustration by Mike Carnevale

Inputs

– All pre-existing youth market research, analysis and segmentation data.

– Documentation of any initial segmentation.

– Responses to the Youth Market Readiness Audit in Chapter 3, and to the 'Pre-Framework' questions at the beginning of this section.

Outputs

– A self-assessment of the niche or broad youth market appeal that your brand and offering have.

– Recommendations regarding the extent of youth culture segmentation need, by each group type, broad to niche.

Stage 2: Brand and youth consumer personality match

Purpose: help brands identify the consumer qualities they should look for in compatible youth and brand-relevant consumer subgroups.

How it works

Step 1: Identify the brand personality traits that represent the essence of your brand to the youth market

Generate a list of personality traits that are intrinsic to your brand. We suggest working with 5–7 traits, but that is entirely up to you. Prioritize these traits in order of most to least important to your brand. Some examples of brand personality traits include: warm, clever, dominant, outgoing, quarrelsome, energetic, predictable, intelligent, attractive, stylish, athletic, plain, healthy, but you can generate your own list of traits that match your brand best.

A few thought-provoking questions about brand personality:

- If your brand were a celebrity, who would it be? What kind of car? What animal, what cartoon character, what archetype? (Pursey, 2016)

- Make a list of adjectives or keywords that best describe your brand.

- If you are looking for a place to start, try using Jennifer Akker's Brand Personality Scale (Akker, 1997). Under each heading, describe how your brand expresses or digresses from the suggested personality trait (see below).

Step 2: Identify characteristics that align with your brand personality traits

Describe each brand personality trait with 3–7 adjectives. These adjectives are also the characteristics that will describe your ideal youth consumer. For example, if your brand personality trait is 'daring', those adjectives might be: bold, experimental, dare-devilish, outspoken, wild and rebellious; or instead: intrepid, brave, valiant, fearless and dauntless. Generate at least five new adjectives per trait, but don't repeat the original brand trait. We suggest some brand trait and consumer characteristic pairings in the list below, but you can generate your own list with adjectives that describe your chosen trait and the compatible youth audience best.

Brand trait/characteristic compatibility examples
Trait: Daring
Characteristics: Bold, experimental, dare-devilish, outspoken, wild and rebellious

Or

Trait: Daring

Characteristics: Intrepid, brave, valiant, fearless and dauntless

Step 3: Prioritize your ideal youth consumer characteristics

Fill in column 1 of the Ideal Youth Characteristic Priority Rating Planning Worksheet (Table 4.1) with the characteristics you have generated, and then rate these characteristics on a scale of 1–5 in column 2. Finally, give the reason why you chose that rating in column 3.

Table 4.1 Use this planning worksheet to identify and rate ideal youth characteristics

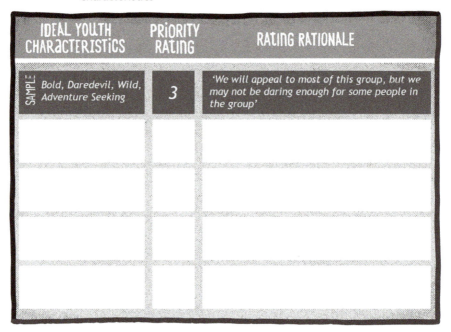

IDEAL YOUTH CHARACTERISTICS	PRIORITY RATING	RATING RATIONALE
SAMPLE Bold, Daredevil, Wild, Adventure Seeking	3	'We will appeal to most of this group, but we may not be daring enough for some people in the group'

SOURCE Illustration by Mike Carnevale

Inputs

– Brand identity and mission statement, and any pre-existing youth market research and analysis data.

– A list of your potential brand personality traits from your brand book or platform.

– A list of ideal consumer subgroup characteristics to be distilled from those traits.

Outputs

– Prioritized core brand personality traits.

– A prioritized list of your ideal youth consumer characteristics.

Stage 3: Youth subgroup opportunity identification and prioritization

Purpose: develop a list of subgroups that share key personality traits and characteristics with your brand; determine subgroup alignment and commercial viability for your brand.

Now that we have identified and prioritized your ideal youth consumer characteristics, we will identify the Gen Z audience subgroups that share those characteristics. We recommend developing a comprehensive list of the groups, subgroups, micro groups and even splinter groups that you feel will best align with your brand. We will then show you how to prioritize this list, based on brand–consumer subgroup alignment, and the subgroup's ability to positively impact the brand.

How it works

Step 1: Generate a list of potential youth audience subgroups

Select the segmentation filters that you will use as a starting point from the potential youth audience subgroups list below. Generate a list of actual groups and subgroups that fit under the filter headings. For example, if we filter for activities, we might start to generate a list consisting of gaming, athletics, playing music, creating art, writing, acting, learning or working. Do the same for Interests, Brand and content affinities, Opinions and Situational Context.

Filters to help identify potential youth audience subgroups

Filter: Activities: Examples: Those involved in these activities: music, entertainment, social events, YouTuber/creator, work, reading, Fortnite, swimming, hacking, painting, binge-watching, etc.

Filter: Interests: Examples: Those who identify according to interests such as: LGBTQ, #BlackLivesMatter, eSports fans, technology, science, etc.

Filter: **Brand and content affinities**: Examples: The brands that youth subgroups relate to and the content that they consume.

Filter: **Opinions**: Examples: Those who identify with opinions such as: social issues, censorship, environment, teen pregnancy, privacy rights, equality, diversity, politics, religion, economics, etc.

Filter: **Situational context**: Examples: Those in life situations such as: live events, prom season, testing periods, frequent travels, weather, etc.

Next, keeping with the above example, explore each type of activity for subgroups (or more niche groups) that participate in those activities, depending on the extent of the segmentation need. For example, the two main subgroups for gaming include casual and core gamers (eSports and other non-competitive genre groups), which can be further divided into both PC and console gamers. Subgroups can be further broken down by game platform and genre, while even smaller sets of splinter groups are defined by levels of gameplay sophistication.

This list of potential subgroups should be long, so you can see as much of the youth spectrum as possible. Go for quantity! Conduct secondary research, brainstorm with teams, and deeply explore the rich texture and spectrum of the cultures within Gen Z. The better you know them, the more effectively you will be able to align. From this list, select your top 20 – or even more, depending on how detailed you want to get. We don't want to lose any potential variety that will be valuable later.

Step 2: Complete Table 4.2 by matching subgroups from your list with ideal youth consumer characteristics from Stage 2

Step 3: Prioritize your subgroups from most to least aligned with your brand

Each subgroup will receive an alignment score that will become the Y-axis of the coordinate graph to be discussed below. On a scale of 1–5 (5 being the best), rate each subgroup on how well each brand personality trait describes them. For example, you may decide that cheerleaders can be a moderately daring subgroup, giving them a rating of 3, while you might give snowboarders a 5. Each subgroup's overall score is then determined by totalling their rating number for each trait. In Table 4.3, the snowboarder's subgroup received a

Table 4.2　Use this planning worksheet to match ideal youth characteristics with targeted subgroups

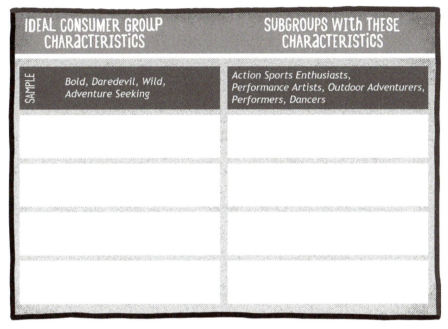

IDEAL CONSUMER GROUP CHARACTERISTICS		SUBGROUPS WITH THESE CHARACTERISTICS
SAMPLE	Bold, Daredevil, Wild, Adventure Seeking	Action Sports Enthusiasts, Performance Artists, Outdoor Adventurers, Performers, Dancers

SOURCE Illustration by Mike Carnevale

total score of 14. They scored higher for daring, but lower on being welcoming and approachable. Beauty vloggers scored much higher (22) on alignment overall. To the brand doing this scoring, beauty vloggers possess more traits in common, and were therefore found to be more aligned.

Step 4: Prioritize your subgroups from most-to-least commercially viable
Each subgroup will receive a consumer viability score that will become the X-axis of the coordinate graph to be discussed below. The list below defines the criteria for viability.

Youth subgroup commercial viability filters

Identifiability: Refers to the extent to which managers can identify or recognize distinct subgroups within the marketplace.

Substantiality: Refers to the extent to which a segment or subgroup of customers represents a sufficient size to be profitable. This could mean sufficiently large in number of people or in purchasing power.

Table 4.3   Use this table to rate and score youth subgroups for alignment potential

SCALE 1–5	DARING	WELCOMING/ APPROACHABLE	VIBRANT	GLAMOROUS	INTELLIGENT	SCORE
PERFORMERS	4	3	5	4	4	20
DANCERS	4	3	5	4	3	19
CHEERLEADERS	3	5	4	3	3	18
SNOWBOARDERS	5	3	2	1	3	14
BEAUTY VLOGGERS	4	4	5	5	4	22
DJs						
OUTDOOR ADVENTURERS						
ENTREPRENEURS						
SNEAKERHEADS						

SOURCE Illustration by Mike Carnevale

Accessibility: Refers to the extent to which marketers can reach the targeted segments with promotional or distribution efforts.

Responsiveness: Refers to the extent to which consumers in a defined segment will respond to marketing offers targeted at them.

Cross-fertilizable: Refers to potential for interaction and influence between different segment categories and cultures, broadening the reach or power.

Influential: Refers to the capability of the group to positively influence consumers across groups, in and outside the youth segment.

Actionable: Segments are said to be actionable when they provide guidance for marketing decisions.

On a scale of 1–5 (5 being the most), rate each subgroup on how valuable your subgroups are from a business perspective, and enter it into Table 4.4. Each subgroup's score is determined by totalling their rating number for each criterion. For example, in Table 4.4, the subgroup of beauty vloggers received a total score of 35. They scored high consistently across the board, in the opinion or experience of the scorer. Dancers scored lower across the board, while performer and snowboarder scores had more highs and lows. To the brand performing this scoring, beauty vloggers present more business opportunity and reach, and are therefore found to be more viable.

Table 4.4 Use this table to rate and score youth subgroups for commercial viability

SCALE 1-5	IDENTIFIABILITY	SUBSTANTIALITY	LONGEVITY/ STAYING POWER	ACCESSIBILITY	RESPONSIVENESS	CROSS-FERTILIZABLE	INFLUENTIAL	ACTIONABLE	SCORE
PERFORMERS	4	3	4	2	4	5	3	3	28
DANCERS	3	3	2	2	3	3	3	2	21
CHEERLEADERS	5	4	2	5	4	5	5	3	33
SNOWbOARdERS	2	1	4	1	4	5	3	3	23
BEAUTY VLOGGERS	5	4	5	4	4	4	5	4	35
DJs									
OUTdOOR ADVenTURERS									
ENTREPRENEURS									
SNEAKERHeaDS									

SOURCE Illustration by Mike Carnevale

Inputs
- Brand personality traits from Stage 2.
- Ideal youth consumer characteristics from Stage 2.
- Potential youth culture subgroups list.
- Youth subgroup commercial viability filters table.

Outputs
- Comprehensive list of youth subgroups that have potential to align with your brand.
- List of youth subgroups that share core characteristics with your brand.
- List of youth subgroups scored by alignment potential with your brand.
- List of youth subgroups scored by commercial viability potential with your brand.

Stage 4: Optimal youth audience definition

Purpose: analyse the relationship of alignment and viability and explore how it creates areas of opportunity for brands.

This is where alignment and viability intersect, allowing a brand to see which youth subgroups are the areas of best opportunity. Brands will find the area of most opportunity in the upper right quadrant (the 'bull's-eye'), medium opportunity in the upper left and lower right quadrants (the rings around the bull's-eye), and the least opportunity in the lower left quadrant.

How it works

Step 1: Plot the subgroups on the coordinate graph (Figure 4.4)

From Stage 3, plot the youth subgroups scored by alignment potential with your brand, and the youth subgroups scored by commercial viability potential with your brand. In this chapter, we have nine scored subgroups for both alignment and commercial viability. Subgroups are scored out of 5–25 potential alignment points and 8–40 potential commercial viability points.

Step 2: Analyse the potential of each subgroup to create opportunity for the brand

Once these points are plotted, we can go back and look at their alignment and viability sub-scores, and integrate this into our strategy. We can look at how best to address these subgroups, to capitalize on their strengths and weaknesses, as they affect the larger target audience. The upper right quadrant is the most useful, the lower left is least useful, but the other two quadrants have a spectrum of usability, depending on what aspects of their alignment and/or viability scores you want to focus on in a particular scenario. Consider in what situations these potential groups of young people might benefit your brand, based on the ratio of alignment to viability.

Step 3: Plot overlap to discover the convergence of supergroups

Once you have determined where on the graph each group lands, and how this can help your brand, consider how many individuals belong to more than just one subgroup. For example, it's not uncommon

Figure 4.4   Plot and analyse each youth subgroup's potential for brand alignment and commercial viability

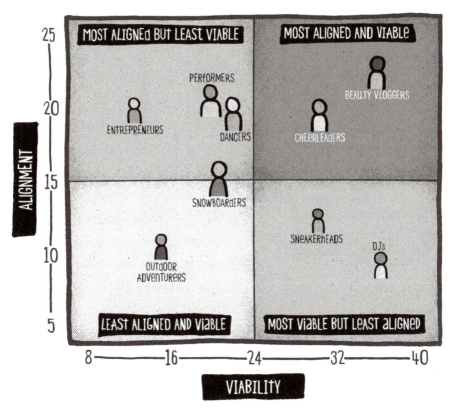

SOURCE Illustration by Mike Carnevale

that dancers or performers also take part in cheerleading for part of the year, while at the same time they can be highly engaged beauty tutorial fans or a vlogger on YouTube. We call this overlap, and when diagrammed, we can more easily see what the separate subgroups have in common (Figure 4.5).

Some subgroups may have more overlap, some less. Sometimes the overlap will be a larger percentage of a smaller group, or a smaller percentage of several groups. Either way, the overlap itself is its own micro group, made up of 2+ subgroups. When we have groups in our graph that overlap, this creates a convergence culture: an opportunity to make powerful cultural connections between multiple youth audiences. However, we must be careful in our approach to these hybrid supergroups, as there is also the potential to alienate those who have

Figure 4.5   The most successful youth brands have discovered where subgroups overlap, identifying a larger converging supergroup relevant to their brand

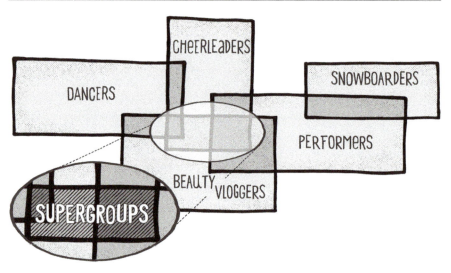

SOURCE Illustration by Mike Carnevale

any conflict of interests or exist outside the overlap. Experiencing how these overlaps behave gives us an insight into the diversified, morphing subgroup that Gen Z can be.

Ask yourself, which groups in the overlapping convergence culture or supergroups do you believe will be most important for your brand? This exercise is helpful to see which subgroups may be most valuable, or drive consumption within the larger context of the group. You can always go back to view the alignment and viability of the overlapping groups to inform decision making. For instance, how did each group score in terms of brand trait alignment or business viability, and how will that influence your decision about which group is the better fit? When would you want to consider emphasizing alignment over viability and vice versa?

Next, think about how closely you want to adhere to brand traits, or to what extent you may be ok with exceptions – sometimes focusing on the core groups at the upper right quadrant, while other times focusing on groups in the other quadrants. Here, groups might be more aligned with less viability, or may have more viability with less alignment. How do you decide which is more important in each situation that arises?

Referring back to your brand guide and the Truths in Chapter 3 will help you make these challenging decisions. We need to know what our most important, vital audience criteria are, and not get distracted: make measured decisions, and be cognizant of the impact your segmentation strategies will have on all audiences. It's critical to understand the way certain groups respond to other groups, and whether this increases or decreases alignment when developing strategies using this framework. We strongly suggest not going so far to appeal to one key group that you turn off an equally important group to your brand.

That said, people still act in unpredictable ways. Even when you follow this directional alignment framework to a tee, you will probably discover outliers and groups you didn't consider that may adopt your brand. By the same token, sometimes groups in the centre of your bullseye may not be as interested as you thought.

While no system can ever predict the exact combination of young consumer groups to target in any given situation, this alignment framework will get you closer to the cultural groups, lifestyles and, in some cases, individuals that matter most.

Inputs

- List of youth subgroups scored by alignment potential with your brand from Stage 3.
- List of youth subgroups scored by commercial viability potential with your brand from Stage 3.

Outputs

- Graph showing overall subgroup alignment and viability potential for the brand.
- Quadrant-by-quadrant view of subgroup alignment and viability potential (each quadrant depicting a different relationship of alignment and viability).
- A highly specified list of groups (subgroups, micro groups, splinter groups) that will align closest with, and be the most commercially viable to, the brand.
- A list of convergence cultures, created when two or more subgroups overlap, and a new hybrid subgroup is formed.

We realize that this is some dense, brain-taxing work. To make it more interesting and bring it to life, try doing the warm-up word game (Figure 4.6): fill in the blanks with the requested information.

Figure 4.6   Word game: complete this activity to assess your brand's youth culture alignment

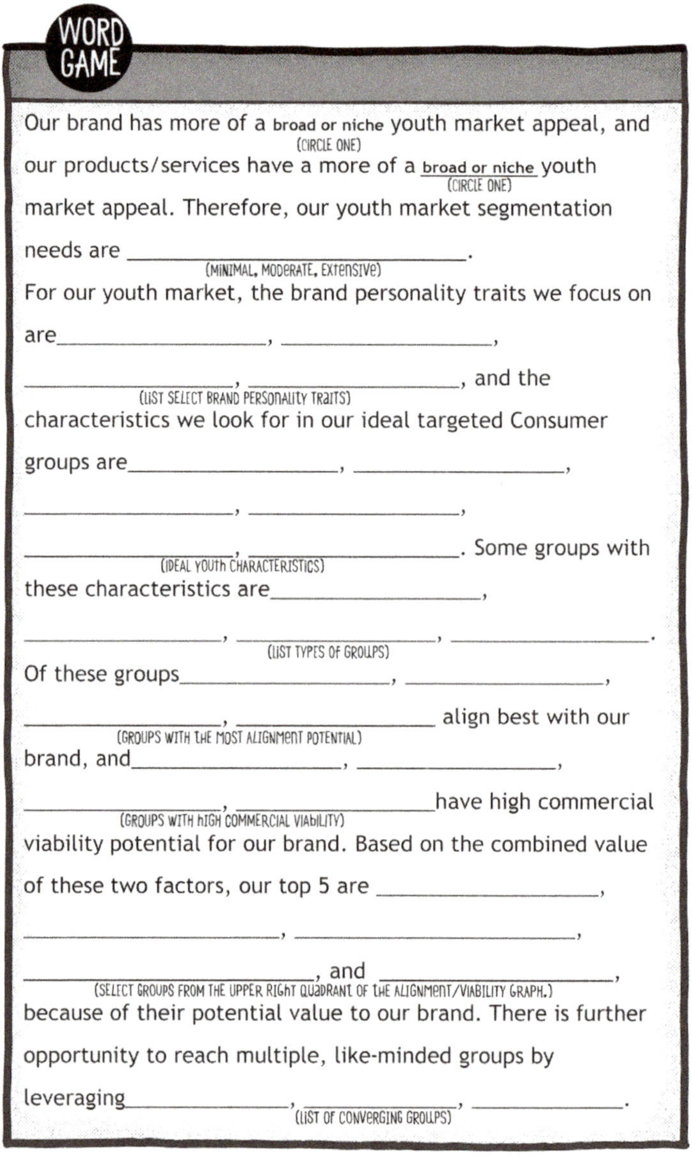

WORD GAME

Our brand has more of a broad or niche youth market appeal, and
(CIRCLE ONE)
our products/services have a more of a broad or niche youth
(CIRCLE ONE)
market appeal. Therefore, our youth market segmentation

needs are _____.
(MINIMAL, MODERATE, EXTENSIVE)
For our youth market, the brand personality traits we focus on

are_____, _____,

_____, _____, and the
(LIST SELECT BRAND PERSONALITY TRAITS)
characteristics we look for in our ideal targeted Consumer

groups are_____, _____,

_____, _____,

_____. Some groups with
(IDEAL YOUTH CHARACTERISTICS)
these characteristics are_____,

_____, _____.
(LIST TYPES OF GROUPS)
Of these groups_____, _____,

_____, _____ align best with our
(GROUPS WITH THE MOST ALIGNMENT POTENTIAL)
brand, and_____, _____,

_____have high commercial
(GROUPS WITH HIGH COMMERCIAL VIABILITY)
viability potential for our brand. Based on the combined value

of these two factors, our top 5 are _____,

_____, _____,

_____, and _____,
(SELECT GROUPS FROM THE UPPER RIGHT QUADRANT OF THE ALIGNMENT/VIABILITY GRAPH.)
because of their potential value to our brand. There is further

opportunity to reach multiple, like-minded groups by

leveraging_____, _____, _____.
(LIST OF CONVERGING GROUPS)

SOURCE Illustration by Mike Carnevale

TL;DR: chapter takeaways

- **After going through the exercises in the Youth Culture Alignment Framework, leverage the final outputs of Stage 4 and put them to work.** You should now have a customized list of targeted groups, subgroups, and so on generated specifically for your brand. They represent the ideal subgroups from both an alignment and commercial viability perspective.

- **This groundwork also serves as a directional guide when developing research studies and building the Youth Culture Engagement Playbook (strategies) in Chapter 6.**

- **Hyper-individualization is the norm: Gen Z expects unique.** When developing creative strategies to reach Gen Z, remember that being highly individualized or even 'weird' presents an opportunity to connect with them on their frequency.

- **Traditional demographic targeting models are outmoded.** If you really want to get tuned in with this group of individualistic young consumers, then focus segmentation strategies on psychographic, lifestyle and situational context as priorities.

- **Embrace the diversity of Gen Z, don't chase the cohort.** If you approach Gen Z as a homogeneous entity, and fail to appeal to the multitude of *'cultural and lifestyle segments'* that comprise it, you will be relegated to a limited view of both their world and the motivations behind their decision making.

- **Identify like-minded subgroups within youth culture that align with your brand, and build relationships with them.** Develop content and experiences that connect to the passions and situations of youth consumers. This human connection helps us to develop true alignment, which fuels the most effective strategies.

Further reading, resources and downloadable materials are available at **www.genzfreq.com**

References

Akker, J (1997) [accessed 15 March 2018] Dimensions of Brand Personality, *Journal of Marketing Research*, August [Online] https://www.gsb.stanford.edu/sites/gsb/files/publication-pdf/Dimensions_of_Brand_Personality.pdf

AwesomenessTV and Trendera (2017) [accessed 5 September 2017] Gen Z: The Audience You Can't Ignore [Online] https://awesomenesstv.com/genz/

French, C (2017) [accessed 15 March 2018] What does Youth Culture Mean in Today's Society, *Doinbits* [Online] www.doinbits.uk

Levinson, JC and Godin, S (1994) *The Guerrilla Marketing Handbook*, Houghton Mifflin Harcourt, Boston, MA

McKibben, B (2007) *Deep Economy: The wealth of communities and the durable future*, Holt Paperbacks, New York, discussed in The Age of Hyper-Individualism – Is the End in Sight? [Online] https://newenglanderbychoice.wordpress.com/2009/06/14/the-age-of-hyper-individualism-is-the-end-in-sight/[accessed 13 March 2018]

Pursey, K (2016) [accessed 15 March 2018] What Are the 12 Archetypes and Which One Dominates Your Personality, 12 June [Online] https://www.learning-mind.com/12-archetypes/

Further reading

Airosus, M [accessed 15 March 2018] Millennials: The Self-Absorbed Generation? [Online] www.porterconsulting.net/index.php/2016/11/30/millennials-self-absorbed-generation/ Akker, J (1997) [accessed 15 March 2018] Dimensions of brand personality, *Journal of Marketing Research*, August [Online] https://www.gsb.stanford.edu/sites/gsb/files/publication-pdf/Dimensions_of_Brand_Personality.pdf

Burrows, D (2015) [accessed 15 March 2018] Is behavioural data killing off demographics? *Marketing Week*, 14 September [Online] www.marketingweek.com/2015/09/04/is-behavioural-data-killing-off-demographics/

Cook, J (2017) [accessed 15 March 2018] Segmentation with Fluid Identities – #3 of 5 Strange Business Strategies from Fernando Pessoa [Blog] LinkedIin, 12 October [Online] www.linkedin.com/pulse/segmentation-fluid-identities-3-5-strange-business-strategies-cook/

Douthat, R (2015) [accessed 19 March 2018] The Age of Individualism, *The New York Times*, 15 March [Online] www.nytimes.com/2014/03/16/opinion/sunday/douthat-the-age-of-individualism.html

Godin, S (2008) *Tribes: We need you to lead us*, Penguin Group, New York

Nick (2014) [accessed 13 March 2018] Society and Hyper-Individualism [Blog], 10 Major Arguments or Ideas Presented in Deep Economy, 23 August [Online] http://deepeconomynvn.blogspot.com/2014/08/society-and-hyper-individualism.html

Portell, G (2017) [accessed 19 March 2018] Demographics: Dead, Dying or Reincarnated?, *Target Marketing*, 11 June [Online] http://www.targetmarketingmag.com/article/demography-dead-dying-reincarnated/

Raphelson, S (2014) [accessed 13 March 2018] Getting Some 'Me' Time: Why Millennials Are So Individualistic, *NPR*, 14 October [Online] https://www.npr.org/2014/10/14/352979540/getting-some-me-time-why-millennials-are-so-individualistic

Semik, J (2016) [accessed 15 March 2018] Product Roadmap Prioritization: Weighted Scoring or the Kano Model, May [Online] www.280group.com/product-management-blog/product-roadmap-prioritization-weighted-scoring-kano-model/

Watkins, JWN (1953) [accessed 15 March 2018] The seventeenth century: The age of individuality, *History Today* [Online] www.historytoday.com/jwn-watkins/seventeenth-century-age-individuality

Yoram, W and Bell, DR (2007) [accessed 15 March 2018] Market Segmentation [Online] www.citeseerx.ist.psu.edu/viewdoc/download;jsessionid=74DDC682D150730B6F276632F3D4ED8E?doi=10.1.1.720.628&rep=rep1&type=pdf

Reveal insights 05
and fuel ideation
with Gen Z

Kids aren't little adults any more than caterpillars are little butterflies. Thus expecting to get great research insights from kids using the same methodologies you use with adults is the equivalent of expecting a caterpillar to fly. It isn't going to happen. However, if you know how kids experience their world you can design kid-centred research that frees them to express their unique perspective, unbounded energy, and joyous creativity. Design kid research with kids in mind. When you do they'll be like beautiful butterflies. They'll dazzle you with their brilliance.

TERENCE BURKE, 2018, SVP OF RESEARCH, EDITOR-IN-CHIEF
KIDSAY TREND TRACKER

Collaboration leads to actionable insights and new ideas

It's not always easy to get the whole story about how young people think, feel or behave. How, then, do we connect effectively with Gen Z audiences and discover what's really on their mind? The motivations of younger consumers are based on an entirely different set of drivers from those of other generations. For example, to understand the purchase decisions of young consumers we can't just extrapolate patterns based on current, older consumers. Assumptions never lead to the truth. Assuming that a particular aspect of youth behaviour or expression might accurately reflect how the generational cohort acts overall jeopardizes the opportunity for truly understanding Gen Z.

It is our experience that deeper insights are revealed through ongoing dialogue and interactive activities, more so than in the more traditional focus-group setting. All too often in this data-driven world, the human element gets lost in the numbers; youth research cannot rely on sterile techniques and environments that might inhibit youth expression. Below we examine the ins and outs of effective youth market research design, and why we believe that research and collaboration methods have to evolve together with youth culture – ultimately adapting at the pace of the generation. As it stands now, when trying to obtain actionable information there is often too much friction in the research and ideation process.

In this chapter, we focus primarily on qualitative approaches to youth research and creative collaboration. Qualitative research is primarily exploratory, and is used to gain an understanding of under-lying reasons, opinions and motivations. It also provides insights into problems or helps to develop ideas or hypotheses for additional quantitative research. It's the ideal method to help us stay tuned in to the perceptions and motivations that evolve and emerge from Gen Z. It helps us approach with an open mind, rather than from a position of authority and expertise: for example, consider going beyond standard surveys or online panels in favour of sounding boards that build 'always-on' dialogues with targeted youth participants. This will inspire *real* insights and start *genuine* communication.

Research and collaboration design for youth participants

We always want to inspire kids to be creative and tell their own stories… giving them the frames of reference and letting them go and create is the goal.

DAN WINGER, 2017, SENIOR INNOVATION DESIGNER AT LEGO

The approach to research and collaboration can make or break a youth-focused initiative. A well-designed process should be an inves-tigatory roadmap, with consistent checks and balances to help us stay on course or pivot when needed. Youth-specific research needs to capture Gen Z opinions and preferences that may not surface with traditional research methods. We have worked with Gen Z for years and have learnt how to learn with them; therefore the majority of our methodologies in this chapter are rooted in some form of interactive study or cultural immersion. Deeper immersion into young people's lives can lead us to create entirely new categories of products, services and content that fundamentally meet young people's needs and wants, provide new value and have the potential to create significant competitive advantages. Does your research or collaboration design facilitate interactions with participants that deliver actionable insights?

Does your research and collaboration connect you to youth culture?

To design and conduct research that reveals Gen Z's opinions, behaviours and preferences, we must have regard for the way they process information and have grown up communicating. Consider the following guidelines:

Establish mutual trust and respect to earn access to the real story: Are you transparent with participants throughout the process? Are you upfront enough to get and maintain their participation? Respect is a two-way street, and Gen Z knows when they are not being heard; they aren't going to give you the unvarnished truth until you earn their trust. Getting closer to the truth means you have to convince Gen Z that you are an ally who wants to listen, and this can be accomplished through interactive and collaborative efforts. If not, their responses are unlikely to go any deeper than a 'sure', or an eye roll.

Select familiar participant environments: Participant experience is critical to reveal insights and facilitate collaboration, so we employ socially powered engagements that are driven by the consumer's perspective and their feedback on the experience. It is critical to make participants feel comfortable; if they feel 'off' they will start to shut down, not express themselves fully (as discussed above), or say what they think you want to hear, to avoid discomfort. Research and ideation is most effective when it integrates input from the full spectrum of consumer experiences.

Collaborate, don't just 'conduct research': Our goal is to be original and in tune with Gen Z. We all know that Gen Z has more options and distractions as they grow up. Is your approach to data collection original and innovative enough to keep participant attention? Does it inspire them to open up and share honest opinions, and want to participate in future projects? For example, we use interactive, often gamified activities and collaboration, rather than one-way questionnaires, to create interactions that don't feel like 'research' to the youth participant, but produce research results for the brand (Witt, 2017).

Elements of youth research and collaboration design

The first element in our process is the recruitment of participants for research and collaboration. This is an important step that is often difficult to navigate, but here we help to map it out. Next, we must consider the environment that a brand and its consumers inhabit: information and trends about Gen Z help us to structure our research methodologies, so that we can customize research or ideation for the consumers that brands wish to reach. Finally, we develop and utilize highly interactive and collaborative methodologies that engage youth consumers and brands throughout the research process. The results are what help form actionable strategies for brands.

Youth recruitment

Collaboration and research are not just challenging to design, they can be a headache to implement. Below we discuss some of the common issues with recruitment and some solutions that can facilitate the task. Reliable findings and innovative ideas rely on feedback from the right young people. The methodologies presented here help eliminate the wild-card so often encountered in digital research: who are the people responding to your questions or tasks, are they really those you want to hear from, and how good are they? The quality of the results is based on the quality of the recruits, whether you are seeking a broad youth population target or a very specific niche cultural profile.

Common snags in the recruitment game

What sources do we use to recruit youth consumers? When we do find a group to participate, how do we ensure that their participation leads to valuable insights? Quality participant recruitment is a significant challenge in research studies involving the kids, tweens and teens of Gen Z.

All of these challenges are complicated, but some are more ambiguous than others: it's not always easy to find sources to recruit from at all; how do we identify, screen and involve the types of individuals we want to recruit, and how do we encourage natural, open and honest participation? Some of the recruitment challenges are less vague, such as obtaining parental consent in compliance with the US Children's Online Privacy Protection Act (COPPA), the European Union's General Data Protection Regulation (GDPR) and Australian privacy laws (see Chapter 9).

Some challenges are downright infuriating. Are your participants focused more on the incentives than they are on sharing open, honest opinions or creative ideas? Incentives can eclipse the true purpose of the research. This is a very fine line we have to walk as we create an adequate level of appeal for participants. Conducting digital research today through mobile surveys and other online research tools has made the process of data gathering easier and more cost-effective, but has opened the door to those who take advantage of incentive offers.

One example of this is a professional 'survey-gamer': one who actively looks for online and mobile app-based surveys offering cash, rewards and other paid incentives for completing surveys. Indeed, there is an entire universe of blogs, sites and social media accounts solely focused on directing people to find surveys for them to deplete your research budget. Another example, not uncommon, is that parents sign their child up, then take the survey themselves, or coach their child through it. Responses that have been adult-washed by parental influence are unusable. Nor do we want a participant who is so exposed to research by parents that they are essentially just 'doing a job', rather than giving real insights.

Solutions to recruitment challenges

Recruitment involves a number of activities: identifying sources, gaining access, outreach, identifying and screening eligible participants, and recruiting an adequate participant size sample based on project goals. With over 20+ years' experience in the field of youth insights, we have developed a set of sources and best practices that we rely on when working with young people.

Focus on building a powerful network of recruitment sources   It's *all* about relationships. Quality participants are only going to be as good as the quality of our sources. Therefore we must ensure that our sources represent real-world environments – or youth hubs – where young people co-exist and interact, and strong connections exist between the sources and the young people involved. Any project should have the highest likelihood of being natural, not interrupting Gen Z's life, so that their participation remains as unaffected as possible.

Once you've established a strong network of sources, large or small, the key is to maintain ongoing expansion efforts. This leads to a diverse conduit for participant recruitment and thus avoids the pitfall of repeatedly cycling through the same people. It's advisable to work with sources who normally have a steady flow or cycle of the young people involved in their organization.

Tips to improve quality participation and responses

Define clear participant selection criteria

Recruit smaller sample sizes (qualitative/ideation only)

Focus on the quality of individual participants

Develop youth-appropriate screeners

Conduct articulation interviews (in-person/mobile video verification)

Involve expert youth facilitators.

Reliable sources for youth participant recruitment

- Schools and after-school programmes
- Influencer networks
- Student clubs and organizations
- Parent meetup groups
- Professional recruiters.

Ideas for participation incentives   Below are examples of gamified incentive ideas for a variety of mobile, online or in-person task-based activities that engage and retain young people in a collaborative way. No youth research and ideation project is game-proof; once you have validated participants and they have met the criteria, you are ready to create and develop an incentive plan for participants.

Thought starters for gamified participation incentives

- Common uses: interviews, ethnographies and mobile video surveys:
  - Lottery draw: after survey or task completion, enter participants into a draw to receive valuable offers from youth-relevant brands. For example, gift cards (from Forever 21, Starbucks, Amazon, Zumiez etc).
  - Once-in-a-lifetime opportunity: for example, when conducting larger studies, offer participants the chance to be guested on a popular YouTuber's livestream.
  - First look: select participants who give the best responses (based on pre-set criteria) and enter them into a draw to receive the new product/sample before launch.
  - Karma bonus: award gift cards for best responses (open-ended questions) or especially valuable contributions. Motivate participants to bring their A Game and get rewarded!

- Common uses: advisory boards, collaborative ideation and testing projects
  - Paperwork palooza: the rewards start now! Encourage the participant and/or parent to sign your consent agreement, join the project group and be entered to win. This type of reward offers immediate recognition and helps motivate participation.
  - Introduce yourself: just for signing up and introducing themselves to the project group, enter the participant into a draw to win one of five gift cards.
  - Chance to be a part of an exclusive new product development: after completion of certain criteria, select participants with the 'best responses' and then further select the chosen few to be included in the development of the next brand-related product.

– Timing is everything: enter the first participant who completes all three tasks as part of the study (Video Qs, messaging feedback and concept ideas) to win one of 15 gift cards. Participants must complete all three tasks by the date listed to be eligible for this prize.

Build the foundation with baseline research

When designing for research or ideation, we need context: it's important to have an overview and understanding of youth culture, the product/service category, current events and the overall media landscape. What are your competitors doing? What are the current technologies, social platforms, worldviews and other perceptions? Ultimately, what is going to affect the way Gen Z will act, interact and interpret their world? Be curious, and come to the table seeking to understand the full Gen Z spectrum. Below are two proven methodologies we suggest using to establish a baseline understanding of the targeted youth market.

Youth and pop culture media scan

What: A youth and pop culture media scan is the practice of scanning youth-related lifestyle media, including: social, video on demand, broadcast news, magazines, books, events and anything that seems like a noteworthy activity within the current and rapidly evolving youth media landscape. Just as satellite images show changing weather patterns, a survey of popular and emerging media is used to identify the frequency of currents (trends) that may indicate hot spots, representing new and noteworthy opportunities (Kumar, 2012).

How: Conduct simple or more sophisticated online research, using social listening tools to identify the topics that need to be addressed.

Why: Youth media scans provide an overview of the latest trends, insights about targeted youth audiences and emerging development of what's new and noteworthy. They help brands gain a general understanding of the youth landscape to lay the foundation to develop campaigns, new products and services. Media scans provide cultural context, reveal patterns and provide direction.

Tip: Conduct mind-mapping sessions to identify the topics of research and set up a digital library of findings (this can be as simple as a cloud or a more robust online dashboard). The key is to observe patterns, look both within and outside of the youth-related lifestyle that may impact your brand.

Trend tracking

What: Trend-tracking research and analysis is a method of obtaining an ongoing quantitative perspective of youth culture. Covering a broad spectrum of categories throughout the year gives a holistic picture of all the critical behaviours, attitudes and aspirations in young people's lives as they are currently, and as they evolve in the context of their world.

How: This is typically done over 12-month timeframes or longer, fielding the surveys 4–6 times a year. Sample size is typically over 1,000 participants per survey (4,500–6,000 youth annually), balanced by US Census-mirrored region and race breakout, and inclusive of mixed ethnicity and gender.

Why: Young people's lives are dynamic, continually morphing as they discover who they are and who they want to become in the context of the world they know. As personalized handheld devices are adopted in greater numbers and at lower ages, the access kids have to knowledge of their world grows exponentially. Trend tracking combines the foundation of the past with a continually updated understanding of the present to enrich your ability to prepare, and even predictively see the future before it materializes into Gen Z's reality. Trend tracking gives you the context to maximize ROI as you produce, price, place and promote your products in an incredibly challenging market.

Tip: Gen Z's preferences, and the way they spend their time, are continually shifting. It is vital to know who they are and how they think to yield the most accurate and articulate responses. Utilizing real kids, not a biased parent speaking for their child, and using a variety of open-ended questions will help to yield a true look at how and what your audience really thinks and why they think that way.

Youth research and collaboration methodologies

We wanted to make sure our prime audience, whom we called the Expressive Creators, had a strong emotional connection with Vans. We wanted to make sure they could relate to the brand's core values of creativity, authenticity, inclusivity and passion. We leveraged consumer insights to understand what made them tick, connect and feel special, and we acted on it to fuel creative expression through content creation, experiential marketing and compelling product collaboration.

SEBASTIEN MARCQ, 2018, FORMER SENIOR BRAND MARKETING
MANAGER EMEA, VANS

Once we have recruited participants and gathered intelligence through a youth and pop culture media scan and trend tracking, we can start to decide how and where to investigate further, and where deeper insights may be needed. Through applying the right mix of methodologies we are able to draw out valuable insights and ideas. We use this mix to encourage participants to be actively involved in select research processes, collaborate – at times even *co-create* – right alongside us.

In order to obtain the best results from our research and collaboration design with Gen Z, we present our research methodologies in all the trappings of youth culture: it's all on their terms, in their space, using language that resonates with them, and in a familiar and accessible format or technology. The way they experience a particular technique can determine that methodology's success or failure, so we take great pains to make sure the participants have a good experience, stay interested, and don't get bored or pushed past their attention span. The more engaged they are, the better the quality of their answers, so we keep realistic expectations of what a particular technique can yield. Below are a few proven, youth-effective methodologies that bring about quality responses from the targeted youth market.

Youth culture advisory boards

What: An online or mobile app-based methodology that allows brands to connect directly with a customized group of experts, influencers and consumers. Youth advisory boards are composed of groups of forward-thinking young people as well as other stakeholders, both of whom fit predetermined criteria that make them valuable to the brand, and deeply connected to youth consumers. They are generally youth subject matter experts, enthusiasts, influencers, rejecters and representative youth – all those who are in or influence your target audience. Groups are typically smaller (ranging from 50 to 100 or smaller), which helps to build a sense of community and commitment to the research study or ideation project.

How: The role of each advisory board is to review and give feedback, or to help collaborate on solving problems and developing new ideas. A well-designed and facilitated youth advisory board engages in qualitative dialogue, in order to enable a brand to develop research or strategies with that brand's target audience. They can reveal key insights, challenge strategic thinking and inspire new ideas to ensure that youth-focused initiatives (messaging, advertising, product development, education programmes, etc.) are infused with youth relevance.

Why: Access to this 'insider knowledge' helps brands to make strategic decisions more confidently. Through insights, ideation and collaboration, or co-creation with the target audience, creative choices are grounded in authenticity and content that will resonate with the target audience.

Tip: Assemble a mix of people, a mashup of talents and personalities, with a variety of roles and experiences. Strive for variety of people and interactions so that there are energy and stimulation within the group. Guide the group experience so that interactions are fun and create a sense of importance of mission within the group.

CASE STUDY   Global cosmetic brand – Gen Z advisory board

Define with us

Fine print: To respect the confidentiality of our client, we do not mention the company name and we have changed the title. The details and outcomes have not been altered.

What we did

As cosmetic use continues to age down, while at the same time rising in popularity and status, cosmetic brands are increasingly focused on the youth market. In order to identify when, where and how to engage teen consumers with their products, we customized a brand-specific advisory board to collaborate throughout the project. The goal was to develop a playbook with a set of pre-approved engagement strategies for the company's internal marketing team to deploy at their discretion, giving them an edge on their competition.

How we did it

We worked closely with the brand's in-house team over a 90-day timespan. The advisory board entailed a group of 92 teens divided into three distinct subgroups of female, male and gender-fluid participants aged 13–18. A range of early adopters, brand rejecters, satisfied customers, influencers and passionate content creators were hand-selected to form a well-rounded group capable of the creative thinking needed. Here's what we did:

- We engaged five beauty influencers who invited teen followers to apply for a VIP experience on a project landing page. At this stage, applicants were qualified before the process of interviewing and selecting participants began.

- We gathered insights via mobile video surveys to determine the engagement channels.

- Participants shared their own ideas for engaging with and experiencing the brand as relevant to each channel.

- We combined everyone's ideas and participants ranked them via a series of fun social quizzes.

- The best ideas were compiled into a virtual catalogue of engagement strategies and tactics.

- We mocked up 10 hand-selected ideas and conducted a caption contest to gauge reactions.

- We continuously tested the content and engagement campaigns on our advisory participants as we developed them, resulting in both validation and course corrections depending on the response.

Why it worked

This company took the time and effort to truly understand what Gen Z audiences were looking for from them by going directly to them, asking the right questions, interacting and *listening*. As a result, they were able to form youth engagement strategies that resonate with the audience and how they want to interact with the brand. They now have a playbook that helps them navigate along the way.

Advisory board best practices

- Launch your customized private mobile community group with a welcome video.

- Start the process by posting discussion topics related to the project in order to get to know each member, build community and spark creativity.

- Each week, post an activity on Monday for the members to do on their own by the following Sunday. Send the participants a notification for the activity and post to the group. Each activity should have a page that walks the participant through the activity steps and stores their responses (text/videos) privately and confidentially.

- During the week, post a few discussion prompts to encourage group discussion related to the activity. These prompts are used to create discussions that probe deeper on the topics, ideas, themes and trends we are seeing from the weekly exercises.

- Ensure each weekly exercise is designed to ideate or dive deeper into ideas that inform, inspire, course correct or validate the direction for your engagement strategies.

- Make sure you involve a range of cultural insiders, from influencers, enthusiasts and extroverts to more introverted creatives and academics.

Mobile video and voice-based surveys

What: A mobile video or voice-based survey is a smartphone, app-based or laptop tool that utilizes video and/or voice instead of text to capture a participant's answers. The majority of communication is non-written, where video allows you to see, and audio allows you to hear, more of the nuances that are often lost in less immediate, text-bound communication. Mobile surveys allow the user to utilize their surroundings and friends, and bring more life and authenticity to the response.

How: The participant is given a question or request, and prompted to create a video or audio response. This technique is most effectively deployed by a mobile app. Typically, participants use a mobile phone, device or computer to take and upload videos.

Why: Mobile video surveys deliver authentic, real-life youth consumer stories and feedback. Because this happens in real time, feedback is not distorted by memory or faded emotions. Mobile responses are often easier to execute for young people, and this means more thorough responses. In addition, because you can actually see or hear a real person giving feedback, you can screen, qualify and cast people for your research, ensuring that they will connect to or represent your target audience. This also provides quality control and limits gamers. Lastly, this affords the ability to get more personalized research when you can't afford to perform research in person.

Tip: At the start of the survey or project, we often use a stimulus video or audio message, in which the question or call-to-action is delivered by someone Gen Z relates to. We find that when the request comes from an insider or non-adult, the trust level and willingness to contribute go up. The stimulation is especially effective when an influencer, creator or a peer, who is either the same age or just a little bit older, delivers the message. It creates familiarity, or more importantly, an aspirational connection.

Social quizzes

What: Social quizzes are a branded or unbranded survey activity, designed to reveal youth insights about your products, their habits and motivations, and to better understand youth perceptions on a national level. However, that's not necessarily how they are designed to come across. They are typically 7–10 questions, presented in a visually appealing way or through voice, instead of a plain text format. They are designed to be fun and entertaining. Social quizzes are often extensively shared and invite tremendous engagement; they can be a cost-effective way to add a layer of quantitative data into a qualitative study.

How: Creating an entertaining and informative quiz is a tough balancing act. Remember that a successful social media quiz needs to be interactive and fun – we've added photos, media files and even co-creative activities to make them more engaging. We've executed them with respondent quotas ranging from 300 to 5,000, so it completely depends on your objectives. They are typically executed on any one of the majority social platforms, or embedded in a landing page.

Why: A social quiz has a similar draw to horoscopes: people are endlessly curious about themselves and their future, or the 'hidden truth' about themselves. They crave the confirmation bias, or controversy, that the results of a social quiz deliver. They seem to be irresistible, so brands can use them to ask questions that the brand finds valuable, disguised in an entertaining format that adds to the social and dramatic aspect of Gen Z's world.

Tip: For the best result, partner your quiz with targeted media or influencers, to embed an unbranded quiz on a website, blog, Instagram ad or Facebook. As much as you can, be creative and tailor your quiz to the target audience – make it all about them!

Influencer mindsharing

What: Influencer mindsharing is a new methodology for both research and ideation that incorporates focus groups, interviews or ethnography projects, all conducted with one or a group of influencers. Think of it as a direct line to the experts on a particular audience or segment. This methodology is primarily used to address more complex problems and ideation challenges than we would with typical participants. It helps brands to leverage influencers to their full potential: beyond just influencing downstream (to followers and consumer audiences), but upstream to brands, in order that we might better understand the target market.

How: In its simplest form, it uses mobile video surveys or voice technologies to facilitate an in-depth dialogue with real youth-relevant influencers. It can also be a multi-phased project, using mixed methods, and can involve a team of influencers who all execute on different projects. It can last several weeks or several months.

Why: Influencers have status and a following, as well as the respect and trust of the audience. They know the target audience better than anyone, and how best to translate and address their wants and needs, as well as inspire and relate to them. They are, therefore, a natural resource for brands hoping to get valuable insights and ideation from that audience regarding their products and services.

Tip: Match your brand with a group of influencers or creators who embody the mindset of your targeted youth audience segment, individuals who inspire the communities you are trying to reach, those with a true passion for your brand or product category, and most critically, people who fit the selection criteria defined for your project.

Influencer – audience collabs

What: An influencer-led survey or ideation project centred around an exclusive experience for targeted youth audience segments (Figure 5.1).

How: The influencer engages a spectrum of your target audience through activities that are fun, interesting and feel 'non-researchy' for participants. For example, an influencer puts out a call-to-action, encouraging the audience to apply, on a custom landing page, for the opportunity to interact as a group with the influencer, and – depending on the rewards for the experience – they might win either products or more personal access to the influencer.

Figure 5.1   Example of an effective youth research and ideation methodology: influencer–audience collabs

INFLUENCER AUDIENCE COLLABS

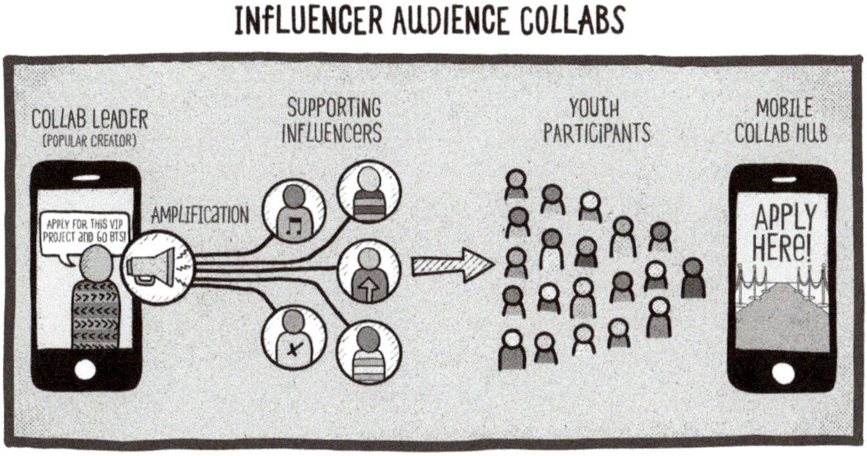

SOURCE Illustration by Mike Carnevale

Why: The organizing influencer embodies the mindset of your audience segment. They inspire: the audience the brand is trying to reach, those with a true passion for your brand or product category, and most critically, those people who fit the selection criteria defined for your project. Additionally, the influencer provides access to a larger, more targeted youth sample size than a typical panel.

Tip: Leverage the expertise of the influencer, allowing them to co-create the experience with the brand, and have creative control over the co-lab itself, making the experience as authentic to the consumer as possible. This will also weed out 'survey takers', so the resultant data and ideas are legitimately coming from the targeted audience.

EXPERT INTERVIEW   Dan Winger, Senior Innovation Designer at LEGO

Young people expect to be increasingly involved with brands and products, and no one understands that better than LEGO. We wanted to know how LEGO meets that expectation and how co-creation benefits both consumers and LEGO, so we went directly to Dan Winger to find out.

Can you give our readers some background to the ways you embrace co-creation at LEGO?

In 2011 we launched LEGO Ideas: a crowdsourcing platform that allows users to submit their LEGO creations, with a possibility of bringing them to market and earning royalties on the sales. The platform creates value for the users by providing a channel to express their creativity through LEGO bricks, share these custom models, get inspiration and feedback from others, engage with a community of passionate building enthusiasts, browse fun and exciting projects and, for a select few, have their creation immortalized as an official LEGO product.

The diversity of projects we have seen on the platform is mind-blowing. Many of the submissions are ones we would probably not have come up with through our internal development process, or creations that would be highly challenging to prove a market viability for without community voting.

The benefit of this endeavour for LEGO is that we have a new line of highly innovative products that have the ability to reach new segments of consumers. The products we have released through LEGO Ideas include an interactive marble maze, The Beatles Yellow Submarine, a trio of realistic birds, and my favourite, Women of NASA.

In addition to LEGO Ideas, we also have the LEGO Life platform. This social network lets users share their creations, be inspired by other builders and safely connect with the community, but also features a variety of interactive content ranging from creative challenges to trivia questions. This product is a more playful and social experience for younger LEGO users (ages 13 and under) to engage with the LEGO brand. Beyond co-creation with users, we also work with various partners to develop new products, entertainment and technology together.

What is your goal for co-creation within the LEGO Creative Play Lab team? What co-creative methods do you employ, and, in your experience, what are the most effective?

Since our core market is boys and girls ages 5–9, not a single LEGO employee is our primary user. Children are the LEGO experts! Therefore the goal of co-creation is to better understand our user: their interests; motivations; pain points; lifestyle trends; fine motor skills for interactions and more. Co-creation sessions with kids are invaluable to define new business opportunities, steer product and feature development, and ultimately determine what they find fun and engaging. Over the years, I have used several different methods which include in-home visits, informal play sessions, formal testing, foundational research, Design Thinking and Lean Startup processes. There is no one method that is more effective than another, they all have their value and use cases. It all depends on the phase of the project and the type of project, along with the expertise and interests of the project team. Personally, I love building things and bringing ideas to life, so I gravitate towards the Lean Startup approach as it focuses on learning through rapid and iterative development. It begins with defining an area of uncertainty and framing a hypothesis (or hypotheses), then building out a minimum viable product for testing these area(s) of focus. The prototype is then brought to a co-creation/test session with users in which we gain validated learnings and reduce the area of uncertainty. The cycle then repeats as the insights help steer the project forward towards the strongest path for success.

How has your role (or process) of co-creation evolved during your time at LEGO?

I've been at LEGO for a decade, so I've seen many changes over the years. From my experience, co-creation has evolved to be more focused and more frequent. We enter co-creation sessions with a clearer vision of precisely what we want to learn (but of course, being open to learnings outside of that scope) and have smaller tests more often.

What advice do you have for brands that are starting out, struggling with, or want to improve their co-creation methods? (Feel free to reference your work with brands outside of LEGO)

Never lose sight of the needs of your user. If you are not within your core market, remember that your opinions may be different from that of the user. So be sure to have frequent co-creation sessions with users and immerse yourself in their lifestyle. Rather than being an outside observer, learn to empathize with them, think like them, and act like them… when appropriate, of course, because sometimes my wife doesn't appreciate it when I act like an 8-year-old.

TL;DR: chapter takeaways

- *Check your assumptions at the door:* forget what you think you know about young people, and involve them as participants in problem solving and ideation. Be transparent, authentic, relevant, respectful, and above all, listen and interact through collaboration.

- *Find reliable sources for youth recruitment:* knowing where to find the right people is one of the biggest challenges. Do the groundwork, build a strong network of youth-relevant recruitment sources, then strengthen relationships with them and maintain expansion efforts. Use our source list as a starting point.

- *Discover the unspoken truths:* insights and innovation are most often derived from what's unsaid. Establish mutual respect, provide a conducive environment and design participant experiences that don't feel 'researchy', in order to reveal genuine insights and bright ideas from Gen Z.

- *Implement research and collaboration around proven methodologies.* Using youth and pop culture media scans, trend trackers and other methodologies, give your research the foundation it needs to be relevant and target the audience you seek. When engaging with Gen Z consumers, explore use of collaborative methods such as youth culture advisory boards, mobile video surveys, social quizzes, influencer mindsharing, influencer–audience collabs and many others.

- *Attracting the right participants and gaining quality responses.* Step outside the cubicle and challenge your insights team to approach data collection and ideation in original ways that encourage quality responses and interactions.

- *Gain valuable insights and ideas, don't get survey-gamed.* Avoid the common pitfalls associated with youth recruitment and research. Take precautions against those who may compromise your research, and game you for incentives.

- *Respect privacy laws and be compliant when it comes to youth data collection.* When engaging with Gen Z consumers, under age 13, know the laws and make sure your interactions are compliant with COPPA, GDPR and Australian privacy laws.

References

Kumar, V (2012) *101 Design Methods: A structured approach for driving innovation in your organization*, John Wiley & Sons, Hoboken, NJ

Witt, G (2017) *A Foundational Guide to Gen Z Collaboration*, Motivate, San Diego, CA

Further reading

Kelley, T (2001) *The Art of Innovation: Lessons in creativity from IDEO, America's leading design firm*, Profile Books, London

Michael, DM (2008) *Qualitative Research in Business & Management*, Sage, New York

Schmidt, S (2017) [accessed 19 March 2018] Predicted Market Research Trends for 2017 [Blog], *Market Research*, 16 December [Online] www.blog.marketresearch.com/predicted-market-research-trends-for-2017

The youth culture engagement playbook

Too many marketers and agencies merely observe culture and react, believing speed is the best practice. But, the brands that will win the hearts and wallets of America's youth are the ones who find authentic ways to actively help make the culture. That's when real engagement happens.

ADAM WILSON, 2018, CARHARTT, FORMER DIRECTOR OF BRAND MARKETING, NORTH AMERICA

What is a playbook and why does it matter?

Playbooks are probably part of your marketing vernacular (or you know them from the sporting world). This chapter is dedicated specifically to developing a *youth engagement strategy* playbook, by laying out and breaking down what we've found to be the key components that help brands connect and build credibility with youth audiences. The good news is that you've already put in a majority of the work for your playbook during the previous chapters: applying the Truths as they relate to your brand, finding your audience alignment, and learning how to approach research for actionable insights. Here, we will focus our playbook on key components and strategies specifically designed for engaging youth audiences.

For all intents and purposes, a playbook is, '[a] way to counteract uncertainty... The playbook and plays in it guide [brands] to make smart, coordinated choices under high pressure...' states Christopher Penn, Marketing Keynote Speaker and Vice President of marketing technology at SHIFT Communications, in a 2017 article (Penn, 2017). As you walk step-by-step through the essential 'plays' (engagement strategies) of the playbook, take the time to understand and practise building the strategies around your needs and audience, until you are ready to build an engagement playbook that works best for your brand. When completed, your playbook will lay out a set of custom-ized engagement strategies that can stand alone, or be integrated to strengthen your overall marketing plan.

Place the focus on consumer engagement and value creation

We are not suggesting that this playbook will be your entire market-ing strategy or plan. In fact, this playbook is specifically focused on *youth engagement*: a crucial aspect of marketing to youth consumers. Engagement means actively contributing to youth culture and involving young people in the content, conversations and experiences along the way – *not* treating youth consumers as passive message-recipients. From a tactical perspective, engagement is the sum of interactions a consumer has with your brand: social likes, comments, video views, shares, user-generated content (UGC), tune-in, event attendance and any direct participation in experiences that a brand facilitates. We focus on this, because authentic engagement is the only proven way for us to get on Gen Z's wavelength, tune in to their frequencies and start forming the relationships that build brand credibility. As you go through the play-book, ask yourself what your brand is doing to celebrate and support what young people are already doing, and how you are creating value.

Components of a *Youth Engagement* Playbook

- Playbook foundation:
  - Brand positioning
  - Target audience

- Research insights
- Youth advisory board
- Business use cases
- Objectives
- Youth engagement strategies:
  - Original content storytelling
  - Influence partner collaboration
  - Live immersive experiences.

How to prepare and get started

In the box above, we've outlined the components of our playbook: the playbook foundation, business use cases, objectives and our three core youth engagement strategies. The first part of this chapter is designed to guide you through the organization and development of the first three components, so that your playbook contains the structure and detail you can rely on to fuel the engagement strategies that make up the rest of the chapter – or final component.

Playbook foundation

1 Complete the Youth Market Readiness Audits (Chapter 3) (Output: brand self-awareness).

2 Develop your brand identity and youth-relevant positioning (Chapter 3) (Output: strong sense of brand that leads to content narratives).

3 Find audience alignment within youth culture (Chapter 4) (Output: know your ideal target audience segments).

4 Apply all available qualitative and quantitative research findings: (Chapter 5) (Output: essential data and key insights).

5 Leverage youth advisory boards during research, planning and evaluation of youth engagement initiatives (Chapter 5) (Output: critical feedback and validation).

Don't go it alone: youth advice makes for better engagement

We discussed the benefits of youth advisory boards in Chapter 5, and there's no better time and place to use them than while developing your playbook. Why go it alone when you can involve participants from your target audience who can help shape the direction of your engagement plans effectively? The case study in Chapter 5 highlights how we formed a Gen Z advisory board to help shape engagement strategies for a global cosmetics brand dominating the industry.

Examples of business use cases

While there is a wide range of use cases that would benefit from a focus on youth engagement, we have put together a list of common ones that we see often, and use to build our playbooks:

- New product launches
- Advertising campaigns
- Social change initiatives
- Subscriber acquisition
- Test marketing programmes
- Seasonal promotions
- Cause marketing
- Education programmes
- Sales events.

Examples of common engagement objectives

Your youth engagement objectives will be unique to your brand, its market position, and how your brand is perceived by young consumers. Below we've included a few examples of consumer engagement objectives commonly applied in our work:

- To attract a younger demographic (be specific) to the brand by focusing on aspirational product qualities.

- To generate awareness and increase brand value across targeted youth segments.
- To create hyper-targeted youth marketing campaigns designed to inspire and motivate customer acquisition.
- To develop and maintain a youth-relevant social change programme that will be implemented by volunteers nationwide.
- To drive higher intent to (purchase, visit, etc.) by strengthening the brand perception directly with young consumers.
- To establish partnerships with popular creators and influencers that produce value, build community and demonstrate ROI.
- To create and deploy youth engagement campaigns that drive sales.
- To build long-term brand loyalty that transcends age and life stage: establishing roots that anchor as they grow.

The worksheet (Table 6.1) brings together the use cases and objectives in a way that illustrates their relationship with specific Gen Z segments. This exercise will help ensure that your playbook is audience specific, and keeps the focus on engagement.

The core youth engagement strategies

Throughout this chapter we focus on three core strategies for youth engagement:

- Original content storytelling
- Influence partner collaborations
- Live immersive experiences.

As we run through each of the engagement strategies, we will take you through a step-by-step process that highlights relevant subject matter, provides thought starters for your brand, takes you through word games, offers insight through case studies and, finally, guides you through a comprehensive planning worksheet. The goal is that the chapter empowers you to develop a playbook with effective strategies that improve youth engagement.

Table 6.1 Use this planning worksheet to identify use cases, objectives and expected outcomes

USE CASES	ENGAGEMENT OBJECTIVES	EXPECTED OUTCOMES
SEGMENT ONE: KIDS AGE 7–8		
SEGMENT TWO: TWEENS AGE 9–13		
SEGMENT THREE: TEENS AGE 14–18		
MIXED SEGMENT: TEENS & YOUNG ADULTS AGE 16–24		

SOURCE Illustration by Mike Carnevale

Strategy 01: original content storytelling

Marketing is no longer about the stuff that you make, but about the stories you tell.

SETH GODIN, 2017

In a world where the greatest prize is attention, content must capture an audience's imagination and get them to tune in. If a brand's content fails to engage youth audiences, then the brand loses the opportunity to tell its story. Content stories can be as short and simple as a meme, GIF or snap, or as developed as an episodic video series, but they must present their key message through a theme/topic, format and channel that is relevant to Gen Z.

Communicate on their wavelength: topics and formats that resonate

Later in this section we will put your stories to the test with our storytelling content evaluator, but first we want to make sure that your content can reach your audience effectively. The following list of popular content topics and formats gives insight into how you can present content in ways that are most likely to intersect with audiences you seek; pair your content with topics and formats that your Gen Z audiences like the most, for maximum impact (Figure 6.1):

- Topics
  - Animals
  - Comedy
  - Education
  - Fandoms
  - Music
  - Gaming
  - Beauty
  - Sports
  - Celebrities
  - Toys
  - DIY

- Format
  - Long-form video (over 5-minute run length)
  - Short-form video (under 5-minute run length)
  - Video story (short length/ephemeral) livestreaming
  - Photo/graphic images and filters
  - Podcast
  - Gamification
  - GIF (animated/static images)
  - Boomerang (forward/backward mini-video)
  - Memes.

Figure 6.1 Favourite video topics and formats among teen girls and boys

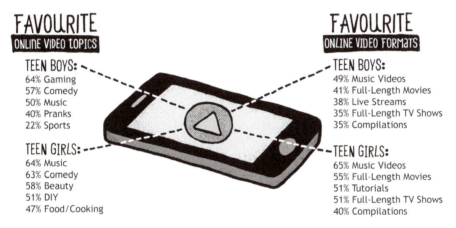

FAVOURITE ONLINE VIDEO TOPICS

TEEN BOYS:
64% Gaming
57% Comedy
50% Music
40% Pranks
22% Sports

TEEN GIRLS:
64% Music
63% Comedy
58% Beauty
51% DIY
47% Food/Cooking

FAVOURITE ONLINE VIDEO FORMATS

TEEN BOYS:
49% Music Videos
41% Full-Length Movies
38% Live Streams
35% Full-Length TV Shows
35% Compilations

TEEN GIRLS:
65% Music Videos
55% Full-Length Movies
51% Tutorials
51% Full-Length TV Shows
40% Compilations

SOURCE Artist's rendering from: Gen Z, The Audience You Can't Ignore study by AwesomenessTV. Artist's rendering by Mike Carnevale

Social platforms for engagement

Social platforms are a critical piece of the youth engagement play-book, so we stress their contribution to content delivery here. The worksheet (Table 6.2) will help to prioritize the best platforms for your audience. (For a more comprehensive look, see Chapter 7 where we take a deeper dive.)

When choosing social platforms for content delivery, think about a day in the life of Gen Z. It's is not just about what platforms youth consumers generally like and use, but when they are active on those platforms throughout their day. If we want Gen Z to engage, then we need to deliver the right content on the right platform at the peak usage times for the target audience.

Table 6.2 Use this planning worksheet to prioritize social platforms by youth segment (Complete the worksheet by generating a list of social platforms and prioritizing them for each audience segment, based on what best fits your brand and audience needs)

PRIMARY PLATFORMS	SECONDARY	TERTIARY	RATIONALE
SEGMENT ONE: KIDS AGE 7–8			
SEGMENT TWO: TWEENS AGE 9–13			
SEGMENT THREE: TEENS AGE 14–18			
MIXED SEGMENT: TEENS & YOUNG ADULTS AGE 16–24			

SOURCE Illustration by Mike Carnevale

Social and mobile moments: a week in the life of a teen

Jake Skoloda, 18-year-old entrepreneur, shed some light on the social media habits of Gen Z by describing a week in the life of his friend Jen Smith, a 16-year-old student:

> When she looks around her classroom at the end of a lesson, pretty much all of her classmates are on their smartphones. They're sending out Snapchat 'streaks', scrolling through their Instagram feed, or looking at YouTube videos their friends sent earlier. Jen and her friends are connected 24/7, *but* [there] are definitely peaks and dips on their social media usage.
>
> Like most of her friends on social media, Jen is essentially marketing her own self brand. She knows that you need to post content between 6 pm and 9 pm on a school night to maximize likes and engagement: any earlier, and she risks her friends being caught up in after-school activities, but any later and she risks people falling asleep. During weekends, she knows her friends are busy and likely not checking social media as much. However, while all of this is true for platforms such as Instagram and YouTube, it isn't true at all for Snapchat. Jen, like her friends, is on Snapchat almost constantly through her waking hours, although her peak times are early in the morning, right after school ends, and again before going to sleep. Plus she also finds time for reblogging on Tumblr, two other finsta accounts and her secret anonymous videos on TikTok!

Put your story to the test

By now, you understand how important content presentation and delivery are to successful audience engagement. Next up, we take you through our storytelling evaluator, to check your content for its youth engagement potential. So go ahead and check your brand's presentation of story, campaign themes, or any communications with the following evaluator to see how relevant it is to youth culture.

Let's say there are five story ideas you think align with your brand and youth audience, but can't decide which one to focus on... Run them all through this test and move forward with the winner/s. Or, evaluate them, get the score, then try to add elements of value to increase your score. Go back and read the questions for inspiration on how you could add more value!

Gen Z storytelling content evaluator: starter questions

Let's evaluate your storytelling for youth relevance by answering the questions below. Give each one a 'NO', 'YEAH' or 'HECK YEAH' and write it down. (A 'No' is worth 0 points, 'Yeah' is worth 1 point, and a 'Heck yeah!' is worth 2 points. If you score more than 20 points, you are on the right track.)

1 Does your targeted youth audience already respect your brand?

2 Will your content feel new, original or interesting?

3 Is the story featuring those knowledgeable or immersed in the youth culture audiences you are targeting?

4 Is your creative team able to make the subject matter look and feel legitimate?

5 Can your story be told effectively across your targeted platforms?

6 Do you think a young person in your targeted youth audience would be perceived as 'cool' by friends if they shared your content?

7 Will your content themes or titles captivate young people's attention?

8 Does any aspect of your brand story, content narrative or communications bring back fond memories of nostalgia for the target audience or those who influence them?

9 Will your targeted youth audience be able to understand the topic and get into it?

10 Can the story or content be customized or personalized by the audience in some way?

11 Will the story incorporate well-known and respected people? (Creators, influential personalities, or celebrities)

12 Will the story be told in a way that avoids long boring load times, or other elements that exceed your audience's patience?

13 Does your story come to life in a way that will have the audience laughing out loud?

14 After experiencing your content, will young consumers be inspired to reach further, do something better or reach an aspirational goal?

15 Will the story have an ending that makes your audience walk away going 'I need more!'

SOURCE Adaptation of/from Game Hook Evaluator by David Perry on Game Design Book

Warm-up word game

Fill in the blanks in Figure 6.2 with information about your brand and your road to original storytelling that you have accumulated along your journey so far. This serves as a warm-up to the more in-depth worksheet that follows (Table 6.3 on page 121).

Figure 6.2 Word game: complete this activity to practise original content storytelling

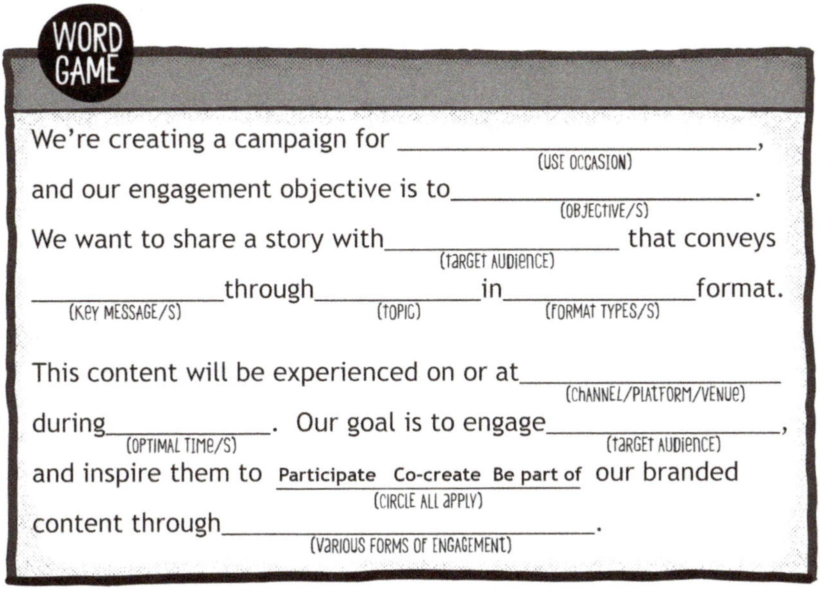

WORD GAME

We're creating a campaign for _____,
(USE OCCASION)
and our engagement objective is to_____.
(OBJECTIVE/S)
We want to share a story with_____ that conveys
(TARGET AUDIENCE)
_____through_____in_____format.
(KEY MESSAGE/S)   (TOPIC)   (FORMAT TYPES/S)

This content will be experienced on or at_____
(CHANNEL/PLATFORM/VENUE)
during_____. Our goal is to engage_____,
(OPTIMAL TIME/S)   (TARGET AUDIENCE)
and inspire them to Participate Co-create Be part of our branded
(CIRCLE ALL APPLY)
content through_____.
(VARIOUS FORMS OF ENGAGEMENT)

SOURCE Illustration by Mike Carnevale

CASE STUDY   Carhartt WIP – the anti-brand story

What they did

Carhartt WIP (Work In Progress) is a clothing brand that has stood the test of time. While you won't see the words 'Streetwear' appear in any of its marketing materials, it is arguably the very epitome of the streetwear movement. Staying true to its roots of ruggedness, collaboration, survival and friendships, Carhartt WIP built a following that is as strong to this day as it was years ago when it was first formed. It has grown beyond clothing to incorporate an in-house music label, a European Skateboard Championships in Basel, Switzerland, and a Carhartt Skate Team, all successful in their own right.

Why it worked

Carhartt WIP defied categorization by refusing to subscribe to any one trend, yet they told their story consistently through channels that were relevant to their target audience. They took a slow and steady approach to brand expansion, and seamlessly wove their story into their various *relevant* collaborations, events and products rather than simply telling it. From YouTube and film documentaries to Carhartt WIP radio (which features DJs, artists, and commentary from those within the Carhartt family) they were able to share their story in ways that were relevant to the brand's consumers. The brand's continual efforts to collaborate with musicians, artists and athletes in their shared space means that they will continue to attract new brand followers.

Strategy 02: influence partner collaboration

Brands are starting to establish longer-term relationships with creators and moving away from the 'one-off' campaigns. Those types of campaigns are proving to be ineffective and no brand loyalty is being built. Instead, brands should work with a handful of creators that hit their demographic and turn those creators into brand ambassadors. Once they become ambassadors, their fans will too.

CHARLIE BUFFIN, 2018, CO-FOUNDER MC PROJECTS AND TALENT MANAGEMENT, YOUTUBE STAR, BRENT RIVERA

Influence partner collaborations (also known as influence or influencer marketing) is as effective in 2018 as it was at inception. It originated when sportswear companies started sponsoring athletes as ambassadors; in fact, the first sponsored athlete was Honus Wagner way back in 1905. However, the sports market is immensely competitive, and athletes were historically locked into exclusive contracts, which forced brands to look outside the world of sports for other sponsorship avenues to influence audiences. That led to the rise of musical artists becoming a hot new sponsorship trend, as marked by Run-DMC's historic deal with Adidas in 1986.

Table 6.3   Use this planning worksheet to develop an original content storytelling strategy

TITLE: *Create a worthy title name*

OVERVIEW: *Briefly describe your content idea and how it's relevant to your brand and targeted youth audiences.*

USE CASE: *What business need does the content support?*   **OBJECTIVE:** *List your key objectives*

TARGET AUDIENCE: *Who is the audience for this content? Kids? Tweens? Teens? Young Adults?*

KEY MESSAGING: *What are the key messages you want young people to remember after viewing this content?*

TOPIC: *What is the topic or theme of this content? Will it resonate with youth?*

CONTENT FORMAT/S:

- ○ Video
- ○ Stories
- ○ Photo
- ○ Graphic image
- ○ Voice
- ○ Animation
- ○ GIF
- ○ AR/VR/MR
- ○ Other_____

CHANNELS:

- ○ YouTube
- ○ Instagram
- ○ Facebook
- ○ Snapchat
- ○ Twitter
- ○ Twitch
- ○ Tumblr
- ○ Musical.ly
- ○ Other_____

OPTIMAL POST TIMES OR CYCLES:

ENGAGEMENT: *How can young people participate or interact with this content?*

ELEMENTS FOR SUCCESS: *Make a detailed list of all the components and resources needed in order for this project to be successful.*

EXPECTED OUTCOMES: *What KPIs will be used to track performance and evaluate the media value for this content?*

RATIONALE: *Why are you creating this content versus something else?*

SOURCE Illustration by Mike Carnevale

Since then, the field of corporate sponsorship of artists and personalities has evolved at lightning speed to include all cultural genres – street artists, designers, gamers, and beyond – to the point where, now, influential figures throughout pop culture have built and normalized mutually beneficial partnerships with brands. With the advent and rapid evolution of technology and social media, it is becoming increasingly common to find individuals who have developed impressive spheres of influence through social platforms. Influence marketing has expanded into a highly competitive field that is open to anyone willing to build relationships and put in the work.

What are influence partners?

Influential people have always helped deepen the connection between brands and consumers, so it's no wonder that influence partner collaboration remains a crucial form of marketing. The influence pantheon includes such a wide array of individuals that to list them all here wouldn't even do it justice. What we can list, however, is the qualities that all of these figures have in common:

- leaders in their field;
- specialists in their area of interest or talent;
- those engaged in youth-relevant communities;
- creators of original content.

These influential figures inspire audiences, who normally might not hear about a particular brand, to pay attention to the influencer's association, thereby offering brands an opportunity to reach untapped audiences. The compounding effect of social and digital media adds fuel to the fire, extending an influencer's reach beyond anything previously seen. The most effective influencers and content creators are those who are able to inspire and motivate their audience to take action. Influencers can be divided into those who *develop a sphere of influence* and those who *develop or create content*. They are two distinct entities, yet increasingly, creators are also influencers, and vice versa (Figure 6.3).

Figure 6.3 Influence partners are comprised of creators and influencers, where the combination has the most value

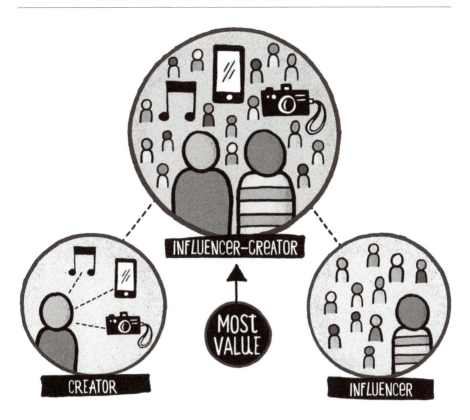

SOURCE Illustration by Mike Carnevale

Brands that develop authentic partnerships with these talented individuals are able to leverage the valuable, and often longstanding, relationships that the influencers have built over time. If you authentically incorporate your brand and offerings in their content, an influencer is uniquely positioned to build trust in your brand. In turn, it's best to trust influencer partners and allow them some creative licence to distribute content in ways that naturally fit their styles, and the styles of the audience. Whether it's through live streaming, video, voice or Instagram stories, the content is told in the first person and in the influencer's own way, introducing a level of credibility missing in any other form of marketing.

The role of influence partners

The power of influence is undeniable. Influencers and creators not only provide highly sought-after exposure and captivating creative content, but also help humanize a brand by putting a familiar, trusted face to the brand's offering. Below you will find a list of what we have found to be the key roles of influence marketing, after more than a decade of managing campaigns and programmes for brands:

- Influencers build trust and credibility through transparency, and by choosing *only* to work with brands that match their ethos and their lifestyle.

- Influencers are often actually part of the brand's audience. Influence marketing, when done right, is a true representation of the audience, reflecting their wants and needs.

- Because influencers live among your audience, they can interact and engage in authentic dialogue directly with your target market.

- Influencers are the ones in charge of creating (or curating) their content, which in turn leads to a greater sense of trust among followers.

Talent selection based on archetype, genre and interactions

We look at influencer partnerships as long-term investments that serve to amplify and strengthen the brand's personality… It's important to align your brand with talent that meets your must-have criteria. We recently walked away from a deal after the talent was unwilling to engage with the brand on social media.

SIMON HUCK, PRINCIPAL OF COMMAND ENTERTAINMENT GROUP

The value of an influencer or creator lies in the attention they can garner for a brand, in an authentic, culturally relevant way. The size of their following indicates their *potential* reach, but the number of actual engagements, or interactions, is a more accurate way to measure how much of your audience they *actually* impact. A quick glance or impression does not hold the same weight as a comment or share. It simply doesn't make sense to find just any influencer or creator who has built an audience – a brand needs to find the influential person or people who will be able to ensure adequate brand exposure, and creators who are able to offer content that is relevant to that brand's audience.

Talent classification: archetypes and genres

For a marketer, one of the most challenging tasks is to identify talented influencers and creators. Below are the main archetypes and genres that we use to describe the 'pantheon of influencers' that we spoke of earlier. Archetypes help categorize the type of influence character by their status or function. The genre is the category that defines what their interest, focus or talent is. Your own lists of influencer and creators will change and depend on your brand, audience and project.

- Archetypes
  - Icons
  - Celebrities
  - Trailblazers
  - Entertainers
  - Insiders
  - Educator
  - Experts

- Genres (by talent/interests)
  - Gaming
  - Beauty
  - Sports
  - Fashion
  - Music
  - Performing Arts
  - Fitness
  - Food
  - Art
  - Comedy.

Talent classification

It is difficult to find a consistent classification system of influencers across the industry. Ask 10 marketers how they would classify the different tiers of influencers and get 10 different answers. The following are some of the ways they are currently broken down:

- micro influencer, influencer, super influencer;
- micro influencer, macro influencer, mega influencer;
- influencer, celebrity influencer.

Regardless of how we label these individuals, the important thing is identifying them by what you can measure. We break them down into four tiers separated into *following* and average *engagement*. When people talk about 'reach' they are typically referring to the number of followers. We believe a better way to classify them is by the number of interactions, as we feel this is the most accurate indicator of their potential brand engagement value. For example, if one influencer has 1.2 million followers, but has an average engagement of under 100 interactions, it wouldn't make sense to rate them above a creator that has 300,000 followers but 200+ quality interactions per average post.

Talent tiers by following size   An older industry method used to organize talent and establish pricing tiers based solely on number of followers:

Tier A: 1 million+

Tier B: 500,000–1 million

Tier C: 100,000–500,000

Tier D: 10,000–100,000

Talent tiers by interactions   At the time of this writing, the most effective way to organize talent and establish pricing tiers is to consider the average number of interactions per social media post (likes, comments, shares, ReTweets or video reviews):

Tier A: 150,000–1 million+ per post

Tier B: 25,000–150,000 per post

Tier C: 5,000–25,000 per post

Tier D: 1,000–5,000 per post

You can't rely on 'impressions' when measuring influence. Impressions don't allow you to understand who is paying attention, who acted on the impression, and how much time was spent with the content. Yet when somebody interacts with content, you *know* they are engaged. Always keep in mind that a large following with low engagement will offer limited dividends to brands. Engagement on the other hand (shares, comments, questions, reactions) represents true value.

While we select talent based on interactions, we recommend choosing influencers who also align with our brand: who are able to balance loyalty and integrity to their followers and their partner brand; who choose partners based on mutual interest and not just for the money; and whose followers represent and make up our target audience. These selections are very personal to a brand's particular initiative, specific use cases and target audience, so there is not an easy cookie-cutter approach. By using the worksheets in this section of the playbook, you will be on the right strategic path towards influencer selection. See the 'Further reading' section at the end of this chapter for more reading.

Tactical partnership approaches

Gifting When a brand contacts an influencer they identify as being aligned with their brand and sends them free products. The goal is to encourage the influencers to post about their product on their own schedule, increasing brand exposure. (Note: we view this as the most productive way to start a brand/influencer relationship.)

- Pros
  - Low cost. Low barrier to entry.
  - Gives brands a low-risk way to assess for true brand fit.
- Cons
  - No guarantee of exposure.
  - Limited brand and product understanding.

Flow When brands send or 'flow' free merchandise, access or experiences to the influencer or creator with an expectation and mutual understanding that there will be reciprocal exposure. This type of engagement typically continues for an ongoing timeframe vs. one-off gifting:

- Pros
  - Effective method to 'seed' products/services in the market.
  - Enables brand a starting point to build an authentic relationship.

- Cons
  - Time intensive, and requires an ongoing commitment.
  - Typically brands require a minimum number of influencers or creators to make an impact.

Sponsored projects   Identify and contract financially with one or more influencers, engaging them in a short-term project:

- Pros
  - No long-term commitment for influencer, creator or brand creating an opportunity to 'test' engagement.
  - Great opportunities to expand relationship with those gifted or part of a flow programme.

- Cons
  - Inconsistent use of influencers or not enough of them is unlikely to produce results (no different from an underfunded media buy).
  - Typically increases financial output, with payment for influencer as well as product.

Influence programme   When a brand identifies and contracts with a group of hand-selected influencers, engaging them in a longer-term partnership with the brand. In combination with flow programmes, this is where we see success rates increased:

- Pros
  - Delivers content and engagement at scale.
  - Opportunities for closer involvement in other activities that the influencer or creator is involved in, which creates value from association and events.

- Cons
  - Larger investment
  - Needs a long-term commitment in order for it to be effective, weaving the influencers into the brand story in the longer term.

Warm-up word game

Fill in the blanks in Figure 6.4 with information about your plans for influence partner collaboration. This serves as a warm-up to the more in-depth worksheet (Table 6.4 on page 131) that follows.

Figure 6.4   Word game: complete this activity to practise influence partner collaboration

WORD GAME

We're developing an Influencer Programme for_____, (USE CASE) and our objective is_____. We'll utilize influencers (OBJECTIVE/S) who _____, specifically_____ (INFLUENCE MARKETING ROLE) (ARCHETYPE/S) who are known for their presence in_____. (GENRE/S) Influencers will have_____and we will choose (AVG. INTERACTIONS PER POST OF___) them based on_____level and alignment. We will (TIER LETTER) collaborate with talent using_____. (TACTICAL PARTNERSHIP APPROACH/ES)

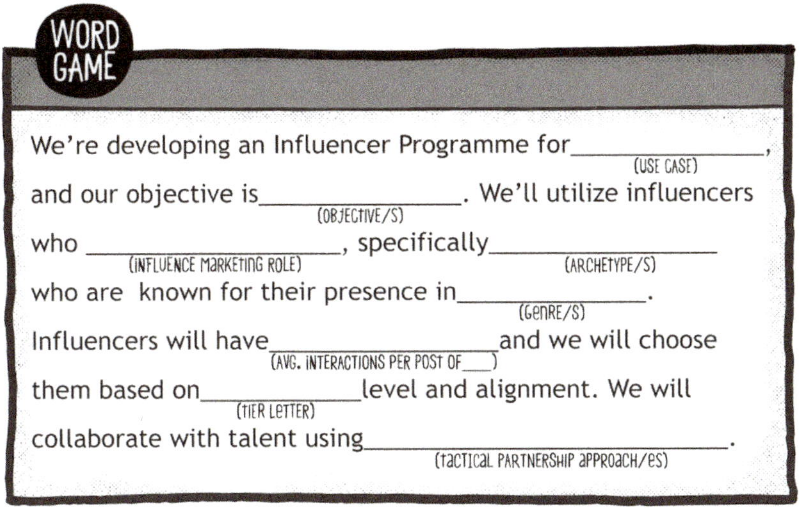

SOURCE Illustration by Mike Carnevale

CASE STUDY   Glossier

What they did

Glossier is a beauty brand that has taken a unique approach to influence marketing. Staying away from the celebrity endorsements typically used by large beauty brands, Glossier has chosen instead to form relationships with customers as brand advocates, as well as with a broad base of influencers and creators. It leverages the loyal following it has grown to generate buzz around its products, flowing new products to influencers among its audience and regular loyal customers before they are commercially available, and establishing a social media referral programme.

Why it worked

By going directly to its audience and treating them like individuals with importance, Glossier has been able to garner organic reviews, blogs and Instagram posts that carry the authentic voice of genuine customers. This in turn has built hype and excitement around the brand, rewards customers for their trust in the brand, and generates an ongoing cycle of brand advocacy, continuously attracting new customers who want to be part of their brand experience.

Strategy 03: live immersive experiences

Every brand wants to forge an emotional connection with its customers. Our brand mission is to inspire a life of exploration, so we felt like this [VR] was a great way to enhance our storytelling, use technology and transport people to the outdoors.

ERIC OLIVER, DIRECTOR OF DIGITAL MARKETING AT THE NORTH
FACE (DUYA, 2015)

In today's digital world, it's become easy to feel less connected with communities in our physical reality, and more engaged with those that social and digital technologies provide. With every new app, device and technology, the digital dominance grows, while actual, real-life human and social interaction has, in many ways, been eclipsed. While technology has fuelled this situation, it also provides infinite ways to change it. Instead of eclipsing real life, social and emerging technologies such as augmented, virtual and mixed reality (AR, VR and MR) are merging live experiences with digital and virtual ones.

Brands such as Nike, Hasbro, Niantic, Estee Lauder and Acura (just to name a few) are already creating revolutionary experiences that are pushing the boundaries of human and digital interaction.

Table 6.4   Use this planning worksheet to develop an influence partner collaboration strategy that will resonate with Gen Z audiences

TITLE: *Create a worthy title name*

OVERVIEW: *Briefly describe your influence strategy approach in a way that your team will understand and young people will care about.*

USE CASE: *What business need does the influence collaboration support?*   **OBJECTIVE:** *List your key objectives*

TARGET AUDIENCE: *Who is the audience for this content? Kids? Tweens? Teens? Young Adults?*

KEY MESSAGING: *What are the key messages you want young consumers to remember after seeing this content?*

CONTENT FORMAT/S:

- ○ Voice
- ○ Video
- ○ Stories
- ○ Photo
- ○ Graphic image
- ○ Animation
- ○ GIF
- ○ AR/VR/MR
- ○ Other_____

CHANNEL/S:

- ○ YouTube
- ○ Instagram
- ○ Facebook
- ○ Snapchat
- ○ Twitter
- ○ Twitch
- ○ Tumblr
- ○ Musical.ly
- ○ Other_____

ARCHETYPES AND GENRES (TALENTS/INTERESTS): *Identify the niche interests or genres that align with your audience and create a list of targeted groups*

SELECT TALENT: BASED ON TIER LEVELS: *Identify talent that aligns with your brand and specific criteria*

CONTENT AND DISTRIBUTION: *What aspects of your campaign will your influencer/creator partner be responsible for?*

- ○ Creating content   ○ Distributing brand-produced content   ○ Both

TACTICAL PARTNERSHIP APPROACH: *How will you structure the partnership?*

- ○ Gifting   ○ Flow   ○ Sponsored project   ○ Influence programme   ○ Other_____

ENGAGEMENT: *How can young people participate or interact with this content?*

ELEMENTS FOR SUCCESS: *Make a detailed list of all the components and resources needed in order for this project to be successful*

EXPECTED OUTCOMES: *What KPIs will be used to track performance and evaluate the media value for this content?*

RATIONALE: *Why partner with influencers and creators versus something else?*

SOURCE Illustration by Mike Carnevale

Acura has used AR helmets that layer graphics over actual terrain to challenge drivers on a contained course, while footage of the experience is live-streamed over social media. Estee Lauder employs a bot called Lip Artist that allows consumers to download a picture of themselves, then suggests styles of lipstick that are applied to the picture, allowing the viewer to virtually test it. Foundation is next for the company. Nike's collaborative next-level contributions are detailed in the case study below. Passive digital experiences are being replaced with consumer interaction opportunities that drive new levels of engagement (Johnson, 2018).

As emerging tech continues to normalize into their daily experience, Gen Z will continue to expect deeper, more enriching communications in every facet of their lives. This offers new opportunities for engagement in ways that appeal to all five senses, enabling brands to bring themselves and their offerings to life in ways that were previously unimaginable. What, then, are the main components of a live immersive experience, and how can you start to create your own that will bring your brand to life for consumer audiences? What follows are thought starters for each of these immersive experiences. Below that, find and use the word game template, and fill in the blanks to create as many different experience outlines as you like, before moving on to the more in-depth worksheet.

Live immersive experience thought starters

- Types of experiences
  - Product drops
  - Pop-up installations
  - Concerts/music festivals
  - eSports tournaments
  - Sporting events
  - Fandom conventions
  - Live performances
  - Opening ceremonies
  - Fundraising events
  - Shopping/Retail

- Locations/Venues
  - Urban spaces
  - Retail stores
  - Movie theatres
  - In-home
  - Shopping mall
  - Concert venue
  - Stadium
  - Theme parks
  - School event
  - Parks and beaches

- Relevant moments
  - Academic semesters
  - Prom season
  - Sport seasons
  - Spring break
  - National holidays
  - Time of a sale or promotion
  - A countdown, or timed event

- Next generation technology
  - Voice AI (artificial intelligence)
  - AR
  - VR
  - MR
  - Chatbots
  - Smart glasses
  - Drone utilization
  - Multimedia event booths
  - Interactive media walls
  - Projection mapping

- Engagement activities
  - Team challenge activities
  - Interactive art installations
  - Product sampling
  - Contests and giveaways
  - Photo/Selfie spots

– Product demonstrations
– Games.

Warm-up word game

Fill in the blanks in Figure 6.5 with your immersive strategy to create a scenario that helps guide the reader's thought process towards creating a live immersive experience. This serves as a warm-up to the more in-depth template that follows (Table 6.5 on page 136).

Figure 6.5   Word game: complete this activity to practise the creation of live immersive experiences

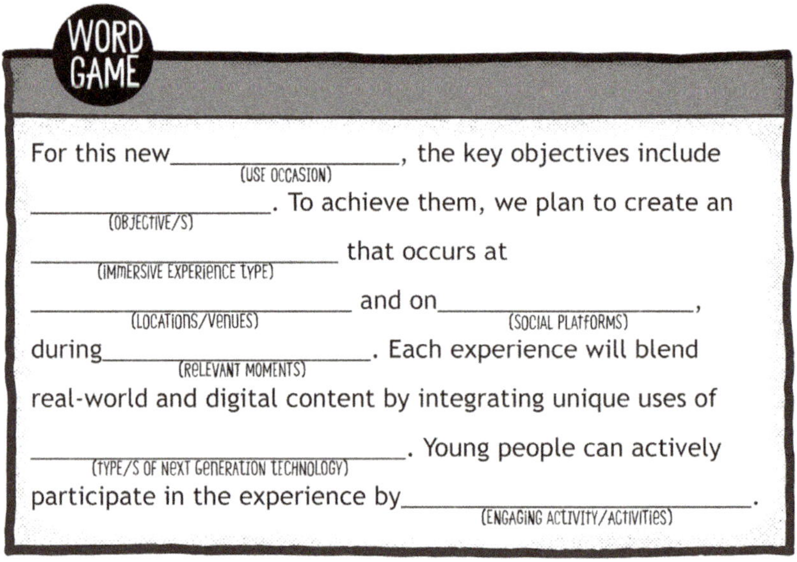

For this new_____ (USE OCCASION), the key objectives include
_____ (OBJECTIVE/S). To achieve them, we plan to create an
_____ (IMMERSIVE EXPERIENCE TYPE) that occurs at
_____ (LOCATIONS/VENUES) and on_____ (SOCIAL PLATFORMS),
during_____ (RELEVANT MOMENTS). Each experience will blend
real-world and digital content by integrating unique uses of
_____ (TYPE/S OF NEXT GENERATION TECHNOLOGY). Young people can actively
participate in the experience by_____ (ENGAGING ACTIVITY/ACTIVITIES).

SOURCE Illustration by Mike Carnevale

CASE STUDY   SOLD OUT in 23 seconds!

'This is the Holy Grail of the experience [Nike is] trying to intend, which is direct to consumer – to the actual consumer, versus a bot, – and same-day delivery', Hnetinka said. 'The Snap code introduces a new paradigm for commerce' (Arthur, 2018).

What they did

Nike's Jordan brand partnered with Snapchat, Shopify, Darkstore and R/GA for a one-off, unique collaboration to celebrate the 30th anniversary of Jordan's now famous All-Star Slam Dunk contest, and the pre-release of the Air Jordan III 'Tinker'. The goal was to enable attendees of the 2018 NBA All-Star game to use a '3D, augmented reality "A/R Jordan" Snapchat Lens' (which could only be obtained before the game at three locations in LA), to view the iconic imagery of Jordan jumping from the free throw line for his dunk, right on their smartphone. As if that wasn't enough, some attendees were able to use the lens to scan a code giving them access to experience an exclusive e-commerce opportunity, where they were able to purchase the Tinker in pre-release in about 15–20 seconds, and have it delivered later that day. The shoe sold out in 23 seconds (Bennett, 2018).

Why it worked

The collaboration created an epic amount of hype and excitement along with a feeling of exclusivity, generating a meaningful and relevant experience for Nike's community. It also allowed a seamless integration of both a shopping and a social experience, bridging the gap between the two until they effectively became one single experience. To complete the frictionless engagement, the same-day shipping and start-to-end in-app process meant that the entire action was fun, easy, and almost instantly gratifying for customers.

Your engagement playbook should help you think strategically, keep your team focused and prepare everyone to take action, so don't forget to actually bring your playbook into your planning meetings once it's completed. Don't make the mistake of letting your playbook collect dust on the shelf. All too often we've seen brands with marketing playbooks get too comfortable and stop referring to them for guidance, taking a detour from solutions already customized to a situation. The chapters that follow provide a deeper dive into the tactical details of the varied aspects of content creation, distribution and social engagement.

TL;DR: chapter takeaways

- **An effective youth culture engagement playbook must emphasize three core strategies:** original content storytelling, influence partner collaboration, and live immersive experiences. After working

Table 6.5 Use this planning worksheet to develop a live immersive experience strategy that will resonate with Gen Z audiences

TITLE: Create a worthy title name

OVERVIEW: Briefly describe/overview your live event strategy in a way that your leadership team will understand and that will resonate with young people

USE CASE: What business need does the live experience support? **OBJECTIVE:** List your key objectives

TARGET AUDIENCE: What are the key messages you want consumers to remember about your brand after experiencing this live event?

TYPE OF EXPERIENCE:

○ Product drops   ○ Pop-up installation   ○ Concerts/music festivals   ○ eSports tournaments
○ Sporting events   ○ Fandom conventions   ○ Live performances   ○ Opening ceremonies
○ Fundraising events ○ Shopping/Retail   ○ Other_____

LOCATION/VENUE: **RELEVANT MOMENT:**

○ Urban spaces   ○ Retail stores   ○ Academic semesters   ○ Prom season
○ Movie theatres   ○ In-Home   ○ Sport seasons   ○ Other_____
○ Shopping mall   ○ Concert venue   ○ Spring break
○ Stadium   ○ Theme parks   ○ National holidays
○ School event   ○ Other_____   ○ Culture-specific
○ Parks and Beaches

NEXT GENERATION TECHNOLOGY: What types of technologies can you use to enhance the fan experience in person or online?

        ○ AR   ○ VR   ○ MR   ○ Livestream   ○ Other_____

ENGAGEMENT ACTIVITIES: How can people who can't be at the live event be included in the experience? What is your event hashtag? How will your brand community be able to participate, in person and online, in this live event?

BRAND-GENERATED CONTENT DURING THE EVENT: Content created by your team at this event can be used to tell your brand story

STRATEGIES TO FACILITATE USER GENERATED CONTENT: Content created by participants at this event be repurposed or used to tell your brand story

ELEMENTS FOR SUCCESS: What KPIs or social metrics does your live event or experience need to meet in order to be deemed a brand win?

EXPECTED OUTCOMES: What is the marketing goal for this live event or experience strategy?

RATIONALE: Why produce this live immersive experience versus something else?

SOURCE Illustration by Mike Carnevale

through this chapter, you'll have a solid directional start on engagement strategies, and tactical approaches for your brand.

- **Place the focus on youth engagement and value creation, not pushing messages.** Focus on authentic interactions to get on Gen Z's wavelength, tune in to their frequencies and start forming the relationships that build brand credibility. This means actively contributing to youth culture and involving young people in the content, conversations and experiences along the way – *not* treating Gen Z as passive message-recipients.

- **Original content storytelling: in a world where the greatest prize is attention, content must capture an audience's imagination and get them to tune in.** Content can be as short and simple as a meme, GIF or snap, or as developed as an episodic video series, but needs to present relevant messages through themes, formats and channels that meet Gen Z in moments that matter. Marketing is not only about what you make, but about the stories you tell.

- **Influence partner collaboration:** Find real creators and influencers that speak to and inspire the youth audiences you're after. Become part of the creator and influencer communities, but let the creator chart the course with your guidance when it comes to content and distribution.

- **Live immersive experiences:** Where the digital world meets the physical. Immersive experiences have always been important to the brand–consumer relationship. Today's emerging technologies bring experience to the next level, exploring the limits of experience and the imagination.

Further reading, resources and downloadable materials are available at **www.genzfreq.com**

References

Arthur, R (2018) [accessed 19 March 2018] Nike Sells Limited Pre-Run of Air Jordan III 'Tinker' on Snapchat, *The Current Daily* [Online] https://thecurrentdaily.com/2018/02/20/nike-air-jordan-snapchat/

Bennett, B (2018) [accessed 18 March 2018] Slam Dunk Commerce: Jordan Brand and R/GA Debut Snapchat Augmented Reality-Shopping

Experience, *The Drum*, 22 February [Online] www.thedrum.com/
news/2018/02/22/slam-dunk-commerce-jordan-brand-and-rga-debut-
snapchat-augmented-reality-shopping

Duya, T (2015) [accessed 18 March 2018] The North Face Brings
Virtual Reality to Retail [Blog] 12 March [Online] www.digiday.com/
marketing/north-face-brings-virtual-reality-retail/

Johnson, L (2018) [accessed 18 March 2018] Why Brands
Like L'Oréal and Acura Are Betting Big on Augmented
Reality, *Adweek*, 26 July [Online] www.adweek.com/digital/
why-brands-like-loreal-and-acura-are-betting-big-on-augmented-reality/

Penn, C (2017) [accessed 18 March 2018] Why We Need a Marketing
Playbook [Online] www.christopherspenn.com/2017/02/
why-we-need-marketing-playbook/

Further reading

Hudson, D (2017) [accessed 18 March 2018] How to Differentiate Social
Media Influencers and Content Creators [Blog] 5 May [Online] blog.
dashhudson.com/influencer-marketing-content-creator-social-media-
strategy-brand-marketing/

Hunckler, M (2017) [accessed 18 March 2018] 3 Strategies for Marketing
Innovation from Former Marketing Exec at P&G and Coca-Cola
Turned VC, *Forbes*, 4 August [Online] www.forbes.com/sites/
matthunckler/2017/08/04/3-strategies-for-marketing-innovation-from-
former-marketing-exec-at-pg-and-coca-cola-turned-vc/#59b99a527e00

Keller, E (2003) *The Influentials*, Free Press, New York

Kumar, P (2017) [accessed 18 March 2018] 21 Beautiful Lessons You Can
Learn From 'Seth Godin' [Blog] 12 June [Online] www.medium.com/
indian-thoughts/21-beautiful-lessons-you-can-learn-from-seth-godin-
7c7d2c22e80

Rock, D (2008) [accessed 18 March 2018] SCARF: A Brain-Based Model
for Collaborating with and Influencing Others [online] www.epa.gov/
sites/production/files/2015-09/documents/thurs_georgia_9_10_915_
covello.pdf

Thorn, J (2014) [accessed 18 March 2018] The Dawn of Athlete
Endorsements [Blog] 20 January [Online] ourgame.mlblogs.com/
the-dawn-of-athlete-endorsements-f504cba917b0

Social strategies and tactical considerations

What social media represents is an evolution in the field of communications, just as the internet and mobility before it. The tools will change, the platforms will evolve, but the way in which people communicate with other people through digital networks and electronic devices has been fundamentally transformed through the development of social media.

OLIVIER BLANCHARD, 2018, SENIOR ANALYST AT FUTURUM
RESEARCH + ANALYSIS

Be where they are

It's clear that social media are an intrinsic part of Gen Z's lives and that refining your social, digital and influence strategy is a top priority. For brands, this translates to needing everything from a mobile-responsive website to harnessing the power of influence. Let's put some context around that statement. In 2017, Variety reporter Susanne Ault reported research finding that Gen Z's emotional attachment to YouTube stars such as Tyler Oakley or PewDiePie is 7× greater than their attachment to traditional celebrities such as Seth Rogen or Jennifer Lawrence. In fact, Ault found that teens perceive YouTube stars as 17× more engaging and 11× more extraordinary than mainstream stars (Ault, 2015). What's more, research conducted in 2016 by Twitter found that digital influencers have nearly as much clout as a friend or family member (Swant, 2016).

All this leads us to realize just how important it is to have the right social media strategy. If we leverage the strengths of each social, digital and live streaming platform by creating poignant and authentic content that will appeal to Gen Z, we stand the best chance of cutting through the noise. The key here is to utilize social and mobile platforms as a conduit for inspiration, aspiration and engagement rather than plain old fashioned selling (Chaykowski, 2015).

Think of each digital platform as a mobile portal for engagement, symbiotically created by brand professionals, influencers and the community. As content creators, influencers have amassed vast quantities of fans, subscribers and credibility within youth culture. They do this by supplying social and digital platforms with relevant, engaging content that accurately fits the medium. By partnering with these creators you take a giant stride towards being able to create authentic experiences for Gen Z audiences.

Know the unwritten rules of social engagement

When it comes to social media, parents often tell their kids, 'Think before you post'. Guess what? The same goes for brands! Do you know and follow the unwritten rules of tween engagement on social media? If not, it's time to start learning because, like most things in life, there are cultural norms. Here's an example we learnt from the Gen Z tweens and teens we partner with as part of our client work: it's just 'not cool' when a friend or brand 'blows up their feeds' with too many pictures, updates or marketing messages. Posting so many photos is considered bragging or showing off, and this violates the emphasis this generational cohort places on inclusion and its rejection of anything flashy or ostentatious.

Another important area to pay attention to is that gender roles – for both girls and boys – are also heightened on social media. Gen Z researcher Devorah Heitner noted in *The New York Times* that many tween boys expressed the need 'to appear masculine' in their choice of Snapchat filters (Heitner, 2017). Tween girls also told Heitner that when it comes to social media, they feel pressure to walk a fine line 'between cute and sexy'. For both boys and girls, there's a keen awareness of body image and they don't like to be 'body-shamed'.

We advise the brands we work with to use social media as an opportunity for 'seeded serendipity', where Gen Z can feel like they 'discovered' a cool video or meme to share with their friends via other social platforms and earn social capital within their community. Given the rise and fall of social platforms (hello, MySpace), our focus is on how social platforms can be utilized to connect with the consumer, not necessarily on a specific platform.

Tuning in to social media

Here are some key strategic approaches to consider when using social platforms, digital media, and influencers to connect with youth culture:

- It's important to have consistent branding, voice and tone across all social platforms.
- Focus on social interaction and storytelling connecting with followers as friends, and sharing experiences with your brand community.
- Choose and secure a vanity URL – your unique web or social account address that identifies your brand, even on social platforms you don't intend to use.
- Create content that is inspirational, relevant and share-worthy so Gen Z looks good sharing it with their friends, and they can inspire others in their social groups.

Social platform considerations

There are a multitude of social and digital platforms that occupy the attention of Gen Z (Table 7.1), but as of the time of publication

Table 7.1 Identify social platforms and assign primary, secondary and tertiary roles

SOCIAL PLATFORMS		
PRIMARY	SECONDARY	TERTIARY
YouTube	Facebook	TikTok
Instagram	Twitch	Houseparty
Snapchat	Tumblr	YouNow
Twitter	Pinterest	
	Kik	

SOURCE Illustration by Mike Carnevale

(2018) we recommend the following platforms. These are the places Gen Z gather and are most likely to partner with a brand to create, engage, build community and share content.

Priority social platforms

YouTube checklist

- YouTube is recommended as a priority platform for driving tune-in and engagement on branded platforms.
- Parody videos are popular, especially when they mock rules, the establishment or popular culture.
- Leverage creators and influencers to develop content that is fun, relatable and focused on the lives of youth.
- Gen Z admires brands that keep their content real. Show the messy, but beautiful chaos that circles around their daily lives.

Instagram checklist

- At the time of this writing, Instagram is a top priority app for reaching all youth segments.
- Don't forget to utilize Instagram Story and Instagram TV video features to share original and engaging experiences.
- Make strategic use of hashtags to find your audience, increase brand campaign visibility and integrate them into your conversations.
- Instagram allows your brand to quickly engage in conversation, storytelling and build a relationship of trust.
- This platform is often parent-approved and has a lower barrier to entry for younger (under 13) kids.

Snapchat checklist

- Snapchat provides your brand with an opportunity to share story-driven experiences with youth audiences.
- Once niche, Snapchat is now mainstream and focused on storytelling and experience-driven activities.
- Consider using Snapchat in conjunction with social media creators and influencers to boost your credibility.

- Use Snapchat to share insider secrets, branded filters, AR stickers, tips and show behind the scenes action at live events.

Tumblr checklist

- Tumblr is a great platform for reaching teens and young adults.
- Tumblr is less structured than other social media platforms, and brands are expected to push boundaries.
- Just about any type of media can be posted on Tumblr. From photos to links, GIFs and video, your brand can maximize creativity on Tumblr.
- Consider using Tumblr as a microsite or 'hub' for teen and young adult campaigns.

Twitter checklist

- Create a persona around your Twitter handle to drive engagement and gain followers.
- Use Twitter as a platform to listen to feedback, resolve issues and solve problems.
- Be personable, share GIFs, images, memes, and videos.
- Use Twitter for product announcements, contests and other brand initiatives.

Facebook checklist

- Facebook is a difficult platform to qualify. It is not commonly thought to be a primary platform for Gen Z. Ultimately, it differs by lifestyle and age.
- Facebook posts can be used strategically to grab attention and inform your community about upcoming events and contests.
- Focus on using Facebook Messenger using chatbots, stickers and other value-added communications.
- Facebook Live is also a valuable media platform to connect with youth.

Messaging apps checklist

- When it comes to Gen Z, messaging apps are a crucial avenue of communication.

- Messaging apps are a vital platform because they are cross-platform and work on both iOS and Android devices.

- Messaging App varies by country. For example, Line is popular in Japan, but not in the United States. The key is doing research to find out what messaging app is most widely used in the region you are targeting for your campaign.

- Chatbots are another key feature of many messaging apps. Both Kik, FB Messenger support the use of chatbots on their platforms.

TikTok (formerly musical.ly) checklist

- TikTok is a social media platform for creating, sharing and discovering short music videos.

- Like Snapchat and Instagram, teens are using TikTok to become internet stars and amass huge followings.

- According to ABC News (2016), nearly 60 million teens (and tweens) are using TikTok to make their own music videos.

Live streaming checklist

- Identify the right live streaming platform (Facebook Live, Instagram, YouTube, Twitch, Periscope, Tumblr), for your target audience.

- Plan out the content for your live stream so that your live event is professional, well thought out and has a specific goal or metric attached to the live event.

- Design for engagement, retention, and interaction with your community by asking and answering questions, having call-to-actions or elements of gamification in your live event.

- Make sure your brand persona and voice are reflected in your live stream event. Live events are also opportunities for your audience to connect authentically, in real time, with your community management team.

Tactical considerations for influence partner collaboration

I feel like everybody, whether you have one follower or a million followers, has an opportunity to either positively or negatively affect people.

TYLER OAKLEY (2015), YOUTUBER, AUTHOR AND INFLUENCER

Reminder: influence marketing isn't a quick fix

Knowing the platforms your audience is most active on represents one of the significant challenges for brands targeting Gen Z. While in 2018 platforms such as YouTube, Facebook, Snapchat and Instagram remain the dominant platforms, other emerging platforms such as Twitch, YouNow and Kik – and other social media, live streaming and messaging platforms that are just off the radar – should also be considered as part of your influence marketing strategy. Gen Z appreciates brands that are on the cutting edge, and where they want to be. In addition, establishing a presence early on will lend authenticity to your usage of the platform later; it's an investment into building brand relevance.

The common misperception is that influence marketing will increase your social media following and engagement over a short period of time. Your brand may experience an initial bump, but developing a consistent following happens at a slow and steady pace. Influencers open the door for brands, but they can't promise immediate acceptance.

Spotlight: Branden Harvey

From *Seventeen Magazine* to *Mashable* and *Forbes*, Branden Harvey tells stories through photography, Instagram, Snapchat, Twitter and any other social media tool he can get his hands on to share good things with his legion of fans. His captions and photos on Instagram have been featured in *Fortune Magazine*, *Mashable* and *Esquire* and he was nominated for a Shorty Award for Snapchatter of the Year. Twice. Branden has leveraged his role as a social media storyteller and influencer to help brands such as Disney, Square, Southwest Airlines, (RED), UNICEF, American Express, The College Board and Coca-Cola tell stories that matter.

In 2017, Branden launched the *Sounds Good* podcast, the *Goodnewsletter* and the *Goodnewspaper*, a physical quarterly newspaper (print is alive!) to widen his media footprint and spread the good news. Branden has amassed over 100,000 Instagram followers and 11,000 Twitter followers, and remains one of the most influential and popular storytellers on Snapchat. He's an influencer who uses social media and his fame as an opportunity to affect people positively.

Learn more about Branden Harvey: http://www.brandenharvey.com
Learn more about Good Good Good: https://www.goodgoodgood.co

Influencers and creators: legal implications

In the early days of influence marketing, there was little regulation around influencer endorsement disclosure compliance from brands and marketers. Often the only disclosure of a paid sponsorship was a hashtag (#collab, #sp, #spon, or #ambassador), often buried deep below the fold of social media posts.

In summer 2017, the US Federal Trade Commission (FTC) began holding influencers, brands and marketers to tighter endorsement compliance, requiring them to be much more transparent in their social media business relationships. Among the fundamental changes to social media endorsement disclosure rules, the FTC now requires influencers, marketers and brands to adhere to a tighter set of regulations (Fair, 2017).

FTC social media influencer recommendations

- The FTC is now holding influencers personally responsible for not clearly and conspicuously disclosing their paid relationships with brands when making endorsements in social media.

- If you hire influencers, you must ensure that they comply with current FTC guidelines and educate them on their duty to disclose and monitor their endorsements for your brand for compliance. If they fail to comply, you must document your efforts to bring them into compliance.

- Influencers must clearly state that they are a paid spokesperson. This can be done through watermarks (even on ephemeral photos on

Snapchat and Instagram Story feeds) or use of above-the-fold hashtags such as #ad #sponsored. 'Ambiguous' disclosures, such as #Thanks or #Ambassador or #Collab, are no longer adequate disclosures.

- Tagging a brand in a photo is now considered an endorsement. As such, brands, influencers and marketers must clearly disclose any relationship between the endorser and brand.

- Don't rely on native disclosure tools on Instagram, Snapchat or YouTube or assume that using these tools puts your brand in compliance.

SOURCE Adapted from Fair (2017)

If you decide to work with influencers, it's important that you find someone who aligns with your brand values, is interested in a collaborative working relationship and committed to complying with all current influencer marketing laws and regulations. This means that even if you are a brand based in Australia who is marketing to Gen Z audiences in the United States, you are bound to follow the FTC social influencer guidelines.

At the time of publication (2018), neither the European Union nor the Australian government has issued any influencer-specific guidelines. It's vital that before you engage with social influencers, you verify what the current laws and regulations are in the countries in which you choose to run campaigns. Influencers should also be reminded that they need to comply with all online privacy and data collection laws, including the FTC's Children's Online Privacy Protection Act (COPPA) and European Union privacy laws under the GDPR regulations. We go deeper into COPPA, Australian privacy regulations and the European Union GDPR requirements in Chapter 9.

Emerging social and digital media

Live streaming

While generational cohorts may be tuning in to Facebook Live, Periscope, Instagram Live, YouTube and Twitch to watch live streaming events, youth culture has its own ecosystem of streaming apps where they can interact with friends, celebrities and online video game streaming. One of the most popular tween live streaming mobile apps is YouNow, which reports that viewers spend more than 30 minutes per day on it and that more than 70 per cent of users engage with the content (Dreier, 2017). Anyone with a smartphone can log on to YouNow and communicate with text messages and animated icons, and exchange real and virtual gifts that can be redeemed for cash.

So why are live streaming platforms such as YouNow, YouTube, Houseparty, Facebook Live or Twitch so popular? Above all, this generation values instant gratification and authenticity, and these live streaming mobile apps provide them with a place where they can feel comfortable in sharing their lives and expressing themselves and connecting with their peers. Brands that choose to host a live streaming event should prepare by having a clear set of content moderation and online safety protocols ready before they turn on the camera. As with any social media event, you will have your fair number of trolls and boorish behaviour to moderate.

Gamification

A powerful social engagement strategy to boost engagement is to integrate elements of gamification into your marketing, social media, community and other digital brand experiences. Gamification is the term used to describe the use of game-design principles (points, levels, leader boards, social sharing, rewards) to drive community engagement and organic growth and to enhance your social reach, achieve marketing goals and build brand awareness.

As a marketing strategy, gamification works because it introduces active elements of fun and competition, taking your marketing from a dull and passive experience and turning it into an inclusive activity that allows any brand enthusiast to participate. Gamification will also enable you to create opportunities for interaction that can help you build trust and create opportunities for authentic and emotional connections with your community. Gamification is now widely used across all sectors, from entertainment to banking and healthcare. For example, Penny is a personal finance app to help track spending habits, and Fitbit uses gamification to help its community reach their health goals through social validation, achievement-based objectives and other gaming mechanics.

Trivia HQ, created by the founders of Vine (acquired by Twitter), utilizes many aspects of gamification to engage its community and build its brand simultaneously. What makes HQ different from other mobile games is that it re-creates the shared experience of watching a TV game show, where people shout out the answers and win actual cold hard cash, right on their mobile device (Baird, 2017).

Here's how Trivia HQ works: Every day the game goes live (3 pm and 9 pm ET), with the host asking a series of 12 trivia questions that players answer in real time. The game mechanics are simple (social validation, leader boards and rewards). If you get the answer right, you move on to the next question. If you answer incorrectly, you're out. At the end of the game, the winners split the cash. If nobody wins, the money rolls over to the next game until there's a winner. The reason HQ is succeeding is that it paired gamification with a screen that's always within reach – the smartphone – to be a conduit for a shared experience, sponsored content and revenue.

Augmented and virtual reality

As new forms of media (AR, VR, MR) begin to mature, they will become commonplace. Millennials were raised with iPhones and touch screens. Gen Z will be immersed in MR experiences. These are new marketing platforms and offer unique methods of engagement that static mediums can't compete with. From a brand perspective, AR offers more accountability, better interactions and quantifiable ROI. All the major tech brands including Apple, Facebook, Google, and Amazon are keenly aware of the power of AR and are developing software that will become instrumental in how they continue to engage with their audiences.

JOSH HASSIN (2018), CEO, LOOKIT AR – AUGMENTED REALITY
PLATFORM

Augmented reality in advertising gives brands an opportunity to flex their creative muscles and reach multiple generations at the same time. Consider the ways a teenager might interact with your print ad in a magazine using the native AR capabilities of their smartphone. While their grandparents might merely read an article (or view an ad) in a magazine, how cool would it be for Gen Z to scan a textbook to unlock videos, sounds or view limited-edition merchandise in 3D? Or imagine using the AR feature on your Facebook camera app to unlock exclusive content, music and video from media embedded in a concert ticket? That future is now, as AR has become increasingly accessible for consumers and more affordable for brands to produce.

PokémonGO set the standard high, with the most downloaded AR app in history. Pokémon inspired millions of young people to get off the couch and head outside to visit PokéStops, PokéTrains and PokéGyms and capture a myriad of creatures from the Pokémon universe. Even brands such as Starbucks have leveraged the popularity of the Pokémon AR gamification to drive sales by allowing users to unlock a unique PokémonGO Frappuccino flavour. Other savvy brands, such as Cinnabon and BestBuy are also piggybacking on the popularity of PokémonGO by making their physical locations PokéStops. They are also placing Pokéballs on the game map to raise awareness of their physical locations and draw players into their business with the hopes of converting them into a sale (Bradley, 2016).

Similarly, Gen Z is among the earliest adopters embracing virtual reality (VR) technology. In 2017, tech giants Apple, Google and Facebook all announced the integration of AR capabilities into their smartphones and/or apps. For most youth, their first experience with VR is using a Google Cardboard VR viewer, not more expensive headsets from Oculus and Samsung. Google is leading the way through the distribution of Google Cardboard viewers that allow thousands of school kids to explore VR content created by YouTube and Google Expeditions that will enable them to explore the ocean floor, or Lockheed Martin's STEM (Science, Technology, Engineering, Maths)-focused VR app that allows students to visit and explore Mars.

The Simpsons jumped into the VR game in 2016 by giving out free branded Google Cardboard VR viewers alongside branded content specially developed for VR viewing. *The Simpsons* turned to VR to mark its 600th episode and include *The Simpsons* fandom in the celebration. Fans could then use their branded VR viewer with a specially designed app and enter a 360° immersive experience that transported them into the world of *The Simpsons*. For the latest instalment (2017) of the *Star Wars* saga, Disney partnered with Google on a branded AR experience. After downloading a free app, *Star Wars* fans could place AR stickers characters from *The Last Jedi* into the physical world.

While we are still in the very nascent stages of the AR, VR and MR revolution, Gen Z is the first generation to grow up with these technologies. Youth brands have a tremendous opportunity to reach out through original, interactive experiences that merge the real and digital worlds. Let's look at how an iconic youth brand embraced and combined the emerging technology of AR with mobile smartphones to create a mobile-first experience that was a hit with Gen Z consumers.

CASE STUDY   How MTV embraced AR

After seeing the success of the Snapchat Dancing Hotdog AR filter, a team at MTV started to think about how they could integrate AR into their fan experience. The key was not just to do it because it was cool or because there was a buzz around what Snapchat was doing. Instead, the MTV team started to brainstorm beyond the gimmicky nature of AR and thought more about how to integrate an MTV AR filter into an authentic, shareable and immersive context.

After much deliberation, and working as a sort of side project, the team came up with the idea of creating an AR filter based on the iconic Moon Person to support the 2017 MTV Video Music Awards (VMAs). The dancing AR Moon Person was launched and engaged audiences far beyond their expectations. MTV reported (De Napoli, 2017) that the AR Moon Person generated almost 20 million impressions and 2.4 million views across social media over the course of one week.

According to the Moon Person project manager, Thomas De Napoli (2017), the critical metric for the AR experience was to test a new digital experience that would increase brand affinity. When the numbers came in, the AR Moon Person experiment blew their initial targets out of the water and served as a roadmap to transition an ageing youth brand into relevance for a new generation.

Chatbots and AI

According to a 2017 analysis conducted by *The Voice Report* (Marchick, 2017), an estimated 25 million voice assistants were expected to sell in 2018 at $40 to $180 – up from 1.7 million in 2015 – and kids are among the most enthusiastic adopters of chatbots and artificial intelligence (AI) voice assistants such as Google Home, Siri and Amazon's Alexa (Rosenwald, 2017). For this and subsequent generations, AI and bots are the new normal. Amazon's Alexa is now integrated into appliances from General Electric (GE), making starting the washing machine as easy as 'Alexa, wash my clothes'. Bots are growing in popularity, primarily driven by this generation's preferred methods of communication and the fact that they are comfortable conducting most daily activities on mobile devices. Amazon's Echo devices are wildly popular with kids who ask Alexa for help with school, jokes, spelling checks and ordering pizza from Domino's (Rosenwald, 2017).

Brands looking to engage with Gen Z have dived into the chatbot pool, launching some of today's most popular chatbots. Sephora and H&M have created bots that share fashion advice, and Saban Brands, with its teen-focused entertainment film and TV franchises, such as the *Teenage Mutant Ninja Turtles*, is offering one-on-one conversations with actors and characters. Facebook reports that developers have created more than 11,000 chatbots for its Messenger platform, and Kik – one of the most popular messaging platforms – unveiled 6,000 new chatbots last month alone (Wirkin, 2016). Kik also has a Bot Shop that, much like Apple's App Store, provides a centralized hub for digital distribution of chatbots.

Sephora, for example, has a Kik chatbot that helps users learn how to apply makeup, with tutorials, product recommendations and video clips. It can even help Gen Z customers in physical stores by providing product information. Even pop queen Katy Perry, Maroon Five and YouTube platform AwesomenessTV have created chatbots to gamify their brand, engage with their fans and build community by providing content that is relevant, useful and appealing to youth audiences.

Privacy and emerging technologies

When it comes to these and other emerging technologies, it's important to remember that, for many consumers, even those in Gen Z, these technologies are not yet mainstream. As such, brands need to educate consumers on the benefits, how the technology can make their lives better and, most importantly, how you will use and protect the personally identifiable information (PII) and other data you are collecting. We go deeper into both COPPA and GDPR and current online privacy proposals in Australia, and how they impact your brand community, in Chapter 9.

Contrary to what you may hear in the news, as a generational cohort Gen Z is very concerned with privacy, even more so than previous generations. Even the US toy giant Mattel, which recently announced (2017) the launch of *Aristotle*, a home baby monitor that 'comforts, teaches and entertains', faced a public backlash for its use of AI and the potential privacy implications. Gen Z takes privacy and data collection very seriously, and if you violate their trust, they will hold it against your brand.

TL;DR: chapter takeaways

- Leverage the strengths of each social, digital and live streaming platform by creating poignant and authentic content that appeals to Gen Z.
- Establish consistent branding, voice and tone across all social platforms.
- Focus on social interaction, connecting with followers as friends, and sharing experiences with your brand and/or fan community.
- Choose and secure a vanity URL – your unique web or social account address that identifies your brand, even on social platforms you don't intend to use.
- **Influence marketing is not a quick fix.** There is a common misperception that influence marketing will increase your social media reach and improve engagement over a short period of time. Your

brand may experience an initial bump, but developing a consistent following happens at a slow and steady pace.

- **Create content that is inspirational, relevant, and share-worthy.** It should help elevate young people's status in youth culture by participating in the conversation and sharing content with their friends.

- **Use digital and social media platforms as tools that help them solve problems, complete a task and connect with friends and entertainment experiences.** If your social media and content strategy doesn't provide them with any of these things, your brand will be filtered out of their feeds, screens and world.

- **Start developing emerging media strategies today** (hopefully, you're already in progress). Do you have tutorials online that could be ported into a chatbot or AI skill? If you're a brick-and-mortar business, is there an AR experience that can bring customers into your store?

- **Legal implications of influence collaboration.** Increasingly, there are more laws and regulations that now require influencers, brands and marketers to clearly state the nature of their relationship through transparent markers such as hashtags and watermarks. It's up to you to enforce and manage influencer compliance with these laws in any country where you are using them to market products for your brand.

References

ABC News (2016) [accessed 27 December 2017] 'Baby Ariel' Talks Musical.ly, the Explosively Popular App for Teens, *ABC News* [Online] http://abcn.ws/1RE6SyU

Ault, S (2015) [accessed 23 November 2017] Survey: Digital Star Popularity Grows Versus Mainstream Celebs, *Variety* [Online] http://variety.com/2015/digital/news/youtubers-teen-survey-ksi-pewdiepie-1201544882/

Baird, D (2017) [accessed 8 May 2018] From Gen Z to Grandma, Everyone is Buzzing About Trivia HQ, *Gen Z Pop!* [Online] https://medium.com/@derekeb/ from-gen-z-to-grandma-everyone-is-buzzing-about-hq-trivia-3653fe7ae7eb

Bradley, D (2016) [accessed 24 December 2017] How Brands Are Using the Pokémon Go Craze to 'Catch 'Em All', *Campaign Live* [Online] https://www.campaignlive.com/article/brands-using-pokemon-go-craze-catch-em-all/1401940#I7UYy9HHAQlEgjmr.99

Chaykowski, K (2015) [accessed 12 December 2017] Twitter Finds Growing Business Pairing Internet Stars With Big Brands, *Forbes*, 17 December [Online] https://www.forbes.com/sites/kathleenchaykowski/2015/12/17/twitter-finds-growing-business-pairing-internet-stars-with-big-brands/#35f0cec37c8d

De Napoli, T (2017) [accessed 1 January 2018] One Giant Leap for All Fankind, *V by Viacom* [Online] http://v.viacom.com/mtv-vma-augmented-reality/

Dreier, T (2017) [accessed 29 December 2017] What the Kids Are Watching: The World of Tween Live Streaming, *Streaming Media* [Online] http://www.streamingmedia.com/Articles/Editorial/Featured-Articles/What-the-Kids-Are-Watching-The-World-of-Tween-Live-Streaming-115773.aspx

Fair, L (2017) [accessed 2 December 2017] Three FTC Actions of Interest to Influencers [FTC Business Blog] [Online] https://www.ftc.gov/news-events/blogs/business-blog/2017/09/three-ftc-actions-interest-influencers

Heitner, D (2017) [accessed 22 November 2017] Rules for Social Media, Created by Kids, *New York Times*, 5 January [Online] https://www.nytimes.com/2017/01/05/well/family/the-unspoken-rules-kids-create-for-instagram.html

Marchick, A (2017) [accessed 15 November 2017] The 2017 Voice Report, *Voice Labs* [Online] http://voicelabs.co/2017/01/15/the-2017-voice-report/

Oakley, T (2015) *Binge*, Gallery Books, New York

Rosenwald, R (2017) [accessed March 27, 2017] How Millions of Kids Are Being Shaped by Know It All Voice Assistants, Washington Post, 2 March [Online] https://www.washingtonpost.com/local/how-millions-of-kids-are-being-shaped-by-know-it-all-voice-assistants/2017/03/01/c0a644c4-ef1c-11e6-b4ff-ac2cf509efe5_story.html?utm_term=.009f9e28ccff

Swant, M (2016) [accessed 22 November 2017] Twitter Says Users Now Trust Influencers Nearly As Much as Their Friends, *Adweek*, 10 May [Online] http://www.adweek.com/digital/twitter-says-users-now-trust-influencers-nearly-much-their-friends-171367/

Wirkin, T (2016) [accessed 5 August 2017] Apps Put on Notice as Study Suggests Teens Love Chatbots, *VB*, 17 July [Online] https://venturebeat.com/2016/07/17/apps-put-on-notice-as-new-study-suggests-teens-love-chatbots/

Content strategies and tactical considerations

Quality, relevant content can't be spotted by an algorithm. You can't subscribe to it. You need people – actual human beings – to create or curate it.

KRISTINA HALVORSON (HALVORSON AND RACH, 2012), FOUNDER
AND CEO, BRAIN TRAFFIC

A crash course in content strategy

Gen Z has been raised on a diet of social and digital content that is engrained in almost every aspect of their lives. For them, content isn't just king, it's like the very oxygen they breathe. It provides them with those most important items they can celebrate and share. Therefore, the stakes are high for brands to create relevant content that breaks through the noise, inspires and encourages engagements. Furthermore, each social platform has a different set of features and a unique culture of its own. Content produced must be platform-specific to stand a chance of resonating.

In this chapter we give a 'crash course' in content development, as well as some tactical content considerations. The purpose is to ground you as you start to successfully navigate the rapidly evolving state of social and digital content. We start by showing you how to apply the Truths from Chapter 3 as content planning guides, which can easily be customized for your brand. We explain the importance of identifying and owning branded social vanity URLs across platforms, and break down a strategic approach to selecting them. A major emphasis is placed on creating content that helps young people elevate their status or 'makes them look cool'. We also share a general guideline for establishing social voice, tone and content styles that fit Gen Z by platform. We include a case study from a major QSR (Quick Service Restaurant) that's dedicated itself to getting 'it' right. Then we touch on a content management as it relates to timing, quantity, and editorial calendar development. While this section could easily break out into its own book, we've focused on some of the key points.

Directional content strategies: putting the Truths into action

When planning and developing content for Gen Z audiences, we revisit the Truths (Chapter 3). The Truths act as a guideline for planning content themes. They help you to consider youth consumer wants and needs, as well as check and balance your thinking, so that you have the right mix of targeted content.

Directional content strategies

Identity: introduce your brand. Create content that shapes the perception of your brand in the minds of young consumers as something or someplace for them. Convey your diversity, excitement, relevance – whatever your identifying traits may be – by showcasing your products and services. Include information about the people behind the brand, and any other educational content leading them to consider your brand.

Trust: prove it. Create content that helps give young people reasons to believe that your brand will deliver what it claims. That it's reliable, has ethical business practices and that an association will be beneficial to Gen Z by exposing/demonstrating 'how it's made', 'behind the scenes', 'demonstrations of...' – it's all about showing, not telling.

Relevance: make people look cool. Create content that positively showcases the coolest, original things your brand is doing in ways that elevate the social status of young consumers who follow you. Even if your brand is inspiring, relatable and trustworthy, it's just as important to be viewed as socially acceptable, and even enviable.

Possibility: provide inspiration. Create aspirational content that shows young people a way forward; that pushes boundaries and motivates them to reach further or improve their lives. Whether it's an immediate solution to a problem or inspires them to dream about future careers, capture their imagination.

Experience: blend their worlds. Create content that celebrates relevant moments that young people can live or re-live vicariously. Experiences should connect them to the rest of the world, whether real or digital.

Identify and secure social vanity URLs

No content plan is ready without establishing your branded vanity URLs across social platforms, websites and landing pages that convey your brand. (A social vanity URL is a unique identifier of your brand, also known as a handle or account, on a social media platform, such as twitter.com/cocacola.) The goal and challenge is to have a unified and consistent vanity URL that represents your brand identity across social and digital platforms.

Ideally, you should sign up for the social vanity URL on every social network to make it easier for your target audience to find your brand. Even if you don't intend to use a social platform, you should secure the social vanity URL so that your brand or organization doesn't get hijacked by a bad player or troll. You may also want to secure URLs that are close iterations of your name, just to avoid confusion, such as twitter.com/coke, twitter.com/therealthing. Select a unified social vanity URL handle that will align with your goals, your brand persona, and position your brand effectively in youth culture. Below are the primary criteria we suggest applying to select vanity URLs that work for you.

Selection rubric: social vanity URLs

Keep it real: If a brand's actual name is available – grab it. Even if it's not a platform you're going to utilize, it's a good idea to catch it while you can and prevent brand identity theft.

Use keywords: If your company name isn't available, choosing a relatable, SEO-friendly keyword phrase is often the next best option.

Be relevant: Choose a handle that makes sense to promote your brand.

Keep it short: This makes it easy to remember, find and also easy for people to mention you in their social media.

CASE STUDY   How to choose a social vanity URL

Here's an example of how we approached vanity URL selection for AMAZE.org, a remarkable non-profit organization that produces 'less awkward' sex education animation videos for tweens, teens, parents and educators.

- Using the social vanity URL rubric, we compiled the following list of potential vanity URLs for AMAZE to use on social networks.
- For each social vanity URL, a supporting rationale is provided. We have also researched the availability of the suggested social vanity URL on the primary social platforms.

1 Social vanity URL

  – Proposed social vanity URL: ***/amazeorg**

- Rationale

  – Social vanity URLs **were** available on all social platforms

  – Features Amaze brand name, SEO + keyword viability

  – Conveys message of the AMAZE initiative

- Social vanity URL rubric

  – Keep it real

  – Use keywords

  – Keep it short

  – Be relevant

2 Social vanity URL

  – Proposed social vanity URL: ***/amzbodz**

- Rationale

  – 'Amzbodz' is derived from popular lexicon

  – Social vanity URLs available

- Derivative, shorter version of #amazebodz
- Fun message helps to take awkwardness out of the conversation
- Rubric
  - Use keywords
  - Be relevant
  - Keep it short

Does your content make Gen Z look cool?

Perhaps the most important content goals, when marketing to Gen Z, is to attract and keep their attention, and help them look cool, *especially* to their peers. They demand instant gratification, 'likes', social post views and personal expression. In a time when they are being overwhelmed by information, and their screens are being filled with images of perfection and curated reality, Gen Z is also seeking interaction that feels real and authentic. In the age of social media, provide them with a way to help build their personal brand and they will embrace your brand.

Look at it from the perspective of Gen Z consumers. They have grown up in a world where they know they are being judged by both friends and strangers, who then use that judgement to define themselves. If your brand is perceived as being too babyish, lame or boring, Gen Z will look elsewhere… and they have infinite options at their fingertips. There's a reason why Gen Z loves Instagram and Snapchat: both brands offer tools (filters, digital/AR stickers, fonts) that provide them with social validation and self-esteem and make them look cool to their friends. In the case of Instagram, the secret sauce is the easy-to-use filters and digital stickers that transform an ordinary smartphone photograph into a masterpiece. A quick double tap of the screen gives them what they crave most – instant feedback and validation.

From dog ears to flower crowns, Snapchat is continually adding new filters that allow Gen Z to share their individuality with the world. This also serves to fill boredom, have fun with friends and connect in 'real life' by sharing their daily life with enhanced filters and digital stickers. Their Snapchat 'messaging streaks' feature leverages Gen Z's need for constant connection to a whole new level. There are lots of ways to convey your voice and brand authenticity to your tween community, but no matter what you do, make sure to create content that serves the community's social needs – content that will make them look cool if they share it with their friends, or that will make them feel as if they have added a layer to their identity.

Mobile first

Any brand seeking to connect with young people must have a mobile-first video strategy. No exceptions. Research conducted by Adobe in 2017 found that 76 per cent of Gen Z inherently choose a mobile device to watch video, live stream, play games and video chat. A survey conducted by Gen Z media platform AwesomenessTV found that 71 per cent of Gen Z's typical video consumption is streaming, and one-third is viewed from a mobile device (AwesomenessTV, 2017). If you want to make them look cool, present content in a format that is current and has social value with their friends. Finally, understand that social platforms also offer an opportunity for 'seeded serendipity', where your audience can feel as though they 'discovered' fresh content that they can share with their peers via their favourite hubs – thus earning social capital in their circle of friends.

Creating a memorable brand voice

A consistent and memorable social voice is key to building relationships with youth audiences. Your followers and community should be able to recognize your content, even when they don't see any branding, because the voice becomes as familiar as their real-life friends. Voice should always remain the same, but tone can change depending on the context. You're always the same person, but your expressions and language should adapt to the social platform.

For teen and younger audiences, an aspirational voice is often recommended. It can have a similar effect to the voice of the cool, popular person in the grade above in school: the kind of person you listen to because you want to be like them and have them like you. Gen Z wants to be liked – rather than a persona too far out of reach, such as the celebrities and influencers they idolize. When creating content that appeals to Gen Z, it's vital that you develop and fine-tune your brand persona, voice and tone across social media.

An excellent example of this is the kids' media powerhouse The Walt Disney Company (TWDC). A brand that once had a reputation as a staid stalwart of old media, Disney found a new formula for success by discovering and embracing a unique voice that resonated with Gen Z audiences. The next step in its transformation was creating and sharing content that reflected this shift in tone. Existing content was reimagined into new formats such as GIFs and musical.ly videos.

Voice, tone and content style guide by platform

Create your content in such a way that it leverages the most popular native product features and storytelling capabilities of social media platforms. Here is an overview of a few voice, tone and content style considerations for several of the top social platforms most frequently utilized by Gen Z.

YouTube

Voice, tone and style

- Humorous, entertaining, authentic.
- On these two Gen Z-centric video platforms, the tone should match the video content. For example, if the video is about visiting VidCon, embrace the idea of 'exploring' and make it fun, silly-dramatic and include Behind the Scenes (BTS) footage and exclusive interviews.

Content considerations

- YouTube is recommended as a top priority for driving Gen Z intent through entertaining, fun and engaging content on a branded platform.

Platform inspiration

- YouTube
    - Tyler Oakley (@tyleroakley)
    - Smosh (@smosh)
    - AwesomenessTV (@awesomenesstv).

Instagram, Instagram Story and Instagram TV

Voice, tone and style

- Creative, aspirational, conversational, kindness.
- Instagram is the highest-priority app for the Gen Z demographic, including kid and tween audiences, regardless of platform age restrictions.

Content considerations

- Your content developed for Instagram, Instagram Story and Instagram TV should be highly creative, story driven and visually stunning. Embrace features such as Boomerang, AR filters and digital stickers.
- Instagram is a very hashtag-driven community, so do your hashtag research to find your audience and be sure to include them in your post.

Platform inspiration

- Adam & Justin (@lankybox)
- Liza Koshy (@lizakoshy)
- Justice (@justice).

Snapchat and TikTok (formerly musical.ly)

Voice, tone and style

- Brief, informal, fun, short video clips.
- The tone for these social platforms is brief, informal and funny. Influencers and brand content on these platforms are highly irreverent, edgy and fun.

Content considerations

- On Snapchat use the 'My Story' feature to create collaborative storytelling experiences, contests, scavenger hunts or other active experiences for Gen Z audiences.

Platform inspiration

- Snapchat

    - Lilly Singh (@iisuperwomanii)
    - Karlie Kloss (@karliekloss)
    - Mitu (@mitu).

- TikTok (formerly musical.ly)

    - Ariel Martin (@babyariel)
    - JoJo Siwa (@itsjojosiwa)
    - Disney platform UK (@disneyplatformuk).

Facebook Live, Houseparty, YouNow, Periscope

Voice, tone and style

- Fun, conversational, informational, fan scoop, BTS.
- Just about every social platform has a live streaming feature and should be utilized to provide real-time access to events, celebrities and aspirational experiences and lifestyles.

Content considerations

- One of the key drivers of these live streaming platforms is to provide fans and followers with BTS access to celebrities, experiences, and events.
- Many of these events are aspirational in nature and provide the community with access even though they aren't able to attend the actual event.

Platform inspiration

- YouNow

    - Zach Clayton (@BruhItsZach)
    - Merrell Twins (@MerrellTwins).
- Periscope

    - Sam Sheffer (@samsheffer).

Twitter, Tumblr

Voice, tone and style

- Informational, meme driven, confrontational, real time, edgy.

Content considerations

- Twitter and Tumblr are both communities that thrive on memes, GIFs, video, hashtags and conversations built around real-time events (sports, breaking news, television) and pop culture moments.
- Consider creating GIFs around your brand persona, or positioning your brand in pop culture.

Platform inspiration

- Twitter
  - Oh My Disney (@OhMyDisney)
  - GraceVanderWaal (@GraceVanderWaal)
  - Better Make Room (@BetterMakeRoom).
- Tumblr
  - Kendall Jenner (@kendalljenner)
  - Amanda Brennan (@continuants)
  - Pixar (@disneypixar).

CASE STUDY   Embrace the fans – Taco Bell

Brand voice and tone

Taco Bell presents Gen Z with the opportunity to align themselves with a brand that is 'young, adventurous and cool'. They can reflect this persona and retain cultural relevance across all the content they share on their social platforms.

Content strategy

Whether it's Snapchat, Twitter or Instagram, Taco Bell creates memorable, share-worthy experiences and story-driven branded content. Their content is like a mini-TV show – it tells a story.

Snapchat

As one of the first brands to embrace Snapchat, Taco Bell uses the platform to test new ideas, connecting with its community through humour and storytelling.

By calling for Snapbacks, it provides co-creation avenues for fans and an opportunity to engage directly in a conversation with its community.

Instagram

Taco Bell is selling the persona that it is fun, hip and cool. It does this by making sure that new food items are Instagram and FOMO worthy. By focusing on the needs of its Gen Z customer, it also fuels innovation and helps Taco Bell stay abreast of current trends and generational sensibilities (Taylor, 2017).

Twitter

Taco Bell leverages platform application programming interfaces (API) to create engaging experiences that make its community look cool. Its #Tacogram hashtag generated a fun Twitter Card to share with friends.

Why it works

Don't market to me

The Snapchat campaign is all about treating Gen Z like personal friends, not consumers.

Make me look good

Taco Bell knows that Gen Z carries smartphones with cameras and its food will end up on Twitter, Tumblr and Instagram. It worked with its food team to get the perfect formula for stringy cheese so that fans who Instagram their food had FOMO-worthy photos (Taylor, 2017). Every single time.

Tell me a story

Taco Bell uses social media and embraces elements of storytelling to weave together a narrative that is often funny, irreverent, collaborative and shareable.

Tactical content considerations

- **Content realness**: Gen Z can smell a half-baked endorsement or brand trying too hard from 1,000 miles away. It doesn't matter how good your production value is if your message doesn't hit the mark. Be authentic, relatable and then be shareable. Simply put, when it comes to authenticity, if you're not trusted, you'll get 'ghosted', or abandoned by Gen Z.

- **Create the right vibe**: Create content and entertainment experiences to stand out, whether it's hilarious, snarky or an 'all the feels' must-see. Giving Gen Z a reason to connect, share and thrive in their community will help make them your ally.

- **Don't be a poser**: Gen Z vernacular is more alien than ever – but *don't* pretend to talk the talk unless your community team or youth ambassadors really walk the walk. Most importantly, give your community the tools they need to take control of their own identities.

- **Be event driven**: Content, especially for younger audiences, is very event driven. Their concept of time is marked mainly by occasions such as birthdays or holidays. It's important to acknowledge these milestones by sharing appropriate event content.

- **Comments are content**: Responding to comments within posts can create a great deal of positive sentiment but can also drive expectations for personal acknowledgement or interaction. However, commenting also drives expectation, which will require you to stay consistent.

Content management basics

Brands need to take the phrase 'acting like a publisher' literally.

DIETRICH MATESCHITZ, FOUNDER AND CEO OF RED BULL

(BRENNER, 2014)

Timing and volume of content posting

When it comes to how often you post content, the best practice is to find the balance between not sharing so much you're beating your audience over the head with content but posting enough to keep them engaged and coming back for more. This is a process of trial and error. Don't be afraid, especially at first, to experiment with frequency and content type.

The best metric for determining how much to post is to have a community management team measure your audience's reactions. If your content elicits lots of likes, reshares or reposts, you're on the right track. Conversely, if you start posting a lot of content and see that your likes and shares are dwindling, or the community tells you in the comments to dial it back, listen to them. Pay attention, listen to, and resolve any community concerns.

The most important thing to remember is to be consistent with your posts. Another consideration to keep in mind is when to post. For example, if you're a teen brand, the majority of your audience is in school during the day, so you'll want to share mid-day (lunch) and after school. In the summer, you may want to increase the frequency of your posts on your social platforms throughout the day. While there's no hard-and-fast rule on how often you should share content, here are some guidelines to start.

Content timing and frequency matter

YouTube   Video content is typically shared a few times per week at most, with exceptions for live events and/or holiday-driven content.

Snapchat   MyStory posts, which tend to be longer and involve multiple types of media, should be posted no more than twice a week. Snaps that include just a picture or 20-second videos that feature characters can be shared two or three times a day.

Instagram

- Instagram photo or video posts are highly curated and should convey your brand tone and voice. You might consider only posting a couple of times a week on your Instagram profile page.
- Consistency is the most important thing on this platform. Instagram Story posts can be pushed daily, give you lots more creative freedom and tend to be less curated than photo posts on your profile page.

TikTok, Houseparty, Tumblr   These platforms provide opportunities for daily interaction with your community.

Live streaming (Facebook Live, Periscope)   Live streams should be built around an event (holiday, celebration, milestone) or fan experience-driven event.

Facebook   Since Facebook is not a primary social platform for younger Gen Z teens and tweens, posting on Facebook three to five times a week will be more than sufficient. The key is to post frequently enough, so they know the Facebook Page is still active.

When it comes to engagement and conversation through social platforms, there's no magic formula for frequency. You read the pulse of the community and respond accordingly. Doing so demonstrates that you are authentically interested in hearing from your community. Just posting content without answering is not an engaging experience for Gen Z. If you post content without engaging with your community, you become a content mill.

The key is to demonstrate that there is a real person behind the social accounts who is listening and responding. If you fail to engage on a personal level, your youth audience will perceive you as actively marketing, and will tune you out. Remember, unlike previous generations, Gen Z has been marketed to their entire lives and are very adept at sniffing out blatant marketing messages.

While having a content calendar is a really good idea, think past a mindset of 'post on Snapchat every Thursday at 3:42 pm'. With social media, you need to be agile and responsive, not simply post and walk away until the next post is due.

Content and editorial calendars

When it comes to engagement through social platforms, there are two critical components to keep in mind: the editorial and the conversational. Both elements play a critical role in youth engagement and will directly impact how well your brand content drives Gen Z intent to align with your brand. It's a symbiotic relationship between the structure provided by the editorial content and the more fun, engaging conversations you have around that content through social platforms. Think of it this way: the editorial content is the structure where content lives, but it's the conversations that occur around your content that compel Gen Z to hang out and return.

The primary purpose of the editorial frequency is to make sure you are producing enough content to 'feed the beast'. By plotting your content out months in advance on your content calendar, you'll be able to guarantee you have a deep repository of material that is topical, seasonal and culturally relevant to Gen Z. It's also important to have a mix of brand-specific and non-branded content. If you solely share your own content, you risk being perceived as being self-centred, 'trying too hard' or being just another cog in the corporate marketing machine. Mix it up. Think about third-party, non-branded or 'neutral content' from brand ambassadors, and moments from pop culture that can be curated and shared with your audience. This may also generate opportunities for reciprocal or fun social media-driven banter between you and other celebrities, brands or the community.

As you fill out your editorial calendar, look to holidays and other events happening in the world and in popular culture. For example, if it's National Ice Cream Day, share a photo of your brand situated with ice cream on Instagram and ask the community what their favourite flavour is to eat. Your social content calendar will highlight holidays and events that occur during each given month. By creating a weekly focus that will repeat each month, you will provide structure and set expectations for content that is relevant and highly shareable. Beyond what we've outlined in this chapter, the key to creating a winning content strategy that will resonate with Gen Z, the most important thing to keep in mind is to make sure your content remains authentic to your core brand identity and values.

TL;DR: chapter takeaways

Identify the content and stories that resonate with your target audience, and create more of it. The first step is to look at how often your content is being shared and how often Gen Z is engaged in the conversation through comments. What does the performance data tell you? If the results don't meet your expectations, your message may not be tuned in with Gen Z and your voice, tone or style needs adjustment.

- **What are the key events for your audience?** Do you have themed content ready for major and minor holidays? Are you thinking beyond the major holidays like Christmas, Boxing Day or Thanksgiving? Gen Z is a global generation, so consider creating content that celebrates Diwali, the Hindu Festival of Lights or Black History Month and other cultural celebrations.

- **Never forget the power of a call-to-action (CTA) – it's as relevant on social media as it is anywhere else.** CTAs within hashtags or digital messaging help connect your audience to a feeling of 'possibility' which can help build a robust, passionate and active community around your content. CTAs essentially allow you to invite the community into the experience.

- **Establish social vanity URLs that position your brand effectively.** Use our social vanity URL rubric to see if your existing vanity URLs on social platforms accurately reflect your brand persona, voice and tone.

- **Create content that resonates with Gen Z audiences by identifying and then consistently applying the same voice, tone and persona.** Your content should also be situated in an authentic context for the social platform or platform you are using.

- **If Gen Z doesn't trust you, they'll ghost you.** This is why creating content that resonates as authentic and is shared on the right social platform is so crucial to building credibility with Gen Z: trust is at the heart of authenticity.

- **Don't be afraid to experiment with emerging media.** Look to emerging technologies such as augmented reality (AR) or new social platforms such as Messenger Kids (Facebook), Houseparty or PopJam (primarily used in the United Kingdom) as places to experiment with existing and original content and as ways to share content and connect with Gen Z.

References

AwesomenessTV and Trendera (2017) [accessed 5 September 2017] Gen Z: The Audience You Can't Ignore [Online] https://awesomenesstv.com/genz/

Brenner, M (2014) [accessed 19 March 2018] Leadership Lessons from Red Bull, *LinkedIn* [Online] https://www.linkedin.com/pulse/20141118162108-951391-leadership-lessons-from-red-bull-media-house/

Halverson, K and Rach, M (2012) *Content Strategy for the Web*, 2nd edn, New Riders, Berkeley, CA

Taylor, K (2017) [accessed 28 October 2017] Instagram Powers Taco Bell's Innovation, *Business Insider* [Online] http://www.businessinsider.com/instagram-powers-taco-bells-innovation-2017-4

Building community with Gen Z

09

Community management is an art, not a science. It requires an iron fist in a velvet glove... each online community decides what it is going to be, and in the end, reflects the people that participate in it. The internet is made of people.

CATERINA FAKE (2013)

Gen Z and online communities

Here's the hard truth: Gen Z doesn't need you to create an online community for them to feel connected to their peers or talk about your brand. Unlike previous generations, Gen Z's online communities are both ubiquitous and focused on niche interests. They can self-organize, and gather and organize knowledge to create online communities around passions, interests and social justice issues that matter most to them and their peers. As a result, they are less interested in joining online communities created by a brand whose sole purpose is to sell them merchandise. While Millennials are very averse to advertising, Gen Z is more pragmatic and don't mind seeing ads for things that help them – as long as it is delivered in a creative way that they appreciate enough to share with friends.

What Gen Z cares about most are your brand values. Building a community around shared values and demonstrating your commitment to those ideals is the key to winning the loyalty and lifelong brand preferences of this generation. Among the values that matter most to them are: inclusivity, acceptance, and plain old being nice.

In addition to aligning values, Gen Z expects three things from your community efforts on social media: acknowledgement, trust and, most importantly, that their association with your brand must make them look 'cool' to their friends. Yet don't fall into the trap of trying too hard to appeal to the Gen Z demographic, because it will come off as just that: 'trying too hard'. The bottom line is – your brand's actions speak louder than your words.

What is community?

In the age of 'always-on' news, mobile phones, media and social feeds, it's easier than ever for young people to feel disconnected from people and things that really matter. To combat this sense of loneliness, the most connected generation in human history is turning to online communities to help foster a sense of purpose where their contributions and passions are valued and shared by others. A community can take many forms. It can exist online or offline. Or both. In either case, a community is a living system of shared interests built around pop culture, photography, favourite brands, geographic proximity, the need for emotional support, clubs, political affiliations or fandom. Some online communities are public and more visible, while others are closed communities where members are vetted before gaining access to the group. Online communities can be built on many types of platform, from social networks such as Facebook, Instagram or Twitter, to curated communities hosted on blogs, Reddit threads, Google Groups, hashtags or other forums. The success of any community rests in its ability to make members feel understood, to be given opportunities to contribute, and to be able to exchange ideas with people who share the same passions and respect for other members of the community.

Community managers who are doing their job well will use social media channels to notify the community of upcoming events, flash sales or concerts. They will also foster community by using social media to share the excitement from a music festival, ComicCon, product release or other events that not all members can attend. Doing so shows your community that you care enough about them to include them even when they can't be there in person. In short, a community can be anywhere that people who share common interests and passions are gathered. Some communities exist only online, while others live in both the physical and digital worlds. For many of Gen Z, joining a community allows them to collaborate with others, shape their own identities, and find, create and negotiate how and when brands, marketers and educators interact with them.

CASE STUDY   Fan community – Taylor Swift

From the very moment she burst onto the music scene, Taylor Swift has had the Midas touch when it comes to embracing social media, fandoms and online community. The key to her success was treating fans not as consumers who would buy her records and concert tickets, but as friends. For starters, Taylor Swift recognized that many of her young fans would be on Tumblr, not Facebook. She embraced Tumblr, leaving comments on fan art, offering advice and engaging with her fandom. Her authentic engagement on Tumblr and Instagram created a sense of belonging and made fans feel as if they are connected to a broader community of support, where they are both valued and understood. Taylor got to know her fans so well through Tumblr that she surprised them with Christmas gifts, and with handwritten notes and cards (Harris, 2014). When a fan reached out to her on Instagram asking for advice on how to handle a bully, Taylor responded and shared her personal experiences with bullying (Quinlin, 2014).

When it comes to marketing to Gen Z, Taylor Swift has understood that this is how you do fan marketing – build relationships, treat fans like friends, empower influencers to spread the word, support your brand ambassadors and engage with them in the places where they feel most comfortable. During the release of her album, *1984*, Taylor Swift took to Tumblr to find fans across the United States and United Kingdom and invite them to hear her new album *1989* before anyone else. These sessions were secret and became known as the 1989 Secret Sessions.

The lucky fans she invited used the distributed hashtag #1989SecretSessions to share their videos and pictures with other 'Swifties' around the world. This brilliant move situated the marketing of the album in a more authentic context, harnessed true fans as influencers and connected fans with the larger Taylor Swift community. Her whole approach to marketing is about the 'fans first'. From her album launch parties, where she baked cookies with fans, to the 1989

Secret Sessions and her authentic embrace of Tumblr, Taylor Swift has engaged efficiently, celebrated her fans and rewarded their loyalty. They, in turn, have embraced her as a person and a brand.

How community fuels innovation

A brand that partners with and supports their online community can tap into a passionate base of enthusiasts who can help to get brand newcomers on board, drive sales, increase engagement and extend customer loyalty and the lifespan of your consumer. Listening to and partnering with your brand community also leads to product innovation and market research. Gen Z, in particular, responds well and rewards the brands that allow them a seat at the table to share their feedback, suggestions and ideas (Lu, 2017). In fact, if you are authentic, stand for something worthwhile and include Gen Z in the conversation, they will respond with their support.

CASE STUDY   Brand innovation community – LEGO Ideas

LEGO is universally loved by Gen Z. The LEGO brand has an enthusiastic community of builders and creators who frequently share their ideas, suggestions and masterpieces across social media platforms such as Twitter, Facebook and Instagram. LEGO has tapped into that passionate and creative energy with their LEGO Ideas incubator programme. The LEGO Ideas community provides a way for anyone to share their ideas for new LEGO sets with the community.

When a LEGO creator submits their concept, the LEGO community (fansites, community boards, Facebook, Twitter, Instagram) starts to vote for the proposal. Once you reach 10,000 supporters, LEGO will review your submission and start the LEGO Review process, which can ultimately lead to seeing your idea make it into production. Just imagine that for a moment – your name could be against its very own official LEGO set! LEGO Ideas is a prime example of how a brand can collaborate with the community to fuel innovation and ideas for new products that the community feel they had a part in creating. This symbiotic relationship benefits both the brand and the consumer (LEGO Ideas, 2017).

Gen Z and communities of support

Gen Z is perpetually connected to their peers, friends, teachers, parents and content through social media apps on mobile phones. They grew up with mobile technology and content creation resources, online communities and digital media, so as a demographic they are open to engaging in communities of support. Online communities provide avenues for Gen Z to find other people who are facing the same struggles or challenges as they are themselves. These communities of support are a vital part of the Gen Z psyche. Reaching out to strangers in online communities is second nature for them. In fact, they've grown up knowing that they can connect with others for emotional support or guidance. A community can also be built around a common hashtag, making it platform agnostic. When people use a standard, distributed hashtag, it acts as a beacon calling those seeking camaraderie, solace or solutions.

CASE STUDY   Community of support –
Encircle: LGBTQ+ Family & Youth
Resource Center

Even smaller brands and not-for-profits are effectively utilizing social media and community to engage with Gen Z. A good example would be *Encircle: LGBTQ+ Family & Youth Resource Center*, an organization that advocates for and works with LGBTQ+ youth. Its outreach efforts are both online and in person at its resource centre in Provo, Utah, where it also holds weekly events.

Utah encompasses a vast amount of land, with LGBTQ+ youth living in rural, underserved areas, including the Navajo Nation. This geographic disparity provides Encircle with a unique challenge: how to serve LGBTQ+ youth in both rural and urban areas. To bridge the urban–rural gap, Encircle uses Instagram Stories as a youth-facing platform designed to keep youth in their local area up to date with upcoming events, resources or messages of support and love (Encircle, 2017a). Its Snapchat stories are highly creative, featuring both photographs and videos to convey its messages.

Encircle also uses Facebook as a way to connect with the broader community on LGBTQ+ issues and events, utilizing Facebook Groups to hold more specialized and specific conversations with its community (Encircle, 2017b).

Facebook also provides a way for Encircle to spread its 'No Sides: Just Love' message to LGBTQ+ youth and their families living outside the immediate Provo metro area (Facebook.com/EncircleTogether).

The Encircle community also rallies around the brand hashtag #EncircleTogether on Instagram, Facebook and other social platforms, where anyone can share their media and connect with others involved in supporting LGBTQ+ youth. Together, this blended approach of both social media and real-world advocacy is laying a foundation of trust that allows Encircle to reach out to LGBTQ+ youth and their families no matter where they live and provide a far-reaching community of support.

Building community

Community managers should focus on creating a healthy environment for the community to take root and thrive. Among their many tasks, they should keep tabs on the pulse of the community, listening to the wants, needs and concerns of the members. They need to be the enforcer of the community guidelines and monitor digital citizenship while working with the marketing team to keep the values of the brand aligned with the values of the community. Think about your existing online community efforts. How could you make them more engaging? Are you meeting the needs and expectations of your community? By asking yourself these questions, you will get closer to building meaningful communities.

There is a social identity within a group that is both individual and collective. As a community manager, you will want to think about how the content you're sharing and the interactions you have with your community appeal to both of those dual identities. In our experience, community managers should let this process happen naturally to allow for the most meaningful communication to occur between peers and give members time to discover their role in the community (Baird, 2010).

Roles in online communities

Each member of your online community will bring a unique set of experiences, sources of information and level of participation in the community. There will be some members who naturally become the group organizers because of their ability to keep track of details, while those who have artistic skills will find their identity as they offer creative input. An active community manager will need to be able to identify these people and then rally them around a shared goal or ideal.

This exchange of knowledge and experience transforms a group of people into a community as members begin to appreciate the expertise and perspective of each member. As members interact with the community, they will develop relationships, shared values and interests. Because of this distinctiveness, members of a group must have an opportunity to discover what their contribution will be and which role they will play by interacting socially with one another (Baird, 2010). Allowing a community to create a sense of identity is critical. An essential consideration in your community efforts is to think about designing an online community, where members are given time to build an identity that aligns with your brand values.

Community management roles

Role: the organizer

- **Task**: Provides an ordered way for the community to examine information.
- **Procedure**: Provides summary of information and community knowledge.
- **Value**: Lead thinker.
- **Example**: Community manager uses Facebook Events to keep the community aware of upcoming live streams and real-world events that may be of interest to the community.

Role: the facilitator

- **Task**: Moderates the community, keeps the conversation flowing, manages trolls and keeps people focused.
- **Procedure**: Ensures all members have the opportunity to contribute and participate in the community.
- **Value**: Inclusivity.

- **Example**: The community manager asks open-ended questions that encourage the community to engage in conversation.

Role: the strategist

- **Task**: Decides the best way to complete a task or drives the conversation through the development and enforcement of the community guidelines.
- **Procedure**: This person is keen on keeping community conversations organized and civil.
- **Value**: Detail.
- **Example**: Community manager recognizes inappropriate interactions among community members and can redirect them into a more positive direction.

Role: the supporter

- **Task**: Provides overall support for specific individuals or the community at large.
- **Procedure**: Looks for ways to help members or community members achieve their goals.
- **Value**: Helpful.
- **Example**: Community manager recognizes and celebrates contributions from other members of the community.

Role: the narrator

- **Task**: Relates information and provides context.
- **Procedure**: Provides the community with a sense of order.
- **Value**: Organizer.
- **Example**: Community manager uses social media channels to keep the community informed and, when necessary, provides a brand mea culpa.

Role: the researcher

- **Task**: Supplies the community with outside resources to provide comparative knowledge.

- **Procedure**: Goes looking for other information to provide credibility and authenticity.
- **Value**: Credibility.
- **Example**: Community manager listens to feedback from the community and, when necessary, researches complaints and provides solutions.

SOURCE Adapted from Fisher *et al* (2006)

Finally, it's important to remember that a community built around a shared set of values is a living entity that is always evolving. In other words, a well-designed community should provide users with the tools and leave it to them to construct their meaning and level of contribution to the community.

Community management

Being a community manager involves some serious juggling. You need to take care of a carefully balanced mix of activities, conversation and content in order to foster motivation and engagement, while also providing members with access to the information and knowledge that motivated them to join the community in the first place. In this section, we will review some of the fundamental roles and responsibilities of a community management team. It's also important to note that some of these functions may overlap.

Community guidelines

Communities flourish when they are rooted in trust, shared community standards and an expectation of reciprocal generosity from all the members. Strangers are connecting with strangers to build experiences that matter to them, and that's what is at the heart of every healthy community. The community manager should encourage people to share concerns when they feel these rules have been violated and be prepared to squash bad actors and trolls. Ideally, there should be a series of warnings leading up to expulsion and an appeals process. Think about your efforts on Facebook. Have you communicated with your community what your moderation policies are?

Community guidelines are an essential part of any gathering of people with diverse beliefs, experiences and backgrounds. These guidelines, ideally created with the input of the community, are the rules that will help foster, grow and protect the members. Think of them as the 'legal system' of the community. While not legally binding, the agreed community norms and acceptable behaviours set the tone, expectation and penalty for violating those rules. Think about your brand values. How might these guiding principles be folded into your community guidelines?

Your community guidelines should be posted on your website, along with your terms of service (TOS), and shared frequently and widely on any social platform your brand has set a stake in. In a similar vein, your brand should also follow the community guidelines of the platform (eg Instagram, Snapchat, Tumblr, Twitter, Facebook) you are using, so before you create that new community hub, be sure to get the rules and make sure you can stay true to your brand values.

Community moderation

If you build a brand community, people will come – and so will the trolls, the drama queens and all the other misanthropes that inhabit the internet. The key here is not to overreact, and instead, have an ongoing conversation with your community on what is appropriate behaviour. Also, by being protective, your community will feel a sense of accomplishment and ownership for the community they are helping to cultivate.

It's also worth making sure your community knows how to report abuse and other inappropriate behaviours to the team. Hopefully, you've outlined the types of actions that will get you banned in your community guidelines. Do you have an internal process for evaluating and handling bad actors in your online community spaces? Create an expectation that the moderation of the community is a collective effort. The more eyes on the end goal (of a successful, mutually respectful community), the better.

Celebrate the community

If you really want to create effective messaging that gives members a feeling of possibility and accomplishment, you need to be the cheerleader for your community. Here are some of the strategies that we advise clients to use to do exactly that:

- **Showcase:** If someone in your community contributes a unique piece of community-generated content (CGC), or great idea, share it with the broader community. *'Hey, @pandajones created this awesome thing, check it out!'*
- **Validate:** If someone makes an astute observation or makes a good suggestion on how to improve your brand or product or gives you a reminder that you're not staying true to your brand values, acknowledge their contribution by providing narrative feedback.
- **Celebrate 'We':** When your community reaches a milestone or does something cool, talk about it! Remember, when the community achieves something you should give them credit for it by talking about how **the community**, not the brand, is responsible for producing the milestone.

Persona, voice and tone

Nothing is more vital to the success of your online community efforts than your persona, voice and tone. Gen Z expects you to have a conversation *with* them, not *at* them. They want to talk to your brand, and you should listen. We delve more into the specifics of how to develop a persona, voice and tone in Chapter 7, but the key takeaway is to develop a persona and then make sure your community management team uses it in a way that is consistent with your brand values, messaging and interactions on social platforms.

Content moderation

No matter how much positive and uplifting content your channels showcase, there will always be uncontrollable, or unexpected, behaviour from the audience-at-large. Depending on the age of the participants, the level of content moderation required will vary.

While sometimes this can make you feel like shying away from social platforms because of the user-generated content (UGC), don't do it! Instead, embrace the platform and create Community Guideline policies that support the unique nature of the platform, your brand values and a healthy community:

- Showcase your community guidelines within the additional details of your channel. These should be expectations for and from the community.
- Content should only be removed due to extreme language, danger, threats, abuse, and references to illegal activity.
- Use negative comments as an opportunity to restate and show your commitment to both your community and brand values in your response to community trolls.
- Decide the level of commitment you have to the audience. Responding to comments within posts can create a great deal of positive community, but can also drive expectations for individual acknowledgement or interaction. Commenting also drives expectation, which means you will have to stay consistent in your timely response to your community.
- Avoid 'robot' responses or non-organic context.

For kid and tween centric communities (under 13), you should expect to moderate more frequently and rule with an iron fist. There should be a zero tolerance for bullying, and again, this needs to be outlined in your community guidelines. For older teen and young adult communities, you can be a little more lenient on content moderation, as long as the 'edgier' content and comments align with your voice, persona and tone.

Digital citizenship and online communities

In our experience, we have found that brands that have been successful in developing a culture of good digital citizenship have done so by creating a relationship of trust where they can have ongoing discussions regarding what is and isn't appropriate online behaviour with their community.

How brands can combat cyberbullying

Learning how to become a responsible digital citizen isn't just a school or parenting issue. As the 'host' of an online community, it's up to your brand to make sure that you are fostering a space that is tolerant of divergent beliefs, supportive and responds to bullying. By doing so, you are promoting a healthy and safe online community. There are many ways to define 'digital citizenship', but we feel that it comes down to three main components:

- Civilly conducting yourself in the online world just as you would be expected to behave in the offline world. Universal rules of social conduct apply in both environments.

- Watching out for each other in your online community, much as you would do in your 'real world' neighbourhood.

- Behaving responsibly and compassionately with your online actions.

Social reporting tools

As we outlined previously, at a very early stage your brand should set the expectation that for your brand to assist community members on digital citizenship issues, they must report abuse to you as soon as it happens. Perhaps one of the most critical ways that both brands and community members can be good digital citizens is by reporting bullying, abusive or inappropriate comments. Every social networking site has social reporting tools. Make sure your community knows that these tools exist and encourage them to use them. Your community members, as well as your internal teams, should know how to report bullying and other negative behaviours directly to the platform.

One of the most important things you can do as the host of an online community, whether it's on a social network or online forum, is establish a protocol to triage any threats of self-harm. Several considerations need to be decided on when engaging with youth communities. For example, who on your internal team should be notified? Are you ready to track an IP address and call local authorities if a member of your community posts a threat of self-harm? What resources do your community managers have to pass along to anyone who threatens self-harm? Interacting with someone threatening self-harm can be very distressing for members of your community management team, so you'll also want to ensure it's also important to provide them with emotional support resources.

CASE STUDY   How Instagram supports the Gen Z community

Gen Z teens and young adults are increasingly turning to online communities on social media platforms such as Instagram to talk about their mental health struggles with social anxiety, depression and bullying (Twenge, 2017). In May 2017, Instagram launched an initiative called Instagram Together to showcase their continued commitment to developing tools that address bullying, mental health, and other topics impacting tweens, teens and young adults. As part of the Instagram Together campaign, several influential members of the community are showcased on a special microsite (https://instagram-together.com/), sharing stories of how they use the Instagram community and hashtags to share their mental health journey with others to build (or find) a network of support.

In the same month, and as part of Mental Health Awareness month, Instagram announced hashtag campaigns called #KindComments and #HereForYou, which highlight how the social network has helped support its community members struggling with mental health issues. The Instagram community was invited to participate and share their thoughts and struggles with mental health issues using the campaign hashtags. The community responded: as of June 2017, over 97,000 images were tagged #HereForYou and over 46,000 images were tagged #KindComments by the Instagram community.

Members of the Instagram community can also anonymously report others whom they feel may be in need of mental health support. The self-harm reporting feature allows users to report a mental health concern to Instagram and send the user a message with mental health resources in their country. These resources also display when someone visits a hashtag for a sensitive topic, such as hashtags associated with self-harm, eating disorders, and suicide. As a result of community managers having an ongoing conversation with the community and keeping a pulse on how the community was evolving, Instagram was able to create a community initiative that supported their needs and aligned with the values of both the community and the brand.

Gen Z and digital citizenship

Good digital citizenship means thinking about the effects on others before posting content or sending messages. It also means standing up for anyone being targeted by bullies – online or off. These behaviours may be challenging for brands to control, but it's an important aspect of running an online community, especially when there are minors involved. The key is to state in your community guidelines that there is an expectation that all community members will also be productive digital citizens. Seizing the opportunity to be a leader on the subject of responsible digital citizenship will help you build credibility with Gen Z audiences and help you earn their respect. As we outlined in Chapter 2, fairness, being inclusive and kind are important values for Gen Z.

It's also important to remember that for Facebook, Instagram or any social channel to assist you on digital citizenship issues, you must report abuse to them as soon as it happens. As a brand, you not only need to model this behaviour, but your community needs to know that you expect this response. Brands that are willing to build a sense of online community and instil responsibility for good digital citizenship on their social platforms find that they are empowering their community with valuable skills that benefit them beyond the physical, social or virtual spaces (Baird and Fisher, 2010).

Guidelines for digital citizenship

Here are three ways you can integrate the principles of digital citizenship into your online, social media and marketing content:

- **Be civil**: Create content that encourages or models interacting with others in a civil manner in the online world just as you would be expected to behave in the offline world. Universal rules of social conduct apply in both environments.

- **Be empathetic**: Lead by example by creating content that embodies the ideals of understanding others, respecting and celebrating our differences and behaving in a kind, compassionate and inclusive manner.

- **Be an upstander**: Think about how your brand can be an advocate for the underdog. Create content that encourages your audience to watch out for each other in your online community much as they would in their 'real world' neighbourhood.

Community management: Gen Z and privacy

The laws that govern children's online privacy, the collection of data, parental notification and rules around marketing to kids vary by country. Laws centred around children's privacy data are at the centre of an ever-evolving and changing public policy debate. For example, in June 2018 China proposed strict new regulations designed to protect children from unscrupulous data collection. And in July 2018, a new law came into effect in California governing the collection of personally identifiable information (PII) and data of its residents, including children. It's important that before engaging in any marketing or data collection activities for minors, you seek legal counsel to advise you on compliance with the laws and regulations around children's privacy and marketing.

In this section, we will take a look at the privacy and marketing regulations in the United States, the European Union and Australia. Generally speaking, the key here is to plan for the data collection of minors before you begin collecting PII from children under 13 and work with your legal team and COPPA compliance consultants to make the right privacy decisions for your community and brand.

United States: Children's Online Privacy Protection Act (COPPA)

It is important to note that with some of the social platforms mentioned, directly targeting the youth demographic under the age of 13 (without proper verifiable parental consent (VPC)) may be a direct violation of the COPPA. This law also dictates how you share these data with third-party vendors, cookies and ad companies.

At the heart of COPPA is a set of legal requirements surrounding how a brand may collect, use and store the PII of minors under the age of 13. Per COPPA, if you are going to collect PII on children you must first seek permission from the parent. To obtain consent, the

Federal Trade Commission (FTC) has outlined the approved ways to gain parental approval, including (but not limited to): 'Email Plus', credit card transactions and faxed consent forms (FTC, 2017).

Several Safe Harbor vendors will walk your brand through COPPA compliance issues. While it may be costly to do so, it's much less expensive than being fined by the FTC for violating COPPA laws. As of June 2017, the law allows for a $16,000–$40,654 fine per individual violation.

European Union: General Data Protection Regulation (GDPR)

While COPPA is narrowly focused on the privacy of children, the General Data Protection Regulation (GDPR) privacy laws are focused on data protection for both children and the broader population. For websites and apps whose audiences are primarily kid-focused, additional requirements apply. These regulations are commonly known as GDPR-Kids (GDPR-K). However, GDPR stipulates that privacy standards and collection of PII must be held to a higher standard when the data come from children. At the time of this writing, it's not clear how Brexit will impact the participation of the United Kingdom in the GDPR privacy regulations.

While the age of consent varies by country, the EU has set a range within which each country can set the age of consent: no lower than 13, but no higher than 16. In Spain, for example, the age of consent was set in law at 14 years old, while the United Kingdom set the age of consent to be 12 years old (SuperAwesome, 2017).

Under the GDPR, any organization or brand that seeks to collect PII from kids is required to secure VPC from parents. To obtain consent, marketers can use methods similar to those used under COPPA, including (but not limited to) the following ways: 'Email Plus', credit card transactions, faxed consent forms and, as they become available, other types of technology that provide parental consent.

Australia: kids and online privacy

As of 2017, the Australian government doesn't currently have any specific laws outlining the collection of data, privacy or marketing to children. However, the Australian Law Reform Commission (ALRC) has two working policy committees who have suggested a specific set of privacy laws modelled closely on the COPPA laws used in the United States.

The Obesity Prevention Policy Coalition (OPPC) and Young Media Australia (YMA) made a joint submission suggesting that direct marketers should be prohibited from collecting or using PII of children without the VPC of any individual under the age of 14 (ALRC, 2017). Like COPPA, the working committees proposed that verified consent can be attained through a signed form sent by mail or fax, provision of a credit card number or electronic signature, or calling a toll-free number staffed by trained personnel.

An additional proposal put forth by the OPPC and YMA committee was a prohibition on making consent to use personal information for direct marketing purposes a condition of entry to the competition, promotion or other activity if the entrant is under the age of 14. However, the ALRC recommends that the age is set to apply to any minor under the age of 18. These regulations are, at this time, under review by the ALRC (2017).

TL;DR: chapter takeaways

- **What Gen Z cares about most are your brand values.** Building a community around shared values and demonstrating your commitment to those ideals is the key to winning the loyalty and lifelong brand preferences of this generation.

- **Brands build community wherever they go.** On social networks, online groups, around a shared hashtag and/or real-world events.

- **Community guidelines are the cornerstone of any good social engagement strategy plan.** Members of your community must know up front what behaviours are acceptable and what the penalties are for violating those common standards.

- **Familiarize yourself with youth-centric community guidelines.** Review guidelines from brands such as YouNow, Flickr, Instagram and YouTube as best practice examples. Pay attention to how they use tone, voice and persona to appeal to Gen Z audiences.

- **Keep your community in compliance with privacy laws.** If you are engaging with children under the age of 13, be sure to comply with all facets of COPPA (as well as EU and UK privacy laws) before you collect any PII without VPC.

References

Australian Law Reform Commission (ALRC) (2017) [accessed 12 November 2017] Particular Privacy Issues Affecting Children and Young People, *Australian Government* [Online] http://bit.ly/KidsPrivacyAU

Baird, D (2010) [accessed 9 November 2017] Social Identity, Knowledge Management & Member Roles in Online Communities, *Social Media Today* [Online] https://www.socialmediatoday.com/content/social-identity-knowledge-management-member-roles-online-communities

Baird, D and Fisher, M (2010) [accessed 22 September 2017] Neomillennial User Experience Design Strategies: Utilizing Social Networking Media to Support '*Always on*' Learning Styles [Online] http://journals.sagepub.com/doi/abs/10.2190/6WMW-47L0-M81Q-12G1

Encircle (2017a) [accessed 12 November 2017] Instagram [Online] https://www.instagram.com/encircletogether/

Encircle (2017b) [accessed 12 November 2017] Facebook [Online] https://www.facebook.com/encircletogether/

Fake, C (2013) [accessed 8 August 2017] Online Communities, 24 July [Online] https://caterina.net/2013/07/24/online-communities/

Fisher, M *et al* (2006) [accessed 15 June 2017] Designing Community Learning in Web-Based Environments: Flexible Learning in an Information Society, *IGI Global* [Online] https://www.igi-global.com/book/flexible-learning-information-society/403

FTC (2017) [accessed 15 June 2017] Complying with COPPA: Frequently Asked Questions [Online] https://www.ftc.gov/tips-advice/business-center/guidance/complying-coppa-frequently-asked-questions

Harris, K (2014) [accessed 12 September 2017] Taylor Swift Surprised Her Fans with Christmas Presents and Their Reactions are Hysterical, *Buzzfeed* [Online] https://www.buzzfeed.com/kristinharris/taylor-swift-sent-fans-surprise-christmas-presents

LEGO Ideas (2017) [accessed 11 December 2017] How It Works [Online] https://ideas.lego.com/howitworks

Lu, Y (2017) [accessed 5 May 2017] Houseparty's Teenage Consultants Help Design the App [Online] http://nymag.com/selectall/2017/04/housepartys-teenage-consultants-help-design-the-app.html

Quinlin, E (2014) [accessed 12 November 2017] In touching personal message, Taylor Swift tells bullied teen fan to 'keep walking in the sunlight', *Today*, 4 September [Online] https://www.today.com/popculture/taylor-swift-sends-touching-instagram-message-bullied-teen-fan-1D80126920

SuperAwesome (2017) [accessed 12 November 2017] What Europe's Data Privacy Laws for Kids (GDPR) Means for Digital Media [Online] https://blog.superawesome.tv/2016/04/21/gdpr-passes-into-law-what-this-means-for-kids-marketing-in-europe/

Twenge, J (2017) [accessed 22 October 2017] With Teen Mental Health Deteriorating Over Five Years, There's a Likely Culprit, *The Conversation*, 14 November [Online] https://theconversation.com/with-teen-mental-health-deteriorating-over-five-years-theres-a-likely-culprit-86996

A primer on social and influence media valuation

10

Here's the deal. If you want to measure social media ROI, stop wasting your time doing software demos and attending webinars. Just figure out what you want to track, where you can track it, think about both current customers and new customers, and go do it.

JAY BAER (2017), FOUNDER CONVINCE AND CONVERT

Social and digital media constantly change, the need for accountability doesn't

All the audience insights, alignment and reach in the world are pointless if you're not getting enough attention and engagement within youth culture to build an audience capable of driving business growth. If there is one thing we want to stress here more than anything, it's the creation of value. Putting your time, energy and resources into creating value for the young people who make up your targeted 'youth market' – the ones you are trying so hard to identify, reach and engage – is the most important thing you can do. If not, then the metrics in this book – or any source for that matter – are meaningless.

This chapter serves as a primer on earned media value (EMV): the measurement and valuation of social and influence campaigns. We discuss EMV in terms of the metrics involved, and how it works with several of the social platforms most popular with Gen Z.

However, the social platforms are constantly in flux. We recommend understanding all the different metrics and analytics features, and how each is a building block, before committing to any one particular social or digital platform, or influencer/creator content performance. An influencer or creator may waver in their potential for earning media value, but if we follow the EMV formula we can identify the platform and talent that have the highest potential value at a given time for a specific brand or audience. The chapter concludes with an interview with the founders of Hookit, experts in the field of data-driven social, influence and sponsorship intelligence.

Earned media value

Social and digital media are where Gen Z lives, and that's where today's brands are trying to reach them. However, while social and digital media have clear pricing structures and valuation standards, it's hard to connect organic social and influencer activity to ROI. How, then, do we measure the effects of social media, specifically influencers and creators – essentially word of mouth, or social endorsement campaigns – on Gen Z consumers? Without a formula for valuation, trusting that the endorsement of a popular influencer or creator will benefit your brand is a gamble or leap of faith. That's where EMV comes in. EMV is the measurement of value generated from the social promotion for a brand based on the quality of promotion and engagement with a social post. It is designed to approximate what a similar post would cost if a brand were to pay for the same level of engagement through a paid promoted post on the same platform. EMV is growing quickly in viability as a method of identifying specific metrics and assigning them to various aspects of organic social media interactions to quantify the benefits of these endorsements. Below are descriptions of our foundational metrics, and a breakdown of the larger family of metrics that can be considered for EMV.

Foundational metrics

Foundational metrics for success

- Reach
- Engagement
- Sentiment

Reach

Reach is not an absolute measure of value, but it factors into value; visibility within your youth audience segment remains part of the equation to gain traction. Reach (post, page, organic, viral or paid) is defined as the number of unique people who actually saw your content. While reach numbers are not the most important, they do have an impact on every other metric you track, including engagement (likes, comments, clicks, shares) and sentiment (negative/positive). When it comes to measuring Gen Z reach, we address and monitor six main metrics: unique visits, how content is being consumed, geography, bounce rate, page views, and SEO and hashtags.

Reach metrics

Unique visits

- How many people in your target audience are viewing your content? Is your content driving visits to your website, campaign landing page, social platforms and/or other digital or physical location?
- What type of content (images, video, GIFs, AR, VR) is driving unique visits to your social channels?

Content consumption: mobile or web

- How is Gen Z consuming your content? Are they using mobile devices (smartphone/tablet) or web to connect with your content and social media efforts?
- How does this knowledge influence your design and use of each social channel/website?

Geographic location

- Where is your content being shared? Is it doing well in some regions, but not others?
- How can your brand best optimize for geographical locations?

Bounce rate

- Is your target demographic spending time engaging with your content? Alternatively, just moving through quickly and going to another site?
- How can content and social efforts be tweaked to keep them engaged longer on your site(s)? Have you struck the right voice and tone for your content?

Page views

- Are they coming back for more? Are they one and gone? What are other sources driving them to your social channels?

SEO and hashtags

- How effective are your search engine optimization strategies for reaching a Gen Z audience?
- Are web searches or hashtags driving Gen Z to your social sites and content?

Engagement

Engagement happens when young people take a proactive action or respond to a call-to-action on your social media channel. It is defined as a user interacting with content in any number of ways, including viewing, sharing, voting, commenting, reviewing, playing a game or taking a poll. For example, they may like a post, click on a link, comment on a video or share or repost your content. Engagement is the best barometer of how well you are aligned with youth culture, how good your content is and how well it resonates. Take an honest assessment of your social media activity: are you posting enough or blowing up your feed with too much information? If you do not see as much participation from your community as anticipated, look at such elements as the voice and tone of your content. The key here is to think about your audience and how you can best add value that enhances their lives. Of the many metrics we use, engagement is the most important. We prioritize the following metrics: direct interactions; social sharing; social velocity; and time spent.

Engagement metrics

Direct interactions

- These include likes, comments, votes, reviews, playing a game, and video views: anything where the person is directly engaging content with a direct personal response.

Social sharing

- Are young people sharing your content? If so, on what platforms are they sharing and reposting the content?
- If your content is being shared, this is a sign that your content strategy has hit the mark! You have curated and created content that is resonating and being recognized as authentic. So much so, your people are sharing it because you are making the sharer look good to their friends.

Social velocity

- Simply put, social velocity is the rate of change of engagement with content on social media – how many new shares, tweets and other engagements the content is garnering over a given timeframe.

Time spent

- How much time is your audience spending viewing your content?
- What is the benchmark for time spent visiting your own (or your competitors') social content?

Sentiment

Social sentiment is a way of measuring the emotions behind consumer interactions with your brand on social media. Feeling adds context to the level of engagement you have with your audience and impacts reach. It is also a reflection and barometer of how successful the tone and voice you have baked into your content has been. It is important to look at the results and think about why a particular person is satisfied, happy, angry or annoyed with your brand.

Most importantly, sentiment analysis allows you to identify general attitudes towards your brand, product or social media efforts. The goal of sentiment analysis is to correlate social media comments with three basic categories: positive, negative or neutral (Stinson, 2017). The sentiment metrics we like to look at here are sentiment type and brand affinity.

Sentiment metrics

Positive/negative sentiment

- What is the ratio of positive to negative comments on your posts? It is essential that you listen to the community feedback and, if necessary, adjust the types of interactions and content you are posting. Voice and tone are everything.
- A large number of positive comments are an indicator that your content tone, voice and mix are on the right path. If you are getting too many 'angry' emojis, think about realigning your content strategy to garner a more positive sentiment feedback. Take it as an opportunity to listen to your community.

Brand affinity

- If your brand is doing good or improving the lives of others, Gen Z will want to be associated with your brand. It makes them feel good, and it makes them look good to their friends. This is a brand win.
- For many influencers and creators, brand affinity is the ultimate metric. Many brands like to align with influencers as a way to boost their credibility. If the influencer has a community around 'good vibes', that can result in huge engagement and positive sentiment by association for your brand (Figure 10.1).

In summation, when it comes to EMV, we recommend organizing metrics into the following categories, then picking the metrics that work the best for brand, offering, youth initiative and youth audience:

Figure 10.1   Earned media valuation model

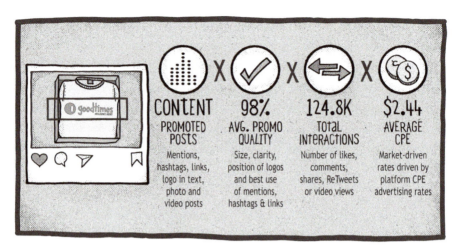

SOURCE Hookit. Artist's rendering by Mike Carnevale

- **Reach:** unique visits, content consumption, geography, bounce rate, page views, and SEO and hashtags.
- **Promotion type and quality:** mentions, hashtags, links, logo in text, photo and video, size, clarity, position of logos and best use of mentions, hashtags and links.
- **Interaction type and quality:** number of direct interactions (likes, comments or video views), social sharing (shares, ReTweets), social velocity, time spent, sentiment of interaction, brand affinity.
- **Cost per engagement:** market-driven rates for a like, comment, share, ReTweet or video view by platform (Hookit, 2017; see interview below).

Social metrics by platform

When it comes to social media platforms, it is essential to understand what native analytic features are available to help you evaluate and choose an EMV formula. In this section, we provide examples of several top social platforms and their different types of native social analytics features that measure value (reach, engagement and sentiment).

For instance, examine your social analytics to see what times you're getting the most engagement on your posts. You might find, if your target audience is school-aged Gen Z, that the best times to post are before school, during lunch and after school. In short, keep tweaking your content until you reach the right balance, voice, time of day and desired levels of engagement. Your metrics for success should not be dependent on any one particular platform: today's 'hot platform' is tomorrow's ghost town (hello, Vine). Instead, develop a strategy that will work utilizing currently popular platforms, and be flexible.

Instagram

Reach

If you have a large number of followers, this is a critical indicator that you have found the correct balance of voice, tone and content. Followers are also considered to be community members who have opted-in or subscribed to your content.

Engagement

To 'heart' an image, video or Boomerang is a way for the community to show you they liked your content. Lots of hearts equates to a positive sentiment and brand affinity. For video and Boomerang content, you will also see the number of views.

Sentiment

An @ happens when someone includes an Instagram handle in a comment on a piece of content. It could be directed at your brand or another community member. The @ reply allows for more interaction and conversation between both the company and the target audience. It is important that your community management team monitor the comments so they can provide customer service and handle the inevitable trolls.

Native analytics

One important thing to do is to make sure that your Instagram account is an Instagram Business account. This will unlock a number of native analytics that can help you track your performance. Having a business account will also allow you to promote your posts, right from the app, more easily.

Value metrics

VPV (value per view), CPM (cost per thousand impressions), CPE (cost per engagement), VPC (value per link click), VPCO (value per comment), VPL (value per like), VPS (value per share), VPPL (value per page like).

Snapchat

Reach

If you have a large number of friends, this is an essential indicator that you have found the correct balance of voice, tone and content. Followers are also considered to be community members who have opted-in or subscribed to your content.

Engagement

A key indicator of high engagement is when a brand issues a call-to-action via Snapchat and the community answers by directing a Snap to the brand. This is known as a Snapback. The MyStory and sponsored filter features are a way for your brand to push their creativity to the max and tell a story that resonates with Gen Z audiences.

Sentiment

When a user takes a screenshot of a piece of content you have sent to your community, you will receive a notification. A large number of these notifications are a key indicator that your content is resonating with your target demographic.

Native analytics

Snapchat provides brands with basic analytics statistics and metrics, including unique views, screenshot figures and on-demand geo-filter performance.

Value metrics

Value per engagement, value per view, cost per thousand impressions.

YouTube

Reach

The subscriber metric is an important measurement that tracks the number of people who have subscribed to your YouTube channel. By subscribing they will automatically receive updates in their feed.

Engagement

The average view metric will help you determine if your viewers are watching your entire video or just the first couple of minutes. This number will help you figure out the sweet spot for video length to keep your viewers engaged and better meet your viewers' needs and expectations. In November 2017, YouTube also added a new 'Community' tab that allows you to share polls, videos, images and text-based content with your community.

Sentiment

YouTube has a thumbs up icon (Like) and thumbs down (Dislike) button that allows users to share their emotional response to your content. The new Community tab also allows your community to leave thumbs up, thumbs down, 'heart' your posts, vote in polls and leave comments on your posts. This is another way for your brand to measure community sentiment.

Native analytics

As part of Google, YouTube has robust analytics features baked into the platform to help track your success and progress in reaching your target demographic.

Value metrics

Value per view, value per click, value per comment, value per like, value per share, value per subscriber, cost per thousand impressions, cost per engagement.

Twitter

Reach

On Twitter, follower count is a highly desirable metric. Based mostly on perception, accounts with large follower counts or a blue 'Verified' check mark are considered to be more influential than those with a smaller following. Hashtags are a vital strategy for increasing your reach, getting your content on the radar and fostering user engagement.

Engagement

Interaction on Twitter is primarily measured by ReTweets (RT), likes and replies. The goal on Twitter is to have a conversation with your community. Brands can also use media such as GIFs and videos, polls and images to increase engagement. In December 2017, Twitter added a new product feature to make it easier to link several tweets together, effectively expanding the ability to contain a conversation in a single thread.

Sentiment

Twitter has a highly confrontational culture, and you should have a communications plan in place to respond to negative sentiment. Sometimes the best strategy is to know when to stop engaging and redirecting your attempts at a resolution to a non-public platform. Hashtags can also be a good barometer of sentiment.

Native analytics

Twitter offers brands a robust dashboard with analytics to measure the effectiveness of your tweets and video content. In December 2017, Twitter rolled out video view metrics for all tweets containing native video.

Value metrics

Value per view, value per click, value per comment, value per follower, value per ReTweet, value per like, value per post, cost per thousand impressions, cost per engagement.

Facebook

Reach

When it comes to Gen Z, common knowledge dictates that they don't use Facebook. The key is to think of non-traditional uses of Facebook. Think about using Facebook Messenger chatbots or Facebook Live to attract Gen Z to your branded content.

Engagement

Facebook is increasingly moving from text-based posts to visual narratives – GIFs, memes, chatbots, AR and live streaming. To garner Gen Z eyeballs, focus on creating quick and immersive experiences utilizing the Facebook platform as a stage.

Sentiment

Brand affinity can be measured by the number of 'likes' and 'followers' your brand page has on Facebook. Sentiment on specific content posts can be measured by a combination of 'likes', Facebook Reaction emojis, and comments.

Native analytics

Facebook provides an in-depth look at your community demographics: from age to geography, gender and device (iOS, Android), you will be able to see if your content is reaching your desired target market.

Value metrics

Value per view, value per click, value per comment, value per like, value per share, value per page, like value per post, cost per thousand impressions, cost per engagement.

Tumblr

Reach

Tumblr is first and foremost a media platform designed to reach the youngest segments of Gen Z. The culture is loose, and just about anything goes. If you use Tumblr, be sure to focus on using interactive media in your content strategy.

Engagement

Users can interact with your content mainly by following, liking and reblogging. Users can also reply and ask questions if you have turned on those options in your Tumblr settings.

Sentiment

Perhaps the most significant metric for sentiment on Tumblr is to have your content become a 'note' (either liked or reblogged by another Tumblr user). A 'like' gives it a little heart and tags it for you; a reblog puts it on your own Tumblr blog.

Native analytics

Tumblr lets brands and content owners filter data to track a specific blog or post and track a topic that goes beyond their content.

Value metrics

Value per view, value per click, value per comment, value per like, value per reblog, value per follower, cost per thousand impressions, cost per engagement.

Read on to hear the perspectives on social, influence and sponsorship media valuation from two leading experts in the field, who are successfully helping companies quantify and improve social, influence and sponsorship return on investment using data-driven intelligence.

INTERVIEW   Hookit founders on social media and influence valuation

SCOTT TILTON, CEO AND CO-FOUNDER, RJ KRAUS, CPO (CHIEF PRODUCT OFFICER) AND CO-FOUNDER

Kraus and Tilton have expertise with technology advances that are shaping the way social media, influence and sponsorship programmes are evaluated for performance. Hookit has built a very powerful platform that we believe is years ahead of the traditional media measurement companies. Hookit tracks, measures and values overall engagement generated around sponsorship assets across digital and social media platforms. Using the *Hookit Valuation Model (HVM)*, the algorithm provides an earned media value (tangible dollar amount) to engagements by combining social interactions (likes, shares, comments and video views) with a content promotion quality score (size, clarity, position of logos), promotion type (hashtags or mentions) and an industry-standard cost per engagement. In addition, it applies computer vision software to measure logos, product placement and other brand information in photos and videos. In total, they offer objective measurement of return on investment (ROI) of influencer, creator and sports sponsorships across digital media platforms.

What are some of the key trends for brands to be aware of when it comes to measuring influential people and event sponsorship performance?

We're seeing a massive shift in the way sponsorships are being measured. In the past, television was the largest driver of value for properties. That has all changed with the rapid growth of the social and digital platforms and the way fans are consuming content. In our world of sports, the athletes, teams and leagues have become their own media properties on social media, with complete control over how they choose to interact with fans and the content they share. This provides huge potential for both the sides of the desk to maximize the effectiveness of sponsorships.

When it comes to measuring performance, Engagement is *the* currency for social and digital media. In social media, you have real-time access to mountains of data at your fingertips to determine which fans are engaging with what properties, what content, the quality of promotion within that context, at what times and on which platforms. Impressions are still the a primary way to measure performance on some platforms, but when it comes to social media, why use eyeballs or make assumptions when you have all that data to measure and make informed decisions?

The next big trend will be measurement consolidation. There is a disparity in the way brands and properties are measuring sponsorship. We spoke with one European football club that was cobbling together data from 26 different tools to produce data and reports to understand and quantify their value. There is a huge need for a single-source solution that consolidates social, digital, TV and other data sources into a single platform or dashboard, which is where our focus has been the past couple of years.

Finally, measurement and information overload aren't enough. You need to extract insights from the data that drive ROI and ROO. The output of those insights will help drive more informed decisions and the context to work with your partners to optimize.

For those new to influence marketing and sponsorship programme valuation, what is earned media value (EMV) and how is it calculated?

EMV is the output to measure the value generated from promotion for a brand based on the quality of promotion and engagement against a post with brand promotion. It is designed to approximate what a similar post would cost if a brand were to pay for the same level of engagement through a paid promoted post on the same platform. We calculate EMV by starting with a platform and engagement type (like, comment, share, view), applying a CPE against the number of engagements on the post and discounting based on a promotion quality score that takes into account factors such as logo size and clarity (we analyse images and videos to identify logos and products), if any other brands are present and placement.

Some traditional media professionals question if EMV is an effective way to measure influence campaigns and sponsorship programmes. What is your expert opinion?

EMV is one component to valuing campaigns and sponsorships. In some cases it's the only means of measuring and comparing value. Ultimately, the value of a sponsorship or campaign is based on the brand's objectives. Do you want to increase brand affinity, drive direct sales, drive landing-page traffic or simply increase brand awareness? Measuring success against the objective or tying it directly back to sales is the holy grail. That is the focus of our platform. Earned media value does provide a very useful means to measure value and more importantly measure how to optimize and improve that value, compare partners to one another or against various indexes (globally, by sport, by league, etc) and track progress over time and against competitors.

Are there any pitfalls or things brands should be aware of when it comes to EMV as a measurement approach?

At the highest level, EMV is merely a total media value equivalent driven by a particular athlete, team, etc. What's becoming increasingly important is… who is the audience engaging with that property? You could have two athletes driving identical EMV, but if one has an audience completely irrelevant to the target demographic you're trying to reach, it ultimately isn't driving value.

Whatever EMV you use, understand how it works so you can explain it and use it effectively. We are very transparent when it comes to our model, because the most important thing for us is how you use it – and knowing how it works helps you to use it more effectively. It is not the only metric that matters. Depending on your objective as a brand, there are other measures that help you determine progress on your path to success.

What strategic advice do you have for professionals of varied levels of experience when it comes to measuring influence campaign and sponsorship performance?

Start with the basics. Know your objectives and measure against that. Work with companies and platforms that help you meet your objectives, that don't just provide data or black box results, but offer insights and recommendations. Not all influence or EMV carries the same value. Audience matters. Affinity matters. Work with a measurement platform that will work together with you to reach your goals. Test and iterate, look for insights that will help drive your business strategies. Most importantly, partner with the influencer, athlete, team, league, event that matches best with your brand from a value, tone, interest and audience makeup perspective. Don't work with someone just because they have a huge following or drive a lot of engagement. Make sure they are the right fit for your brand and your objectives.

Sports sponsorship is one of the few transactional marketplaces that haven't seen a major evolution in the way transactions are made as a result of technology. Increased data from platforms will drive decisions in real time much the way adtech and martech have done. As a result, sponsorships will evolve from Responsive to Predictive and soon Prescriptive using big data, machine learning and AI, which will transform the way sponsorships are bought and sold. Clients always come to us to measure 'what happened?' The more progressive ones come to us and say this is our target consumer and general strategy… who should we be working with to maximize our ROI/ROO. This is the future.

TL;DR: chapter takeaways

- **Focus on creating value before measuring it.** Putting your time, energy and resources into creating value for Gen Z is the most important thing you can do. If not, then all the metrics and media valuation in the world aren't going to help you.

- **Get back to the basics of measurement.** Clearly define what you want to track, align metrics with your objectives and measure those.

- **Develop influence marketing programmes sponsorship strategies around an earned media valuation model.** Evaluate the performance of earned social and influence marketing programmes based on actual engagement and promotion quality, never assumptive impressions.

- **Know the reporting analytics for youth-relevant social platforms.** Are you reaching Gen Z audiences? Are young people actively part of your conversation? Is the sentiment positive or negative?

References

Baer, J (2017) [accessed 19 March 2018] Not Tracking Social Media ROI is Your Fault, *Convince and Convert* [Online] http://www. convinceandconvert.com/social-media-measurement/not-tracking-social-media-roi-is-your-fault/

Stinson, E (2017) [accessed 18 March 2018] Facebook Reactions, the Totally Redesigned Like Button, Is Here, *Wired*, 24 February [Online] www.wired.com/2016/02/facebook-reactions-totally-redesigned-like-button/

Conclusion 11

Tune in to the frequency of Gen Z

Whether you are an educator, entrepreneur, advertising agency, manager of a charitable organization or part of a global brand targeting youth, we all have one thing in common: the need to get tuned in to the frequency of Gen Z. The Gen Z frequency is the voice of an individualized generation; one that is made up of the many distinct voices that represent its cultural groups, subgroups and individuals. The frequency itself is the wavelength on which the generation and its converging subgroups communicate and interact with each other. It represents their essence. For brands, tuning in allows us to listen to the unique voices within the generational cacophony, and realize that Gen Z is not simply one homogeneous whole. When we tune in to the Gen Z audiences that best fit our brand, we are enabled to create mutually beneficial consumer–brand relationships, based on the wants and needs of that audience.

The goal of this book has been to offer a practical means for brands to get immersed in youth culture and build credibility. Throughout the book, we offer principles and practices that lead and inspire you to discover the particular frequencies of your target audiences. The Five Foundational Truths, the Youth Culture Alignment Framework and the Youth Engagement Strategy Playbook all focus on genuine connection and informed engagement that create real relationships between brands and consumers. While we've laid out action plans, step-by-step guidelines and checklists for you in this book, we're not saying we've provided everything. In fact, it's just a starting point. Our decades of experience working within the youth market have shown us that it doesn't matter whether you are a startup or a multinational company; even some of the most influential brands have failed to listen carefully enough to the signals coming from this group. After

Figure 11.1 The Gen Z frequency is defined by the ecosystem of youth cultural groups and the wavelengths they use to identify and communicate with their world

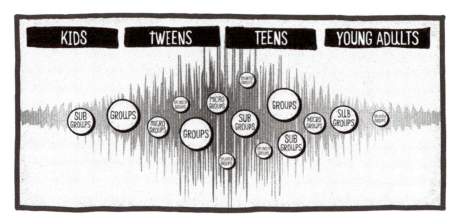

SOURCE Illustration by Mike Carnevale

reading this book, we hope that you are further on your way towards cultural alignment and have tuned in to the frequencies that will help you successfully connect with Gen Z.

The story doesn't end here, though. Let's continue the conversation. We would love to hear your feedback, your unique stories and any questions you might have. For additional resources, insights and downloadable materials, please visit us at **www.genzfreq.com**

Epilogue

Stories from the youth marketing trenches

We know most of you have paid your dues in the trenches of business, marketing, education or advocacy in some way, shape or form, and so you know it can be as challenging as it is rewarding. We've dedicated our professional lives to helping brands tune in to the many frequencies of youth culture: to stop broadcasting static and build credibility. We've boldly stood in front of clients – sweat dripping from our brow – prepared to walk away from a project rather than compromise on what we know is right. We've spun our wheels through all-nighters and weekends, trying to find that sweet spot of connection and engagement, especially with a constantly changing market of young consumers who are frequently mis-targeted. We've leveraged years of experience, failures and successes to guide brands, whether pioneering startups or global corporations, to re-evaluate the boundaries of their marketing rules, in order to actually be heard by the young consumers they want to reach.

We hope this book helps you tune in deeper to the frequency of Gen Z, or any range of frequencies relevant to your work.

It's not easy. Sometimes you win, sometimes you don't. Sometimes brands get it, and get on the right wavelength, sometimes they don't. One thing's for sure: as marketers, you learn something new and crucial every time you step onto the battlefield. The truth that gets revealed to you along the way is where victory can be found. Because there's no better way to communicate a message than to tell a story, here are a few of our own *Stories from the Trenches* of youth marketing.

National non-profit organization

Just say no to outdated marketing

And yes to motivating young people to open up.

It was inevitable. When youth engagement is an intrinsic part of your DNA, eventually someone is going to ask you to work on an initiative focused on social change. When a non-profit organization focused on teenage drug and alcohol abuse risk reduction came to us with a proposal to develop a programme, we were ready to jump in. *This* was the real, life-changing stuff we signed up for.

What we didn't sign up for, though, was the next step: the brief. It turned out the grant for the project had been written for a PowerPoint presentation and a convincer video – our assignment for the contract. It didn't take long for us to see that the angle wasn't going to work. With a target audience of middle and high schoolers, and a goal of getting teens talking, we knew we couldn't do a PowerPoint presentation: we had to talk in their language and on a frequency they could relate to, otherwise we risked them shutting down entirely.

We were in a sticky situation. We were about to tell a client who had already been through a strict approval process via the Department of Justice, that they needed to re-evaluate their approach in order for this to work – *in order for us to even take on the project*. It was the only reasonable, ethical and slightly intimidating option available. Armed with an alternative concept, that's exactly what we did, and we believed in our youth marketing truths so strongly that the client was convinced and went back to the drawing board with a new approach.

We created an interactive card game and online platform as a forum for teens to express their attitudes towards drugs and alcohol. It encourages dialogue between peers and adults about substance abuse issues by talking through scenarios – real and made up – and helps young people understand the risks of drugs and alcohol in a way that is engaging and familiar to them. To this day, it is a nationally recognized programme for teen substance abuse risk reduction.

However, *what* we did is less important than *why* we did it. It would be easy to follow a brief from a client, cash the cheque and move on, but in the long run it doesn't help anyone. We are immersed in the convergence of youth cultures. We see it from the inside out and understand what needs to be done in order to be relevant, to interact in ways that are respected and to effect positive change. We couldn't sit quietly and take on a project that we knew wouldn't work. **In this world of marketing hit-and-misses, you've got to know when to stand up to a client and push back.** You've also got to be prepared to find a compromise that doesn't compromise the end result if they're not prepared to listen. However, those times that they do? That's when you know you're on your way to winning.

Global entertainment company

Timing is everything

A tale of acceptance, diversity, and missing the boat.

It's 2010, and we've been working in youth culture for a long time now. So has a certain Middle East educational and computer-generated imagery (CGI) animation company, and they are brewing up a very interesting and convention-challenging children's edutainment show. The show follows the adventures and developing friendship of two young boys from the United States and Jordan, and is heading into the new and uncharted waters of East–West diversity, acceptance and understanding. When they come to us to build the marketing plan for the US market, we are all in. Tolerance, diversity and respect are right up our alley, and if we can help add authenticity to the show's US release and create a demand for it within our own market – bringing these values into US homes – we are fulfilling our mission. What's more, they have voiceovers from some of the most familiar actors in the industry, which makes this all the more exciting. We dig in, do our research, and lay out a solid go-to-market plan for North America.

The year 2010, however, is not an age of tolerance, and not a climate that wants to embrace and explore the budding friendship between these two cultures, as seen through the eyes of young people. It hurts to say that out loud, but this book is, after all, about truths. As ideal as the concept was, the networks viewed the portrayal of acceptance and diversity in this context as a liability, not an opportunity to attract customers. No matter what an individual's personal convictions might be, the mindset of the North American market at that time did not fall in line with the show's overarching goals. It was decided. The show would not be aired.

We knew the project would be challenging, but we didn't predict that it would end up on the chopping block. We were in the thick of it, working out how best to market this incredible product to our target market. If it were today, we believe this show would be streaming on devices throughout North America, with parents across the country using it as a launch pad for conversations about diversity and acceptance – but it wasn't today, and the content was too far ahead of its time. There is at least one lesson to be learnt from every project you work on, and there were no doubts about the most valuable one here: in the world of marketing, timing is everything.

Global consumer-packaged goods (CPG) brand

The world's most interesting mouthwash

And how we co-created it.

How the heck do you create an innovative mouthwash for any market, let alone Gen Z? That's the question we were left asking ourselves when a global consumer products company came to us to develop an oral care line for the tween segment. It's hard enough for us as adults to remember to floss on a routine basis, so how are we supposed to get tweens to put down their phones long enough to do the same, let alone get excited about an oral hygiene product?

We instinctively knew there was only one reasonable path to take, and it involved turning to the most qualified experts we knew: tweens. They also happen to be the most difficult group to get talking about topics such as body health and hygiene, which led us to realize another truth. We had to listen to them in a way they felt comfortable expressing themselves, which meant – you guessed it – gamification!

Through our virtual flavour lab and the related gamified experiences, tweens went to the store, bought and mashed up ingredients and videoed the process. They also created digital collages as a way to visually share ideas or favourite flavour recipes. **Gamification helps lower some of the barriers for adults working with youth. It distracts and challenges them in a way that allows them to forget their self-consciousness.** For us, it created a forum in which we were able to extract incredible insights, from how often tweens floss right through to more subtle nuances about body health and hygiene concerns for this age group. We segmented our tween advisory group by age, region, geolocation, ethnicity, gender, and daily routines, which helped us identify more specifically how different groups could improve their habits and be incentivized to do so. They knew the goal they were working towards and they threw themselves in with full collaboration, aware they were effectively co-creating a brand-new product. **All throughout the project, we tuned in, we observed, and we *listened*. Because we were under no illusion that we could do this without their direct input.**

All this collaboration led to the creation of mouthwash flavours and a format that resonated with tweens so much that they became a globally successful product for one of the largest companies in the world. Our advisory group helped us break through a saturated category to define an untapped product need, proving there is still blue ocean out there, waiting to be explored.

If you are genuinely willing to collaborate with real users and listen to the feedback of a niche group of consumers, that is.

US-based clothing company

Everything that glitters is not gold

But your core market is 24 carat.

Sometimes, when a contemporary music icon and a clothing brand collaborate, the sonic boom of success reverberates throughout the globe. Sales enter levels never seen before and, typically, the brand leaves a permanent imprint on our consciousness. The following story is not our own but belongs to a close colleague of ours, and highlights how, sometimes, you've got to check yourself to see if the sparkly object in front of you is real gold or just something shiny.

Not so long ago, a *very* well-known music mogul approached a US-based clothing brand he had loved his whole life. He wanted to do a collaboration with them, and get his name, face and fame aligned with the brand. With the phenomenal success of his recent partnership with a global footwear company, it was an easy next move. Except it wasn't. Because the brand said no. That's right. *No.* Just think about that for a second. A collaboration of this magnitude would have skyrocketed sales to numbers never seen before, and taken the brand recognition to an entirely new market. But, you see, that was the problem. This brand had been around for a long time, and although it's worn by all kinds of people today, its core is still as hard and true as the day it first hit shelves decades ago. That core is not the kind of market segment to appreciate having their signature look appropriated by a rapper whose values were far removed from their own. **If the brand took the short-term gain – no matter how monumental it would be – they risked losing their core audience base.** Like a house with an unstable foundation, the rest would eventually crumble. It might not happen all at once, but it would happen. The company ultimately decided they were in this for generations to come and had to take the gut-churning but incredibly brave decision to turn it down.

Recognizing the right decision is not always easy. Standing up for that decision can be even harder, as this company experienced first hand. With push back from every angle, be it agents, managers, internal pressure and even the musician himself – incredulous that they would turn him and his brand equity down – they still stood their ground. They did so because they knew that the short-term gain of the collaboration might well be cancelled out by the risk of disenfranchising their core customers, and that was a chance they couldn't take.

To know a brand and its consumers this intimately, to think of long-term success over short-term gain, and to fight for what is right... that's a lot of youth marketing truth right there.

Energy drink company

You can license authenticity, but you can't buy relevance

There's no shortcut to building trust.

Once upon a time in the far north of North America, there was a grocery brand that saw a golden opportunity to market an energy drink. By licensing what was, at the time, arguably the biggest action sports brand in the world, they believed they would be able to become culturally relevant and cash in on a highly lucrative trend. But it was all the stuff of fairy tales, because **there is no shortcut to relevance, and no faking your way into the frequency.**

It seemed like a good plan at first. License a globally recognized brand, slap its name on an energy drink targeted at that brand's market, and instantly take market share on the shelves. With the brand equity they were acquiring, it was surely a no-brainer, right? Wrong. Unfortunately, nothing in this world comes without a little sweat, tears and hard-earned insights, and that was something the company had breezed right past. With the belief that they could simply waltz in and let the branded equity from the licence do all the work, they went full steam ahead to market. They jumped in without clear insights into the consumer market, paid little attention to their creative execution, and were so far disconnected from the culture they were selling into that they missed the mark entirely.

As it turned out, *every* facet of their frequency was off. **It's not easy to just show up and capture the attention of young consumers, especially those who love action sports.** In fact, as a community, they are probably one of the hardest to gain loyalty among. If you lack authenticity in your marketing, speak off-tone or post a whacky image, it's all over. They will call you out faster than you can strap into your snowboard.

As a result, the brand was dead within a year. By relying on purchased brand equity and failing to invest in the culture, they never earned the respect of the very people they were expecting to buy their product. They clearly brought no youth advisors into the project to make sure they were communicating on the right wavelength and hitting the right tone. The lack of market research was evident in the way they simply bulldozed through. Learning about the needs, wants and frequency of your consumer base is not rocket science, but it does take time and thoughtfulness. If they'd made the effort to align with their audience and build genuine relationships with them, they would have gained their trust, and that's where they would have found sales. Unfortunately, in this instance, they missed the mark on all of them.

World-renowned entertainment complex

The magic power of tweendom

Embrace it, or face the music.

Amusement parks. Who wouldn't want to visit them? Well, as it turns out, a significant number of tweens back in 2015. Tweens – that tricky 9–13-year-old age group that has one foot in the innocence of childhood and the other in teenage cool – are often overlooked as a unique market. **Yet with their influence over family decision making and their developing self-awareness, smart marketers should never underestimate the power of tweens.** If you've ever made the mistake of assuming your own pre-teenage kids will still find something that was beyond awesome last year even slightly cool this time round, you'll know exactly what we are talking about.

Which brings us back to a world-renowned US-based amusement park. Tweens simply weren't viewing it as cool. With its marketing heavily focused on cartoon characters, this opinionated age group perceived it as too young for them, and their lack of engagement was negatively impacting family vacation decisions. Because of this, when we were approached to drive higher visitation intent and strengthen the brand perception within this group, our first step was to go directly to our mobile youth community for some deeper exploration. We worked side by side with our Gen Z advisory group as they participated in a different brand-related project each week, then voiced their opinions and feedback using our online community. They also took part in gamified ideation projects, such as voting on characters and acting out concepts. We didn't just ask for feedback, we asked them to create, apply originality, and express themselves verbally and visually. It was with these thoughts and judgements from our youth group that we were able to develop a culturally relevant action plan. We listened closely to understand their motivations behind wanting or not wanting to go to the park, which allowed us to develop and refine the park's social channel voice to be more relatable and youth-centric. We co-created a tween engagement strategy playbook for both Instagram and YouTube and, because we're still talking preteens here, we created a hub on the company's own website targeting parents of tweens.

This age group grew up communicating differently from us. They skipped the e-mail era, barely hold a phone call and won't admit going near Facebook, but they can be found heavily engaged on Instagram, Snapchat and YouTube, so with insights from our youth advisory group we were able to create marketing campaigns such as targeted Instagram contests, which in turn helped grow the park's tween-focused Instagram following from zero to 238,000 in 18 months. The 24 million views their YouTube channel received in the same time period were additional proof of the impact of insight gathering, ideation and audience validation.

Aristotle may have been right when he said that knowing yourself is the beginning of all wisdom, but knowing others and how to communicate on their frequency? That's the heart and soul of youth marketing.

GLOSSARY

application programming interface (API): a term used to describe the protocols and tools required to build apps and software and specify how they should interact. Example: social platforms such as Snapchat and Instagram provide third-party developers with an API so they can build on top of their platform.

augmented reality (AR): use of a device, such as a smartphone, to create an enhanced version of reality. Most commonly a digital overlay on an image of something being viewed.

Behind the Scenes (BTS): Behind the Scenes is a popular content theme that offers select fans with insider access to a special event or a creative process.

Bones Brigade: Bones Brigade is the professional team name for the Powell Peralta brand, a US skateboard company founded by George Powell and Stacy Peralta in 1978. A shortlist of legendary members (professional skateboard athletes) include Steve Caballero, Tony Hawk, Mike McGill, Lance Mountain, Per Welinder, Tommy Guerrero and Rodney Mullen.

Boomerang: a photograph technology created by Instagram which creates mini videos that loop back and forth.

brand audience disconnection disorder (BADD): slang to describe a condition that often develops when a brand is not well positioned or effectively aligned with youth culture. Typically used when referring to messaging, content and consumer engagement activities that feel disconnected from the target audience.

call-to-action (CTA): content designed to motivate consumers to do something specific, such as download an app, sign up, 'Like', comment, share a post, or any desired action.

Children's Online Privacy Protection Act (COPPA): COPPA is a US law that governs the collection of PII for consumers under the age of 13 years old.

co-creation: a research, product development or strategic initiative that brings different groups together as participants (for example, a brand and a mix of consumer groups, subgroups and micro groups), to enable consumers to co-construct something of mutual value. Co-creation provides a unique blend of insights and ideas directly from consumer participants.

collab: this is shorthand to describe 'collaboration'. It is typically used when referring to brands, creators and media who are working together to create something unique and youth-relevant.

community guidelines: the rules and 'legal system' that specify the acceptable communications/interactions for an online community as well as behaviours and consequences for violating the community standards.

consumer trend tracking: the widespread practice of collecting consumer information over a period of time in order to identify patterns that may have positive or negative implications for a brand.

convergence culture: this is the intersection of two or more cultural subgroups whose combination creates a 'supergroup'. Supergroups provide brands with opportunities for cross fertilization and to reach a larger audience of like-minded people. Also referred to in this book as (subgroup) overlap.

cost per engagement (CPE): CPE pricing is the cost paid when an ad is engaged with. An engagement can be anything from viewing, pausing or muting a video to submitting contact details.

creators: talented individuals who actively create and publish original content for an audience on one or more social and digital media platforms. Creators are also increasingly classified as influencers (*see* influence partner).

digital citizenship: a term used to describe behaviour norms that foster a sense of safety, engagement and kindness within an online community.

DIY: this means do-it-yourself – the act of decorating or making things for yourself, community or environment, instead of paying a third party to do it for you.

EMV: a measurement of value generated from the social promotion for a brand based on the quality of promotion and engagement with a social post. It is designed to approximate what a similar post would cost if a brand were to pay for the same level of engagement through a paid promoted post on the same platform.

engagement: this means actively contributing to youth culture and involving young people in the content, conversations and experiences along the way – *not* treating youth consumers as passive message-recipients. From a tactical perspective, engagement is the sum of interactions a consumer has with your brand: social likes, comments, video views, shares, user-generated content (UGC), tune-in, event attendance and any direct participation in experiences that a brand facilitates.

eSports: an abbreviation for 'electronic sports', which are multiplayer video games played competitively for spectators, typically by professional gamers.

fear of missing out (FOMO): an acronym for the cyberculture term 'fear of missing out', often associated with anxiety after viewing posts on social media.

Federal Trade Commission (FTC): the FTC is the US government agency that oversees enforcement of COPPA.

Five Foundational Truths: we define Identity, Trust, Relevance, Possibility and Experience as five foundational guideposts used to keep brands grounded in youth market realities as they relate to their products and offerings.

Gen Z (Generation Z): born between 1996 and 2011 (approximately), the first generation to become a true global culture as their characteristics are more uniform. Gen Z is expected to account for about 40 per cent of all consumers by 2020. Commonly subdivided into Kids, Tweens, Teens and Young Adults.

Gen Z frequency: the wavelengths or frequencies that young people use to communicate and express themselves. Gen Z has a generational voice, their own frequency, which is made up of many distinct voices. Each youth segment, group, and subgroup – right down to the individual – has a voice that identifies what makes it unique. Each of these voices or frequencies tells an important story that helps us to understand, engage and build credibility with Gen Z.

ghosted: a term used by Gen Z to mean 'giving a cold shoulder' or 'the silent treatment'.

GIF: a type of photograph file format used to create a looping video image, often used in memes on social platforms.

hashtag: word or phrase preceded by the symbol # that categorizes the text and makes it easier to find other people posting on the same topic.

influence marketing: a type of marketing that focuses on collaboration with cultural leaders (influence partners) to distribute your brand's message to the targeted audience and drive authentic engagement.

influence partner: cultural leaders who can be divided into those who *develop a sphere of influence* and those who *develop or create content*. They are two distinct entities, yet increasingly, creators are also influencers, and vice versa. Influence partner characteristics include one or more of the following: leaders in their field, specialists in their area of interest or talent, those engaged in youth-relevant communities, and creators of original content.

influencer: individuals who have *developed a sphere of influence*. Influencer characteristics include one or more of the following: leaders in their field, specialists in their area of interest or talent, those engaged in youth-relevant communities, and sometimes creators of original content. Influencers may also be referred to as influence partners.

influencer mindsharing: a youth engagement methodology for both research and ideation that blends aspects of focus groups, interviews, ethnographies or co-creation projects all conducted with one or a group of influencers. Think of it as a direct line to the experts on a particular audience or segment.

meme: a hybrid of cyber and pop culture, a meme is a visual narrative (image with text, GIF) that may pass from one individual to another through social networks, often in real time.

mixed reality (MR): mixed reality is superimposed content that is anchored to an object and interacts with the real world. The main characteristic of MR is that the superimposed content and real-world content are reacting to each other in real time.

MyStory: first introduced by Snapchat, but now a mainstream feature on social media platforms that allows users to share images and video in real time using a story narrative format.

personally identifiable information (PII): this acronym refers to any data point that can be used to identify a particular person.

qualitative research: this is a research method that emphasizes objective measurements and the statistical, mathematical or numerical analysis of data collected through polls, questionnaires and surveys, or by manipulating pre-existing statistical data using computational techniques.

quantitative research: this is a research method designed to reveal a target audience's range of behaviour and the perceptions that drive it, with reference to specific topics or issues. It uses in-depth studies of small groups of people to guide and support the construction of hypotheses.

ReTweet (RT): when you post a 'tweet' on Twitter, other members of the community can share it on their timeline. This is called a ReTweet.

ROI: an abbreviation for Return On Investment. The earning power of assets measured as the ratio of the net income (profit less depreciation) to the average capital employed (or equity capital) in a company or project. Expressed usually as a percentage, return on investment is a measure of profitability that indicates whether or not a company is using its resources in an efficient manner.

ROO: an abbreviation for Return On Objectives.

safe harbour: the FTC's COPPA Rule includes a 'safe harbour' provision that allows industry groups and others to seek Commission approval of self-regulatory guidelines that implement 'the same or greater protections for children' as those contained in the COPPA Rule.

segmentation: the method of dividing a marketplace into parts, or segments, which are definable, accessible, actionable, profitable and have growth potential. In other words, a brand would find it impossible to target the entire generation or market, because of time, cost and effort restrictions. Common segmentation bases are: Demographics, Geographics, Behavioural, Psychographics, Situational and Contextual.

Snap: the photo and video messages that users send to friends using the social media messaging app, Snapchat.

Snapback: Snapback is a type of call to action (CTA) on Snapchat where one person responds to a Snapchat message with a reply. Brands often use this as a way to engage with their communities.

sneakerheads: a formal definition of a sneakerhead is a person who collects, trades and/or admires sneakers as a form of hobby.

social vanity handle: a vanity social handle is a unique identifier of you and your brand, also known as a handle or account, on social media (eg twitter.com/cocacola).

Streaks: Snapchat Messaging Streaks: to get a Snap Streak, you and another person need to send each other at least one Snapchat in 24 hours.

tl;dr: acronym for 'too long; didn't read', used when sharing content that you did not read.

User-generated content (UGC): acronym for user-generated content; content created and submitted by members of a social community.

verifiable parental consent (VPC): part of the US COPPA law requires that brands secure VPC from any user under the age of 13, using one of three specific verification techniques.

VidCon: a popular annual conference of the video content creator and influencer community, held each June in Anaheim, CA.

virtual reality (VR): computer-based simulation of an environment that users can interact with in a seemingly real or physical way by using specialized electronic equipment, such as a helmet with a screen inside, or gloves fitted with sensors.

visual narrative: a visual narrative is the primary form of communication used by Gen Z, usually in the form of emoji, GIFs or memes.

youth cultural groups: a way to segment a cohort into subdivisions that are similar in specific psychographic, situational and contextual ways relevant to marketing, such as interests, lifestyles, brand and content affinities. This hierarchy includes groups, subgroups, micro groups and splinter groups, which are all categorized by their size and degree of unique characteristics.

youth culture advisory boards: typically an online, mobile app-based methodology that allows brands to connect directly with a customized group of forward-thinking young people, as well as other stakeholders, both of whom fit predetermined criteria that make them valuable to the brand, and deeply connected to youth consumers.

youth engagement playbook: a set of customized marketing strategies designed to drive engagement and build credibility within youth culture. Typically engagement strategies can either stand alone or be integrated to strengthen your overall marketing plan.

youth and pop culture media scan: the practice of researching and scanning youth-related lifestyle media, including social, video on demand, broadcast news, magazines, books, events or anything that seems like a noteworthy activity within the youth media landscape.

INDEX

Note: Numbers in headings, 'Mc' and @ are filed as spelt out in full; acronyms are filed as written. Locators in *italics* denote information within a Figure/Table.

CPSIA information can be obtained
at www.ICGtesting.com
Printed in the USA
BVHW02s1425190918
527935BV00014B/173/P

9 780749 482480